OFF AND RUNNING

The Prospects and Pitfalls of Government Transitions in Canada

One of the most pivotal events in the electoral cycle is the transition of a newly elected political party from opposition to government. The incoming prime minister or premier must assemble a team of ministers, advisors, and staff that is competent and ready to govern, without disrupting the day-to-day functioning of their country or province.

Off and Running sets the stage for successful transitions by describing the best practices from Canadian federal government transitions from 1984 to the present day. It draws on a number of sources: the author's own career in public affairs, including his significant role in the transitions of both Chrétien governments in 1993 and 1997; extensive interviews with more than forty key individuals in the last eleven federal government transitions; and the international literature on government transitions, public administration, and management.

Zussman goes step-by-step through the transition process, from the pre-election stage to transition planning, to implementation and consolidation of the new government. This book is ideally suited to those seeking an understanding of how government works during one of the most crucial points in its life cycle.

DAVID ZUSSMAN is Jarislowsky Chair in Public Sector Management in the Graduate School of Public and International Affairs at the University of Ottawa. He served as Assistant Secretary for Program Review and Machinery of Government at the Privy Council Office.

IPAC — The Institute of Public Administration of Canada

IAPC — L'Institut d'administration publique du Canada

The Institute of Public Administration of Canada Series in Public Management and Governance

Editors:
Peter Aucoin, 2001–2
Donald Savoie, 2003–7
Luc Bernier, 2007–9
Patrice Dutil, 2010–

This series is sponsored by the Institute of Public Administration of Canada as part of its commitment to encourage research on issues in Canadian public administration, public sector management, and public policy. It also seeks to foster wider knowledge and understanding among practitioners, academics, and the general public.

For a list of books published in the series, see page 301.

Off and Running

The Prospects and Pitfalls of Government Transitions in Canada

DAVID ZUSSMAN

IPAC
The Institute of
Public Administration of Canada

IAPC
L'Institut d'administration
publique du Canada

UNIVERSITY OF TORONTO PRESS
Toronto Buffalo London

ISBN 978-1-4426-4709-1 (cloth)
ISBN 978-1-4426-1527-4 (paper)

∞

Printed on acid-free, 100% post-consumer recycled paper with
vegetable-based inks.

Library and Archives Canada Cataloguing in Publication

Zussman, David, author
Off and running : the prospects and pitfalls of government
transitions in Canada / David Zussman.

(IPAC series in public management and governance)
Includes bibliographical references and index.
ISBN 978-1-4426-4709-1 (bound). – ISBN 978-1-4426-1527-4 (pbk.)

1. Prime ministers – Canada – Transition periods. 2. Canada – Politics
and government – Decision making. 3. Canada – Politics and government –
1984–1993. 4. Canada – Politics and government – 1993–2006. 5. Canada –
Politics and government – 2006–. I. Title. II. Series: Institute of Public
Administration of Canada series in public management and governance.

JL97.Z88 2013   352.230971   C2013-906011-1

University of Toronto Press acknowledges the financial assistance to its
publishing program of the Canada Council for the Arts and the Ontario
Arts Council.

Canada Council   Conseil des Arts
for the Arts   du Canada

ONTARIO ARTS COUNCIL
CONSEIL DES ARTS DE L'ONTARIO
50 YEARS OF ONTARIO GOVERNMENT SUPPORT OF THE ARTS
50 ANS DE SOUTIEN DU GOUVERNEMENT DE L'ONTARIO AUX ARTS

University of Toronto Press acknowledges the financial support of the
Government of Canada through the Canada Book Fund for its publishing
activities.

Contents

Foreword   ix

Preface   xiii

Acknowledgments   xix

1 Introduction   3

2 The Context of Transitions: Setting the Stage   14
  Introduction   14
  Types of Transitions   14
  Phases of a Transition   18
  Key Players   23
    Political Leaders   23
    Political Advisors during the Transition Period   30
    Cabinet Secretaries   33
  The Media   35
  Conclusion   37

3 Pre-Election Phase: Kick-Starting the Transition   39
  Introduction   39
  Transition Team   40
    First Principles   49
  Important Working Relationships   52
    Election Team   52
  Readying the Leader to Govern   53
    Role of Spouses   55
    Public Service   57
  Preparing for the Personal Side of Transitions   68

Principles into Practice   70
Conclusion   72

4 The Transition Plan   74
Introduction   74
Key Elements   74
Prime Minister's Office   76
   Chief of Staff   79
   Executive Assistant   80
   Senior Policy Advisor   80
   Head of Communications   80
   Caucus and Party Liaison   81
Ministers' Offices   81
Governor-in-Council Appointments   82
Cabinet-Making   86
Key Cabinet Positions   92
   Mandate Letters   93
Cabinet Decision-Making   94
Machinery-of-Government Considerations   95
Key Public Service Appointments   98
The Media   101
Conclusion   103

5 Election Phase: Putting the Building Blocks in Place   105
Introduction   105
Political Perspective   110
Public Service Perspective   113
   Privy Council Office   113
   Departments and Agencies   114
Information   118
   Transition Documents   119
Conclusion   124

6 Post-Election Phase: Electioneering to Governing   126
Introduction   126
Post-Election Environment   126
When the Rubber Hits the Road   128
   Security Takes Over   134
First Meetings   135
   Prime Minister–Designate Meets the Transition Team   138
      Transition Team Meets the Clerk of the Privy Council   139

Prime Minister–Designate Meets the Clerk of the Privy
Council   140
Prime Minister–Designate Meets the Governor
General   144
Prime Minister–Designate Meets the Outgoing Prime
Minister   145
Swearing-In   147
Pressing Issues   149
Outgoing Governments   150
Public Service in Transition   150
Conclusion   152

7 Post-Election Phase: Getting the Fundamentals Right   154
Introduction   154
Cabinet Selection   155
Candidate Interviews and the Vetting Process   160
Ministerial Behaviour   162
Conflict of Interest   163
Ministerial Staff   163
Informing Individuals Who Are Not Selected for
Cabinet   168
Staffing   168
Prime Minister's Office   168
Ministers' Offices   172
Key Appointments   174
Conclusion   174

8 Consolidation Phase: Making the Transition a Reality   176
Introduction   176
Mandate Letters   177
Cabinet Meetings   180
Early Days as a Minister   185
Learning on the Job   185
Orientation: Training and Mentors   188
Prime Minister Meets the Deputy Ministers   193
Caucus Management   200
Dealing with Failed Cabinet Candidates   200
Evaluating Past Performance   201
Conclusion   203

9 Conclusion   204
  Introduction   204
  Personal Reflections   206
  Key Elements in Transition Planning   208
    Developing a Leadership Style in a World of Inexperienced
    Politicians   209
  Understanding the Emerging Importance of Political Advisors   210
    Establishing Respectful and Trusting Relations among Key
    Players   212
    Selecting the Right Transition Team   214
    Making a Virtue of Planning   214
    Consolidating the Transition by Training and Mentoring   215
  Outstanding Issues   215

Appendices   219

Notes   261

Select Bibliography   277

Index   287

Foreword

Assuming the role of government is a lot like a novice rider approaching a horse for the first time in that both take equal measures of firmness and sensitivity. One nears the animal (and the state) with purpose – after all, one should have maps and destinations – but not without intimidation. Here is the problem: the horse has a mind of its own, even though it is willing to recognize direction. Like the state, it has a powerful sense of itself, and, while it is sure-footed, it has an innate sense of risk and feels danger acutely. It can be obedient, but must feel that it is taking orders from a rider who knows what horses can do and cannot do.

So, here you are: approaching a horse you have never ridden. Actually, it is worse, because you likely may have never ridden any horse (or been in government). The first step, as in governing, is to control the head. One is always well advised to start with a mint to nudge the horse into believing that the process will be painless. After a good brushing of the animal, you stand next to it (always on its left – pay attention!), and in one fell swoop you hoist a saddle on its back (for your comfort, not the horse's), and secure it with a girth that fits under the belly. This installation of the "cabinet" must be done gently, so as not to alarm the horse with the revelation that its destiny is not all its choosing. With your back to the horse, you gently insert the bit (a cold steel bar) into the horse's mouth, hoping it will take it in, and not your hand. Carefully, you slip on the bridle over its sensitive nose and head, cautious not to pull the horse's mane. This is an important instrument of control on communications and priority setting: the bit plays the role of the Prime Minister's Office. You speak to the steed softly, encouraging, not threatening. You are slowly harnessing this ton of muscle, but you don't want to assert your authority too aggressively, not yet.

Once buckled in, that saddle must be mounted. Now comes the hard part, the phase of the exercise that can cause you real embarrassment. You put your foot in the left stirrup, grab the mane and the reins in your left hand, and jump up with all your might, swinging your right leg over the animal and hoping the process will land you in your seat. People are watching. The opposition is licking its wounds, but occasionally looks up, hoping you have missed your step, praying that you are not strong enough to lift yourself into the saddle. The media is quick to comment on every detail: your boots are cruddy, your horse's mane is messy, you look like you are going to fall off.

You have made it. You sit atop a still horse. Slowly, you grab the reins and begin your command. The horse does not move. Gently, squeezing your fingers only, you pull on the leather straps and make contact with the bit, forcing the animal's head to turn down slightly. Simultaneously, you are pressing the government's sides with your calves, showing it your political clout. You are nervous, but it would be your downfall if you showed it. You dig your heels a little and you pull harder, using your arms and shoulders as the PMO asserts itself on the beast's head and mouth. The horse moves, tentatively, experimenting with you. You have the reins. In Canada, you shall reign. Soon enough, you will be using your spurs and, likely, your whip.

This volume is about the art of getting on the horse of government and forcing it to move in a favoured direction. Readers could not be better served than by a winning coach in the art of "getting on the horse" and assuming power. David Zussman is a political horseman of the first order, but, better still, he is a generous instructor who shares his experience in detailing the steps to assuming the role of government at a time when the state is at its most vulnerable.

Canadians are very good in the art of government transition. Our culture, by and large, assumes a certain civility in this process, and the respect we give to democracy dictates that power will be surrendered quickly and without fuss. That being said, it has not always been a well-prepared exercise. Conscious of this reality, the Institute of Public Administration of Canada (IPAC) published a breakthrough collection of essays under Donald Savoie's editorship in 1993. *Taking Power: Managing Government Transitions* was a bestseller; even ten years after publication IPAC received calls after elections from legislative libraries looking for photocopies to replace chapters that had been razored out of the volumes on their shelves. The book was very useful, but, with time, it was clear that the practice of government transitions had evolved and that the sophistication of the exercise was no longer reflected in that great work.

Hence the turn to Zussman, the guru of transitions, who had participated in three himself and who had made a sport of watching others approaching their mount. Zussman invites his readers to consider the riders, the nature of the horses themselves, the variously good-willed attendants, and, not least, the spectators. He examines all the equipment, pointing out strengths and weaknesses, and suggests particular exercises that will strengthen the shoulders, the arms, the legs – all the right political body parts that communicate – and, most important, the mind that strategizes.

This volume is about politics, for sure, but more important it is about governing. Any student of politics and government will win in reading this book, but just as importantly public servants will benefit greatly from its how-to features. Zussman demonstrates that the keys to success are careful preparation and the need to surround the process with people – politicians and public servants – who have been there, and who have observed horse behaviour up close, so to speak, for many years.

A great coach is a great teacher, and in this book readers get both. David Zussman is that trainer, a scholar-practitioner par excellence, a mandarin of the finest ancient Chinese traditions. Combining the sharp eye of a keen student of politics with the skills and knowledge of public administration, Zussman delivers here a bible for assuming power. By carefully detailing the steps, he presents a product distilled from years of experience and research in all the Canadian capitals. With this book, he serves the public administration and the political community exceptionally well. More than that, he serves Canadian democracy.

Patrice Dutil
Editor, IPAC Series in Public Management and Governance
Ryerson University
October 2013

Preface

In 2006, Michael Fenn,[1] chair of the research committee of the Institute for Public Administration of Canada (IPAC), approached me to write a book about government transitions in Canada. At that point, I had been teaching graduate courses in public policy, governance, and public management since the 1970s and had had some practical experience as the head of the Chrétien transitions in 1993, 1997, and 2000. As well, I had served as assistant secretary to the Cabinet (program review and machinery of government) at the Privy Council Office in Ottawa and had also worked in the Treasury Board Secretariat and Statistics Canada during an earlier stage in my career. While my background gave me some preparation for a book in this area, I was not yet convinced that there was enough material available for a broad discussion of best practices for transition planning.

Two recent political events prompted me to propose to the Research Committee that we dust off the original idea. The first was the swearing-in of the minority Harper government in 2008. Surrounded by political neophytes without any practical experience in governing, Harper took the reins of power with ease and a sense of purpose. The smoothness of the transition was hardly noticed by the media, but to government watchers it was a sign that this was a government that had a clear agenda and knew where it was headed. As Canadians subsequently learned, the successful transition was managed by a professional team under the direction of Derek Burney and with the strong support of the Privy Council Office, at that time led by Alex Himelfarb.

The second recent example of effective transition planning took place across the Atlantic, where, as a result of the May 2010 election, David Cameron and Nick Clegg were locked in a battle for the political leadership of the United Kingdom. Given the prospects of a hung Parliament, the two negotiated for a remarkable five-day period until an agreement was reached. Their deliberations, with the support of the Cabinet office, led to the fashioning of a most improbable coalition government and further demonstrated the importance of government transitions to a well-functioning democracy.

With these two independent events serving as useful illustrations, it seemed a propitious time to explore the question of how transition planning is done in Canada and whether there are best practices to be championed and issues to be resolved in order to improve on current ways of managing governmental transitions. As a consequence, I have written this book.

This book is dedicated to the memory of Bill Neville and to the memory of Jean Pelletier – two individuals who worked in the rough-and-tumble world of partisan politics but always in the more important pursuit of good government and integrity in public life. The book is also dedicated to the public servants who have made their contribution to good government by preparing newly elected governments for the unknown challenges each one of them has faced in taking over the reins of government.

I first met Neville in the early 1990s. He was already an icon in the government-relations industry in the early 1990s. He had established a reputation for honesty and integrity and provided mentoring to many of the former political staffers who were entering the government-relations sector at that time.

I knew Neville only by his reputation. Thankfully, when I confided in Torrance Wylie, a well-respected government relations expert and former advisor to Prime Minister Pearson, that I was doing some work on the Chrétien transition, he suggested that I visit Neville, whom I knew well. Neville welcomed me into his impressive office, which was filled with political memorabilia and photos of some of Canada's most illustrious politicians.

After closing his door to the outer offices, Neville reached into his drawer, pulled out a massive three-ring binder, and handed it to me with the following observation: "This is the book that I prepared for Brian Mulroney in 1984 and it should give you a good appreciation of what we had in mind when the transition was done for Brian's first government. While we didn't implement everything in it, it was the basis for all that happened in the early months of his mandate."[2]

With that, he proceeded to describe the mechanics of transition planning and the need for precise preparation and anticipation. Our conversation continued throughout the morning. As the lunch hour approached, he suggested that I would benefit from reading his transition materials more carefully, rather than simply skimming them, as we had been doing during our meeting.

The transition book for the newly elected Prime Minister Brian Mulroney in 1984 begins with encouraging words: "Congratulations. Now the real fun begins."[3] Mulroney had just won a bruising and mean-spirited general election against John Turner, who himself had been recently crowned leader of the Liberal party and successor to Pierre Trudeau. The tide of blue-tinged victories across the country produced more than two hundred Conservative seats in the House of Commons and secured more than 50 per cent of the popular vote. The election catapulted the ambitious Mulroney into the Prime Minister's Office without his having had any parliamentary experience and reduced Turner's once-dominating Liberals to a rump party of only forty dispirited members of Parliament.

However, Neville's welcoming words also contain an ironic twist. Knowing Mulroney's scant experience as a parliamentarian and as a political leader, Neville, with tongue firmly in cheek, knew that Mulroney would have little appreciation of how much "fun" he was about to have. Fortunately for Mulroney and for all who have been involved in transition planning since that time, Neville was about to launch a transition exercise that would smoothly guide the newly elected Conservative party into the Langevin Block, the home of the Prime Minister's Office, and into 24 Sussex with a level of sophistication and professionalism that had never before been experienced in Ottawa. In his choice of Neville as the head of his transition team Mulroney was most prescient.

While Neville was well known in Ottawa as an effective lobbyist and background speechwriter, he had also been responsible for Joe Clark's 1979 transition to power in a minority government. From this experience, he learned how little newly elected prime ministers know about governing, even when they may have had previous experience as ministers in another Cabinet or as long-standing MPs. Neville also appreciated the importance of planning and the need to understand the character of the person he was preparing to become prime minister of the country.

Ten years before leading the transition exercise for Mulroney, Neville had witnessed a Conservative electoral loss and afterwards saw the transition material that had never been put into use. "I went into Stanfield's office after the '74 election and I saw what had been prepared for him. It was about six pages. I mean, I remember laughingly saying, 'Thank God you didn't win! You'd be in deep doo-doo'!"[4] Neville recognized the need for and the importance of a structured, disciplined approach to the transition exercise. Possibly unknown to subsequent transition planners working in the political arena or in the public services of Canada, they have all modelled their work on the templates that he established in 1984.

In the winter of 1993, Jean Pelletier asked me to take on the responsibility for preparing Chrétien to become Canada's twentieth prime minister. While my appointment as head of the transition team came as a surprise to many when it became publicly known after the election, it was, for those who knew better, a typical Chrétien decision. I had studied, taught, and written about public management since the mid-1970s; however, the prospect of leading a transition team was daunting – I had little practical experience in the field and no partisan political leanings. Moreover, at that time there was only a very short list of published material on transition planning in Canada. This problem was quickly remedied when I met with Bill Neville.

While Jean Chrétien was best known as a wily political player and a master tactician, he was not particularly known for his interest in management and governance. However, those who had worked for him at any point during his eight ministerial portfolios in the Pearson and Trudeau era were well aware of his particular interest in good management and strong working relationships between his political staff and the public service. As a result, it wasn't particularly difficult in early 1992 for his chief of staff, Jean Pelletier, to kick-start planning for a government transition that was more than a year away.

Typically, political leaders are suspicious of any formal process that prepares them to govern. Those competing to become prime minister have resisted setting a transition team in place because they fear being perceived by the public as arrogant if it becomes known that they are overtly preparing to take office. Moreover, they are also sufficiently superstitious about "challenging the election gods" by appearing to take victory for granted in advance of actually winning the election. Despite the usual reticence of prime-ministerial hopefuls, Chrétien knew that preparedness was crucial.

In the early 1980s I was working in the Privy Council Office in support of the Cabinet Committee on Communications. In the course of my work I interacted with Chrétien on a number of occasions around Cabinet committee work and had a number of conversations with him about the state of the country in a post-1980 referendum context. While I had no political experience, he was always interested in chatting with the public servants around the committee table. Coincidentally, at that time, Chrétien was looking for a new policy advisor, and he was intrigued by my interest in public opinion research, in my experiences teaching public policy at the University of Victoria in British Columbia, and work reorganizing the Cabinet office of the British Columbia government. Coming from British Columbia, I was especially impressed with his pan-Canadian views and also his passionate articulation of Canadian values, so when invited by him I left the PCO for a stint in the minister's office.

We worked well together. Equally important, I also worked well with Eddie Goldenberg, who had recently rejoined the office after spending some time as a private-sector lawyer. He and I were able to share the policy work and to establish a most agreeable working relationship. After a few very pleasant years working in the minister's office and having experienced the exhilaration and emotional roller coaster of a leadership campaign, I returned to university life in 1984 by joining the public management group in the business faculty at the University of Ottawa.

Over the years I stayed in touch with my former colleagues on the Hill and I took on a number of organizational tasks, notably managing the policy process, during Chrétien's 1990 leadership campaign. After that, I returned to the university, where I continued to work with him on organizational issues, including the restructuring of the Office of the Official Opposition and the recruitment of his chief of staff, Jean Pelletier.

Pelletier's arrival signalled a new way of doing things in the Office of the Official Opposition. Pelletier was disciplined, a gifted manager, and a man deeply committed to Canada. He also was very systematic in his approach to his duties as the person quarterbacking, with Eddie Goldenberg, and John Rae, Chrétien's bid to become prime minister one day. At a point in 1991, after consulting with Chrétien, he asked me to plan the transition for a Chrétien government.

The writing of this book has been a particularly enjoyable experience. It has given me the opportunity to interview (and to interact with) a wide range of political players and public servants who have, to various degrees, participated in federal transitions since 1984. As mentioned earlier in this preface, this work has also given me the opportunity to highlight the contributions of Bill Neville and Jean Pelletier, who recognized the importance of transitions in good governance and were prepared to commit themselves to ensuring that this important link in the democratic process was done as well as possible.

Acknowledgments

This book is dedicated to the many individuals working within the world of politics and public service who have helped to make transition planning a professional activity in their areas of responsibility. In so doing, they have strengthened one of the key features of all democratic states: the seamless transition of power from one political leader (or party) to another.

While many people have had a hand in transition planning since public administration was professionalized in the 1960s in Canada, two individuals, in particular, have changed its nature and quality and moved it from an ad hoc activity to a structured and substantial endeavour.

Bill Neville and Jean Pelletier came from different backgrounds and political persuasions but they shared a passion for good government and the value of professionalism over partisanship in the political world.

One could argue that Bill Neville has written the book on transitions. His briefing book for the incoming Conservative government in 1984 is a remarkable political document that contains frank, unvarnished advice to the incoming and inexperienced prime minister. It also demonstrates a profound appreciation of Canadian institutions, especially the value of a professional and non-partisan public service in Canada. Sharing his transition materials with me in 1992 was a generous act from someone who has been a long-standing champion of good government in Canada.

Jean Pelletier became chief of staff to the leader of the opposition in 1991 and, within weeks of his appointment, the political fortunes of Jean Chrétien began to steadily improve. Pelletier was a particularly able administrator who greatly appreciated the value of planning, meticulous preparation, and steadfast implementation. His steady hand during crises and during the day-to-day operations of government set a standard of professionalism for his colleagues. Although he passed away a few years ago, the memory of his commitment to professionalism lives on.

Both individuals had an important influence on my work. Most important, Bill and Jean taught me that politics can be a noble profession that must be practised with integrity if our system of government is going to be effective.

Patrice Dutil and Wendy Feldman as directors of research at IPAC first proposed that I consider preparing a book on government transitions. Since that time, the IPAC team has been a constant help in the development of this book project and I am grateful for their encouragement and support.

At the University of Ottawa, colleagues Jim Lahey, Greg Fyffe, and Robert Asselin have provided insights and solid advice about the workings of government during our many conversations at O'Dell House around the conference table.

In the course of the past eighteen months, I have been very ably assisted by a number of graduate students in the Graduate School of Public and International Affairs who served as research assistants. Kieran Bergman, Caroline Andison, and Graeme Esau helped with the literature review and read early drafts of some chapters. As has been the case for more than a decade, Susan Snider, a former student of mine with a unique understanding of government organizations, provided much-needed help in organizing the research material.

In the early stages of developing the methodology and framework, I benefited from two roundtables, the first, hosted by James Lahey at the Centre on Public Management in the Graduate School of Public and International Affairs at the University of Ottawa, and the second session, hosted by David Mitchell at the Public Policy Forum. The insights from the people around the table were very critical in deciding to expand the number of interviews and to ensure a balance between politicians and public servants.

Jackie Jantzen performed an outstanding job transcribing more than five hundred pages of text based on interviews with the key players in transition planning since 1984. As well, Howard Yeung, Kate Layton, and Mary Conway at Deloitte Touche were invaluable in preparing the tables and figures and in editing the text. As well, Joan Harcourt and Barbara Feldman provided crucial editorial input that helped to shorten a very long draft and sharpen the messaging throughout the manuscript.

Since the book is dependent on archival information, I am very appreciative of the work provided by Maureen Hoogenraad at Library and Archives Canada, who was responsive to my frequent requests for information about transitions planning and who also helped me access the more than twenty boxes of information that I had deposited there more than fifteen years ago.

Jean and Richard Van Loon, Alan Nymark, Joseph McDonald, and James Lahey read early drafts of the manuscript. I am thankful to them for their many comments, since reading early drafts of any book can be a most daunting experience. Their frankness during our feedback sessions helped me refocus the book on many occasions and probably reduced the production time by many months.

Under the direction of Daniel Quinlan at the University of Toronto Press, the two anonymous external reviewers provided a long list of improvements to the manuscript, which added greatly to the overall quality of the finished product.

Given the centrality of the interviews in this project, I am very indebted to the more than forty people who were interviewed for this book project. All of those whom I approached to participate were willing and insightful interviewees. Despite their very busy schedules they were very accommodating in making themselves available for a discussion about transition planning. All of those who were interviewed are listed in Appendix 9, but it is worth noting that Derek Burney, Richard Dicerni, and Michael Wernick agreed to be interviewed a number of times in order to ensure that I had a better understanding of transition planning from their perspectives.

Finally, the conceptualization, data gathering, and writing of this book consumed most of my non-teaching and administrative time at the University of Ottawa from October 2010 until March 2012. In reality, it caused my golf game to suffer unfairly and, more important, it consumed big chunks of family time. Despite this intrusion, my wife, Sheridan Scott, was a constant source of encouragement and she made sure that I had the writing time that I needed to complete this book. As always, I want to thank her for her customary good humour and, most of all, for being there.

OFF AND RUNNING

The Prospects and Pitfalls of Government
Transitions in Canada

1 Introduction

There is a tide in the affairs of men,
Which, taken at the flood, leads on to fortune:
Omitted, all the voyage of their lives
Is bound in the shallows and in miseries ...
And we must take the current when it serves,
Or lose our ventures.

— William Shakespeare, *Julius Caesar*

One of the most vulnerable and meaningful moments in a constitutional democracy is when one political party loses and voluntarily – peacefully – gives up power to a political opponent.[1] Change is never easy, and there is no more difficult change to experience in government than a transition from one political party to another at the senior-most levels of political leadership. The mere possibility of a change of leadership sets into motion a complex series of activities that can make or break the effectiveness of a government's first weeks and months in power.

In changing power, there is a whole human drama. The hopes and dreams of a lot of people rest on how a transition will unfold. In the office of every member of Parliament of the government soon to be sworn in, members are asking themselves, "Will I be a minister? Will I be important in this government? Will I have a role to play? What happens if I don't get appointed to the Cabinet? What kind of signal is being sent about me to the public, to my friends, to my family, to the people in the party?" If power is the ultimate prize in our system of government, then the process of organizing to take it over and to manage it effectively is a particularly important element in politics.

And it is always important to remember that even among the newly elected members of Parliament and their supporters there will be many disappointed people once the transition is complete. Put simply, there are too few jobs for the governing members of Parliament and for the party faithful to satisfy everyone. As a result, in the wake of a successful election campaign the prime minister will have to deal with anger, dissension, and pushback from those not included in the leadership team that will govern the country.

Transitions give tangible evidence that power has been effectively transferred from one government to another. In some cases, the power has been returned to a government from the same party and with the same leader, as recently occurred at the federal level with the re-election of Stephen Harper and the Conservative Party and in six provincial elections in the fall of 2011. But regardless of what type of transition we are witnessing, the concept of "power transfer" is very real.[2]

In fact, government transition can occur within three different scenarios. The most frequent type of transition is through an election resulting in a change of the governing political party, either as a majority or minority government. This results in a wholesale change of leadership across all political positions. Alternatively, a transition can take place when an election brings the same government back into power. Although this means the same political party retains power, it will still always result in shifts in individual leadership positions and potentially in the person of the prime minister. The third scenario involves a change in the leader of the governing political party without an associated election. Surprisingly, research has shown that this third type of transition can be the most challenging.

For those who look at politics as a human drama, transitions can be seen typically as the third act in a Shakespearean play. Following this analogy, act 1 ends with the election of the leader of the party after a vigorous leadership campaign, and the second act describes the national election campaign, with election night bringing act 2 to a resounding close.[3]

The transfer of power known as the transition period can take up to eighteen months. It begins in the months leading up to the dropping of the writ and then moves through the election campaign. The transition continues in the days between the electoral victory and the swearing-in of a new government (typically two weeks in Canada), followed by a period of consolidation often characterized as a government's first hundred days. The most intense phase takes place between the tally of the electoral votes and the swearing-in of a new government, generally two weeks in which a new or returning leader has the opportunity to put his or her personal stamp on the government after battling an exhausting election campaign. This is the leader's opportunity to select a new Cabinet and to institute a decision-making system that reflects his or her needs and approach to governing. It is crucial that a leader take control of the machinery of government during this phase and take the first steps towards keeping the commitments that were made during the election.

Regardless of how we define it, power acquisition always occupies the intermediate step towards the ultimate goal to implement, change, improve, make over, transform, or move the ideological dial for a democratically elected government. Those who are afraid to admit they seek power in order to effect change or those who are unwilling to use power in order to accomplish their objectives are going to have great difficulty being effective leaders and, more important, will likely fail to effect much change. Too many political leaders (and their party members) have learned after they have won the leadership of their political party that they have little appetite for exercising power by imposing their vision or will on their political colleagues.

As David Cameron and Graham White have pointed out in their description of the Harris government transition in 1995, a successful transition is inherently a function of extensive and thoughtful preparation.[4] It is the creation and execution of a strategy and the logical sequencing of events. The transition strategy provides a road map – a step-by-step guide – to identify how the leader intends to reach his or her goals. It should serve as the foundation for the relevant players, so that everyone knows what will happen and what is expected of each of them. When things go wrong, as they must from time to time, the transition strategy keeps the team on track as they work towards the swearing-in date.

One characteristic of a newly elected government is that it is rarely ready for the demands and decisions that are required during the post-election period. Tony Blair is one former prime minister who is willing to admit to the difference between being prepared for an election and being prepared to govern. In his 2010 memoir he writes, "When John Major called the election we were ready and waiting. We were ignorant of what lay ahead after we passed the winning post, but we had built up near-irreversible momentum towards it."[5] Blair continues, "The disadvantage of a new government is lack of experience in governing. It is also the advantage. Its very innocence, its immaturity, the absence of the cynicism that comes from perpetual immersion in government's plague-infested waters, gives it an extraordinary sense of possibility. From start to finish I never lost my optimism, self-belief or objective belief in what could be done, but you can never quite recapture that amazing release of energy and boundless 'derring-do' that comes with the election of a fresh team – especially when it comes after eighteen years of one party's rule."[6] The importance of a smooth transition and the ability to demonstrate a capacity to govern effectively in the first months of power cannot be overestimated. The appetite for change will never be stronger, but the challenges are considerable.

In the United States, transition planning is a recognized profession, and experts are routinely employed to transfer power from an outgoing administration to a new one. Many books have been written, and academics have devoted careers to American transition planning. In 1976, Jimmy Carter was one of the first presidential candidates to create a transition office during his national campaign. He experienced no adverse electoral consequences due to the existence of his small transition office in Atlanta, but it did create a "hammer-and-tongs" battle between his transition staff and his campaign staff. Ronald Reagan learned from Carter's lesson and devised a formula that worked well: by giving the ultimate power to a member of your inner circle whose decisions are understood to have your full support, you leave no room for infighting. Unfortunately, Bill Clinton did not learn from the Carter experience, and following his victory in 1992 he presided over a highly acrimonious and poorly executed transition that stands as an example of what not to do when planning a transition.[7]

The 1976 U.S. presidential transition is especially notable for the fact that Carter began transition planning well before election day – indeed, steps were taken shortly after his victory in the Pennsylvania primary, with a major effort commencing at the Democratic Party convention. According to John Burke, "Whatever their particular efforts before the first Tuesday in November, what is accomplished during this period directly bears not only on how quickly the actual transition is up and running after election day but also how smoothly and effectively it will operate."[8]

As Clinton's second chief of staff, Leon Panetta, observed at a 1999 conference on government transitions when asked to discuss transition planning among Democratic presidents, "The sooner you start this process of dialogue, you are hitting the ground running if you're elected, as opposed to starting from scratch. You have to have grown-ups in the

White House. By grown-ups I mean people that have experience, that have been around, that bring a level of stability and management to the operation so that you have a disciplined operation."[9]

In recognition of its importance in the political cycle of a government, the U.S. government passed the Presidential Transitions Act in 1963 to provide funds for transitions when a new president comes into office. "Once there is a president-elect, the transition takes on a formal shape with office space in Washington, funds available for staff, and funding for staff training, as well as monies for the outgoing president. In 2001, the General Services Administration (GSA) was authorized to spend $7.1 million in funding for the presidential and vice-presidential transitions, with $1.83 million for President Clinton's transition out of office, $4.27 million for the transition of President-elect George W. Bush, and $1 million for the GSA to provide additional assistance as was required by law."[10]

For this reason Tony Blair created a transition team led by David Miliband and Jonathan Powell, who worked for six months to prepare for the Labour Party transition. In their view, Blair's lack of experience would make him vulnerable to fast-developing events, so they wanted to be prepared to govern. One important feature of their preparations was to meet occasionally with Cabinet Secretary Robin Butler, with the approval of Prime Minister John Major, to learn about the Westminster system of government and to test the viability of some elements of their election platform.

In Canada, however, the transition experience is limited to a small, relatively secret team of people who work in isolation and away from the public eye.[11] Our media often characterize a political party as reckless if it dares to prepare to take over the reins of government before knowing the outcome of an election. We've created a no-win situation. On the one hand, parties are blamed for being arrogant if they prepare; on the other, they are criticized if they are not ready to govern only days after winning an election. Pre-election transition planning is seen as bad politics: you don't want voters to feel that you are taking them for granted. As a result, transition planning is relegated to the shadows, with little expertise passed on from one team to the next. This book attempts to shine a light on the Canadian transition experience as a contribution to good governance and the responsible management of the affairs of our country.

Typically, political leaders are suspicious of any formal process that prepares them to govern. Those competing to become prime minister have traditionally resisted creating a transition team because they fear being perceived by the public as arrogant if it becomes known that they are overtly preparing to take office. Moreover, they are also sufficiently superstitious about "challenging the election gods" by appearing to take victory for granted in advance of actually winning the election.

It is always difficult to get at the heart and soul of a political issue where the outcomes are played out in the public arena but where the preparatory work is conducted out of the public eye. Given the reluctance of governments-in-waiting to acknowledge that any work is being done on their transition, it is not surprising that there is so little written material on transition preparation. However, secrecy does not explain why former politicians and their senior officials who write memoirs of their time in political office devote so little attention to transition planning or to the actual swearing-in.[12] As mentioned earlier, neither former prime ministers Mulroney nor Martin wrote about the planning for their transitions. Only in *The Way It Works*, Eddie Goldenberg's 400-page bestselling account of his ten years with Jean Chrétien, do we find a detailed accounting of the complex exercise of Cabinet-making.

I suspect the reluctance to write about transition planning is due to three factors. First, the official transition process in Canada is a relatively short event measured by the period of time that follows a hectic five-week election campaign. So much energy and time have gone into the election itself that most political chroniclers have tended to skip over this relatively out-of-sight and politically safe honeymoon period.

Second, the key players are often so exhausted (and at times so incoherent) that they are at a loss to remember the events that took place over the transition period. And third, the heads of transition teams rarely stay to work in the Office of the Prime Minister or Premier, so their attachment to the world of public politics is usually short-lived and episodic. Some are fortunate to head more than one transition team, but they rarely see the role as central to their life's work.

Transitions have received some interest in a number of jurisdictions that are of interest to Canadian scholars and researchers. For example, recent work in the United Kingdom and in Australia has improved our understanding about transitions, especially how they relate to caretaker conventions in a minority government/hung Parliament context. Just as important, transitions in the United States have a very well-developed literature that takes full advantage of the strong interest in the presidency in the academic and business communities and in the think-tank world. Given the characteristics of the presidential system, with its fixed-term mandates and three-month transition periods (from the first Tuesday in November to the third week in January of the following year), there are many first-hand accounts of the American transition process as well as historical analyses of trends in transition planning.

This book asks the fundamental question, "How do aspiring heads of governments in Canada prepare themselves, their advisors, their parties and other constituent parts to take over the reins of power in quick order, and without any disruption to the overall functioning of the nation?"

This is not a book about election preparedness and how to win a national or provincial election campaign. It is also not a "how-to" guide for designing and choosing a Cabinet. And most importantly, it is not a "tell-all" retrospective about who did what to whom. There are already many excellent books written in Canada about how elections have been won and lost, and there is no need to duplicate that work here. Rather it is intended to help political leaders maximize the potential that the transition period offers, with essentially three objectives.

The first is to provide first-time transition planners either working for a political party or the public service in the federal or a provincial government with a primer on "smart" practices based on the experiences of those who have worked on transitions since 1984.[13] The second purpose is to fill a gap in the literature by peeling back the secrecy around the transition process to better appreciate the dynamics that surround transitions in a Westminster system. Finally, the third objective of this book is to make a simple argument: transitions need to be well planned and coordinated on the political and public service side in order to set the stage for the successful launch of a newly elected government.

Given these objectives, the book is intended for a few discrete audiences. First, for political players who one day would like to be involved in a government transition, this book can offer some instances of best practices and some examples of what did not work in during past transitions. A second audience for this book is the thousands of public servants in the federal and provincial governments who must learn to work with an incoming or re-elected government but who have had little experience in this unique exercise. And a third audience for this publication is the academic community and those of the general public who are intrigued with questions about how government works.

I have chosen a rather unconventional approach in writing this book, given the unique opportunity that I had to lead transition teams in 1993, 1997, and 2000. As a result, the chapters were shaped by these experiences, and the structure of the book mirrors the way in which we were organized over those three transitions. However, the strength of the book is derived from the interviews with the key senior public servants and transitions team members of the eleven governments that were elected since 1984. The interviews that were conducted for this publication add a level of detail and elaboration about transition issues that go well beyond storytelling. Those interviewed have all played a significant part in transition planning, and their views represent a wide range of ideological and public management perspectives and a unique opportunity to explore the memories, the briefing materials, and the notes of those who were so intimately involved in such an important stage in governing.

In addition to the published research, I also decided to explore the archival material I had delivered, in my effort to clean out the clutter in my basement and garage, to Library and Archives Canada more than fifteen years ago, as a possible source of information for researchers who might be interested in the efforts that went into the Chrétien transition planning. My purpose in retrieving the materials was particularly to find as many publicly accessible illustrations as possible of how a transition really works.

While I was interested in documenting the characteristics of recent transitions in Canadian politics, I was also determined from the outset to write a book that highlights Canadian smart practices. To that end, I was very fortunate to be able to meet with the key players on the political and public service side in eleven transitions.[14] In all, forty-three one-on-one interviews were conducted and recorded, with more than five hundred pages of transcripts generated from the interviews. The key members of the transition teams for all of the nine general elections and two intraparty leadership changeovers since 1984 were interviewed, and an almost equal number of senior public servants who worked in the Privy Council Office, as deputy ministers, or in other relevant roles over the same period of time. In addition, a meeting was held with six deputy ministers who had worked in various capacities on various aspects of the first Harper government transition.

The book covers mainly transitions in the government of Canada, with references to transitions in Ontario, the United Kingdom, and the United States. These examples describe the activities that take place in large governmental systems and will not necessarily reflect the transition work that takes place in smaller provinces and other Westminster jurisdictions. Generally, "transitions in smaller provinces are far less planned and elaborate than in larger political systems."[15] Provincial governments are less bureaucratic, less paper driven, and rely more on face-to-face interpersonal relations. Moreover, at times the political advisors and senior public servants serve on the transition team, creating an interesting intermingling of political and bureaucratic actors.

As a consequence, the "smart practices" described in this book apply to larger Canadian jurisdictions, since the smaller provinces will not necessarily have the capacity to generate the volume of paper and analysis that characterizes the work of the federal public service. In the absence of a systematic examination of the transition work of small jurisdictions, this book can serve as an example of what is possible when resources are not a constraint.

To round out the information-gathering phase of the study, in the fall of 2010 and the early months of 2011 two seminars were organized at the University of Ottawa with colleagues and former senior public servants who had worked on federal transitions in their previous jobs. As well, in the spring of 2011, another roundtable was convened with Ontario deputy ministers to discuss transition planning in the Ontario government. The intention was to discuss features of the federal government's approach to transition planning and to solicit reactions from the perspective of provincial officials who were themselves preparing for an upcoming transition.

Finally, the Public Policy Forum convened two meetings on the theme of "Government Formation" in Canada. The date of the second meeting, 1 June 2011, was expressly chosen to coincide with a visit to Ottawa of Sir Gus O'Donnell, secretary of the Cabinet and head of the civil service of the United Kingdom. The roundtable was particularly interested in caretaker conventions and the recently released U.K. *Cabinet Manual*, used by the incoming Cameron government.[16]

In summary, the book is based on personal experiences and interviews with key participants since 1984 who have worked on the political side or at a senior level in the federal public service. It has also benefited from a review of the transition literature in the Westminster countries and in the United States that has a very well-developed published tradition regarding transition planning.

The book is organized around the four phases of transition planning, beginning with the pre-election decision to strike a transition team and to prepare materials before the governor general sets the date for the general election, to organizing during the election period, to the tumultuous period between election day and the swearing-in of the government and the final consolidation phase, once the government has been launched.

Specifically, chapter 2 sets the stage for the discussion of government transitions by describing the types and stages of transitions as they occur in the Canadian version of the Westminster system of government. It also explores the role of the key players on the political and public service side of the transition and looks at the psychology and dynamics of transitions from the perspective of the incoming prime ministers and their advisors. The chapter also provides a brief conversation about the role of the media and the current rules at the federal level to regulate behaviour during election campaigns. Further background information about transitions is found in Appendix 2 that analyses the nine Canadian federal elections and eleven transitions that have taken place since Brian Mulroney's 1984 election win.

Chapter 3 describes in some detail the way in which political parties prepare to govern. Given that a change in government with a new prime minister is usually the most transformative of the three transition types, it is the one that receives the most complete coverage in this chapter. Included is an overview of the key decisions to be taken during a transition, a discussion of the need to appreciate the style of the incoming government, especially its leader, the importance of building strong working relationships, the need to create a transition team separate from the campaign team, and the value of determining a strategy for working with the public service. The chapter concludes with a discussion of the role played by the secretary to the Cabinet and the central agencies, the meetings between the public service and the transition teams, and the preparations of briefing materials and mandate letters.

Chapter 4 covers the key elements in a typical transition plan. This includes determining the leadership skills and approach to governing of the incoming (and usually inexperienced) prime minister, Cabinet-making and settling on a workable decision-making process that is designed to take advantage of the characteristics of the prime minister and his style of governing. The chapter also explores the role of the secretary to the Cabinet, staffing the prime minister's and ministers' offices, caucus management, and the appointment process. The chapter also looks at media management and the role of the spouse during a transition.

Chapter 5 provides an overview of the transition activities that take place during the election period by the political parties and by the public service who are working along parallel tracks at this point. In addition to describing the evolutionary nature of the transition exercise, the chapter also looks at the "caretaker conventions"[17] that a number of Westminster countries use.

Chapters 6 and 7 examine the post-election period that leads to the swearing-in of the government. This brief implementation phase – about two weeks in Canada – is especially busy, as the defeated government copes with the effects of the electoral results and the exuberant winners begin to come to grips with the responsibility of governing.

Chapter 6 looks at a number of logistical issues, first meetings with the prime minister–elect, transition teams, and the public service. In addition, this chapter examines the challenges of Cabinet selection, the swearing-in process, staffing considerations, and media relations.

Chapter 7 continues the transition story by describing how key elements in a transition concretize the decisions that were taken around the formation of the Cabinet, the organization and staffing of the Prime Minister's Office, offices of the other members of the ministry, and the appointment process.

Chapter 8 moves past the swearing-in and looks at the first Cabinet meeting, initial meetings with officials, mandate letters from the prime minister, and orientation and training programs for the Cabinet and key political staff.

Finally, chapter 9 concludes with a brief overview of the key findings and observations about the Canadian scene on transition planning and implementation for political parties and the public service. Given the scale of the discussion, it concludes with a series of recommendations on future transition planning in Canada.

2 The Context of Transitions: Setting the Stage

I had an agenda. It was a very smooth transition.

— Frank Press, senior advisor to Jimmy Carter, 1976–80

If you don't know where you are going, you will wind up somewhere else.

— Yogi Berra

Introduction

This chapter captures the elements of a transition plan by first describing the three types of transitions that are possible in the Canadian system and then describes the four phases of the transition process that all transitions are subject to, regardless of the political persuasion or the inclination of the incoming prime minister. This chapter also highlights the importance of the leadership qualities and style of the prime minister and the way in which style interacts with the changing role of political advisors,[1] the clerk of the Privy Council, and the media.

Types of Transitions

Transitions occur within three unique scenarios. The most dramatic transition takes place when a new party wins an election and takes over the reins of power from the outgoing party. The Mulroney Conservatives lived through this experience upon winning the election in 1984, as did the Liberals in 1993 and the Conservatives again in 2006, when the Harper Conservatives won the election. Each of these transitions involved a changing of the guard between the Liberal and Conservative parties. Gordon Ashworth, who served as a political strategist for many Liberal Party elections, feels that this type of transition offers the "most transformative opportunities when there is a real change in government because political parties are not organized to do big things – only government can do that, so the transition represents a chance to start the machinery of change."[2]

The second scenario also occurs as the result of an election, but in this case the governing party remains in power and the leader remains constant. Mulroney's Conservatives won a second mandate in 1988 and Chretien's Liberals succeeded with a second and third mandate in 1996 and 2000. Stephen Harper's Conservative government also transitioned into a second mandate in 2008, governing with a minority during its second consecutive term, followed by a third victory in 2011 in which it won a majority in the House of Commons.

The third transition scenario is characterized by a change in the leadership of the governing party outside of the electoral context. For example, Kim Campbell was chosen as the leader of the Conservatives in 1993 and immediately became prime minister. Similarly, Paul Martin won the leadership contest within the Liberal party in 2003 and led the party into the general election the following year.

On the surface, the re-election of the governing party may not require the same transition discipline as that warranted by a change of government. But in some respects, the transition faced by a re-elected leader can be the more difficult of the two. A new prime minister can build the government from scratch – a blank slate can be intimidating, but the opportunities are endless. However, the re-election victory endorses the performance of the government of the day, which makes it difficult to justify making significant changes. Re-elected parties have often won elections based on a "stay the course" strategy. If ministers have been performing well and the machinery of government is running smoothly, why should a returning prime minister make major changes?

Table 2.1. Types of Transitions

Outcome	Prime Minister	Process
Change in government	New	General election
Re-elected government	Same as before election	General election
Leadership change	New	Leadership convention

Arguably, however, this is the best time to make key changes in personnel and to specific portfolios and by taking advantage of this unique situation to make changes at one time. After an election, the caucus, the media, and the public expect changes, so it is a missed opportunity if the returning government decides to stand pat with their current line-up of ministers without having prepared for this opportunity. So even a re-elected government provides a special opportunity to implement a transition plan, even though there will be great pressure from the current Cabinet members and their staff to maintain the status quo.

Kevin Lynch, the former clerk of the Privy Council, maintains that the transition related to returning governments should be as disciplined as one enacted by a new government, if not more so. But more often than not, a re-elected leader engages in a less rigorous transition exercise with the second electoral victory. "That's the wrong way to operate because you don't renew and rethink," Lynch argues. "You actually, in many ways, get more locked into the status quo when leaders should be taking the opportunity to make a fresh start."[3]

By all accounts, however, transitions within a party have proven to be the most complex to lead and implement. This third type of transition scenario occurs without an election and instead is the result of a leadership race within the governing party. Tim Murphy, who was in the thick of the leadership transition between Prime Ministers Chrétien and Martin, remembers, "There were a lot of odd tensions around, and intense media efforts to get Paul to be in opposition to Prime Minister Chrétien, but those issues were still within Chrétien's bailiwick as prime minister."[4] At what point does the transition of power shift from the sitting prime minister to the leadership contender? No prime minister wants to be seen as a lame duck leader, and the transfer of power necessarily occurs upon the swearing-in of a new prime minister. However, the anticipated transfer of power starts to tear away at the leadership hierarchy of the party, and the leadership scenario can begin to have the appearance of a two-headed monster.

A political party's leadership race develops in an environment that aligns supporters with specific leadership candidates. All members of the party are part of a "family" that presumably subscribes to common values and interests. But in reality, the choice of a new leader necessarily means there are winners and losers within the party. To the Canadian public, the government hasn't changed. But moves that are being made behind the scenes can mean significant promotions and demotions within the caucus. For the elected representatives, a lot is at

---

**Behind the Scenes: Trying to Represent Change during
Intra-Party Transitions**

There was a desire to try to find things that would demonstrate change. Prime Minister Martin introduced a democratization package that aimed to change the role of Parliament, to increase the number of free votes in Parliament, and to reduce the power of the prime minister. This democratization package was developed with the clerk over the transition period. There was also a feeling on the part of the incoming prime minister that he had to have a new-looking cabinet. The very delicate nature of cabinet-making was critical, as many people who had been significant players in the previous administration were now not a part of Prime Minister Martin's plans. Not surprisingly, this made for some very difficult conversations in the days leading up to the new government's swearing-in.

– Mike Robinson, head of the Paul Martin transition, 2003

---

stake, because the success of their careers as parliamentarians hangs in the balance. Ministers who have faithfully executed their duties leading up to a leadership transition can find themselves sitting on the back-benches overnight. As expressed by one former minister, "In the end we are all sacked and it is always awful. It is as inevitable as death following life. If you are elevated, there comes a day when you are demoted. Even prime ministers."[5]

Both Kim Campbell and Paul Martin had the unenviable task of attempting a break from the past while still maintaining a sense of continuity as the government of the day. Again, it is hard to argue that major organizational changes are needed, but the incoming prime ministers like to see themselves as agents of change and, more important, would like the public to see them the same way. The 1993 Conservative leadership race saw Kim Campbell campaigning to "do politics differently," leaving the impression that she intended to make dramatic changes. The leader of her transition team, Jodi White, attests to the challenge this presented: "We were looking for some thoughts on things a new prime minister can do that aren't a total outright denial of the last government and what it was doing. I'm pretty sure it was the public service using the DeCotret report that came forward with proposals that contained many good machinery changes. Reorganization of the machinery of government is a place to go that doesn't repudiate the past policies during an intraparty transition, while still demonstrating a commitment to doing politics differently."[6]

In her short tenure as prime minister, Kim Campbell made wholesale changes to the machinery of her government, reducing the number of departments from thirty-two to twenty-three and restructuring the ministry. Eight departments were newly created or fundamentally redesigned, three received new mandates, and fifteen were merged or broken up. All minister of state positions were terminated and six Cabinet committees were eliminated. In hindsight, White recognizes that "there were a lot of people around Ottawa [in 1993] who thought it [the reorganization] was done too quickly and that we were trying to accomplish too much organizational change."[7] This may have been a case where the need to demonstrate that there was a new leader at the head of the government trumped good public management.

Phases of a Transition

Regardless of the type of scenario at hand, all transitions move through four distinct phases of operation. Phase One sees the leader of a party creating a transition team sometimes months in advance of an election. The focus of this phase is on preparation, and the key task is the creation of the transition strategy and plan that will guide the activities of the party, should an electoral victory occur. This preparatory phase also has parallel activities occurring across the street, so to speak, within the public service. The secretary to the Cabinet will be assessing the leadership scenarios of each party and setting the foundation for a smooth transition, pending an election. The secretary, as a neutral player, has a responsibility and loyalty to the government of the day, but also must prepare for a transition, should a change of leadership or re-election occur. The clerk, at this point, will retain responsibility for transition preparations at an almost personal level. The duty to serve the government of the day remains paramount, and the involvement of other public servants in the preparation phase is generally limited to a few senior leaders who support and advise the clerk.

The planning phase can begin as early as a year before an election and continues until the writ is dropped. The second phase spans the entire electoral period, lasting at minimum thirty-six days, and ends on Election Day. Assuming a transition team has effectively prepared, very little change occurs on the political side of transition planning during an election. The transition team, distinct from the campaign team,

Figure 2.1. Phases of the Transition Process

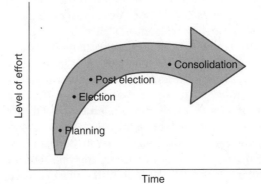

remains behind the scenes, closely monitors changing realities, and continues to move through the necessary activities that will ensure a smooth transition of power.

At this juncture, the public service kicks its transition planning into high gear. The clerk will appoint a team to lead the transition on behalf of the public service writ large, and each deputy minister will also be leading a transition exercise across each department and agency in the government. Regardless of the "expected" outcome of the election (if there is one), the public service will prepare for most eventualities by monitoring the election platforms and promises made by the campaigning parties and assessing their implications for existing operations.

The chances are always good that a new minister will be appointed to a department or agency, and one never knows how much or how little experience this person will bring to the position. It is the question of experience that often marks the starting point for transition preparations across the public service. Politicians who have been in Parliament for many years and who have Cabinet experience understand how a Westminster style of government operates.[8] Graham White explored this issue in greater detail at the provincial level when he analysed the career patterns of 1,375 individuals who held ministerial office in the ten provinces between the mid-1940s and the mid-1990s. His key finding was "the remarkable and most lamentable lack of previous parliamentary experience (especially on the opposition benches) on the part of newly appointed ministers."[9]

This has a direct impact on how the clerk of the Privy Council is able to discharge his or her duties during the transition exercise. Kevin Lynch, serving as clerk to the Harper government, believes that "the transition process is now more complex than in previous years since there are currently fewer experienced politicians being elected."[10] He maintains, "It is a good idea to seek a meeting of minds, in terms of not what a newly elected government does as a government, but actually how it plans to operate."[11]

The "merging of agendas," a phrase used by the late John Tait, the highly respected deputy minister of justice and deputy solicitor general, captures one of the most critical elements of the transition exercise.[12] There is a point, during the end of the planning phase or the beginning of the election phase, when the clerk, with the permission of the prime minister, meets with the transition team of the major opposition parties (i.e., the ones that could form a government in the judgment of the secretary to the Cabinet). Should an opposition party eventually win the election, this single meeting can set the tone for the entire transition exercise and the first months of operations of the government.

At the point where the election results are announced, the post-election phase begins and the transition team takes centre stage in the critical first days following the election. This phase lasts an average of ten to fourteen days in Canada and moves the party through to the swearing-in ceremony and the first days in power. It is an exciting time for the transition team and an exhausting one for the politicians. The process of building a Cabinet is a major preoccupation and it depends to a very large extent on the profile of the MPs from the winning party. Behind the scenes, methods are developed to identify potential Cabinet ministers, judge their suitability for Cabinet, negotiate the swearing-in ceremony with the governor general, set the agenda for the first Cabinet meeting, and prepare the mandate letters for each minister. This brief period also includes the creation of the Office of the Prime Minister and the critical first governor-in-council appointments that have been waiting the arrival of the newly elected government. Proper planning and preparation by the transition team and the leader in advance of the election will ensure Phase Three runs as smoothly as possible.

First meetings are now underway between the clerk, the prime minister–elect, and their respective teams. The deputy minister community is also making last-minute adjustments to briefing books based on the outcomes of the election and are eagerly awaiting the announcement of ministerial portfolios.

Phase Four begins the day after the swearing-in ceremony and the first Cabinet meeting. It runs through the early days of governing and gives the new government an opportunity to consolidate its hold on the levers of power by monitoring the implementation of the transition plan and adjusting it to the reality of governing. The politicians and public servants are now working closely together to ensure that the promises made during the election campaign are being addressed. Ministers are attending orientation sessions, and their ministers' offices are being staffed and trained. The consolidation of power and the ability to effectively govern during these first weeks and months are a direct outcome of a well-prepared transition strategy and the ability to build new relationships between the politicians and the public service.[13]

Most newly elected prime ministers don't realize, or appreciate, how crucial the transition is to their own success. They are exhausted from the election campaign and undoubtedly feel the transition to power is unfolding in a blur. At the same time, they are excited following the win and want to get started as soon as possible. If the newly elected party has been in opposition for a long time, it knows little about governing, and the key players across the political and public service spectrum have had almost no interaction with each other. The learning curve is steep. As the transition unfolds and a new Cabinet is sworn in, experience really does make a difference.[14]

Often an election emboldens the members of a newly elected government into thinking it knows all the answers. After all, what better proof is needed of their political prowess than winning an election? As a general rule, transitions take politicians outside their comfort zone, in part because elections are often a once-in-a-lifetime experience. In reality, party leaders spend the vast majority of their time shoring up support for their leadership and seeking votes and support from the public, with little time or energy left over for transition planning. This behaviour is completely understandable, since a well-prepared transition is irrelevant if they lose the election. But in the event of victory, the period of time between the election and the swearing-in ceremony is very short in Canada, and if the proper planning is not done in advance, a leader will quickly realize that the opportunity for a sure-footed launch into power has passed.

Upon winning an election, the prime minister is faced with an enormous array of decisions that need to be made in a rapid and timely manner. He or she has exclusive jurisdiction over the appointment of the Cabinet and of decisions to change the machinery of government, which need to be made simultaneously. The decision-making process needs to be outlined along with a committee system that will support the work of the Cabinet. To ensure that ministers understand their responsibilities, mandate letters for each minister must be written that describe the prime minister's expectations and the measures that will be used to assess the minister's performance. The organization and staffing of the Prime Minister's Office needs to move forward quickly, along with guidelines for the staffing of ministers' offices. In the days immediately following the election victory, the prime minister also meets with the clerk of the Privy Council, to begin building a new relationship with the public service. All these activities need to be supported by a media strategy, with briefings and announcements made regularly. Since all of them interrelate with one another, the prime minister and the transition team need to give considerable thought to making the transition as seamless as possible.

A well-organized political party will appoint a transition team months in advance of an election. As a general rule, this team will lead the transition exercise from start to finish, with extensive preparations made long before the writ is dropped, although, as we will see in later chapters, some prime ministers have used a double transition team approach. The team will continue to plan the transition through the election period and will lead the execution of the transition plan through to the swearing-in ceremony and the first weeks in power.

Behind the Scenes: Transitions Are Secret

It's very exciting to be involved in a transition, but it's a little like working in CSIS, given the confidentiality of the work. You simply cannot talk about it to anyone. That makes it very hard on the ego – you're working on one of the coolest, most fascinating things and wow, if people only knew. Your ability to maintain confidentiality at all times gets tested regularly, as does your ability to check your ego at the door, because this exercise is not about you.

So when I look back on all the jobs I've had in my career, my work on the transition team has been the most difficult to characterize. As a result, it is the one I've never put on my résumé.

Simone Philogène, staff member of the transition team, 1993

When the transition team is working for a political party that at the outset maintains opposition status, the planning requires a certain amount of delicacy.

As previously discussed, leaders do not want to be seen as taking the outcome of an election for granted. But at the same time, they have a duty to be prepared to govern the country, should the opportunity arise. As a result, a transition team will invest many hours during the months before an election, often in total secrecy and cloaked with the utmost discretion, since there are extensive consultations to carry out and basic research must be completed before the work is done.

Key Players

In effect, the transition exercise revolves around three key participants. In later chapters, other participants will be introduced into the conversation, but at the outset the transition revolves around three kinds of people: the prime minister (or leader of an opposition party), political advisors who may be few or many, depending on the leader's preferences, and the secretary to the Cabinet.

Political Leaders

One of the most important tasks of a transition team is to understand the leadership style of the prime minister. This is the starting point upon which the transition strategy and plan will rest. Developing a generic, off-the-shelf transition plan will fail. The plan must be grounded in the leadership style, approach, strengths, and preferences of the prime minister. And the ability to do this depends on the creation of a transition team that has sufficient time and energy to devote to the task in the months leading up to an election. It will be during these months that the leader can take the time to think through strategy and approach, and to encourage the transition team to reflect this style in the plans for the new government.

This is one of the few occasions that advisors will have the luxury of time to rethink the role of government and chart the course of a new government. For those involved, this is very exciting stuff, since planners are seldom given a blank slate to explore changing the machinery of government. And these debates run in parallel to complex decisions about Cabinet, leadership potential within the party, and the implementation of new policy ideas.

Incoming prime ministers bring with them a particular style and tone to governing that sets them apart from their predecessors and consequently forces the public service to make their own behaviour changes. Leadership style arises from a combination of the leader's personality and ideology, as well as the circumstances and institutional factors that each leader faces.[15] Leadership style is especially difficult for new prime ministers, since "managing the more complex relationship with the electorate that government demands can be one of the most difficult challenges for prime ministers whose leadership style is usually forged in opposition."[16] Or, as the British academic Mark Bennister describes it, individual leadership style is subject to "location, relation, environment and events."[17] As a consequence, most elected officials who become leaders exercise a management and leadership style that is often different from their style as an MP or in an earlier work environment. Leading a government and a political party at the same time and under the watchful eye of the national media places extraordinary demands on individuals and requires them to act in a way that is different from when they were in a more collegial environment.

Experience shows that there is no ideal or perfect leadership style. In large part this is due to the circumstances in which the prime ministers find themselves, coupled with their own management and leadership attributes. As Paul 't Hart notes, prime ministers "need to adapt to the circumstances in which they find themselves – the Cabinet they (partly) inherit, the economic and social circumstances of their era and, importantly, the problems that arise through the behaviour of their Cabinet colleagues. How prime ministers exercise these judgments and how skilfully they use their style vis-à-vis their Cabinet colleagues affect the fates of their governments as well as their own political futures."[18]

Jonathan Powell argues that, on the basis of his observation of Tony Blair and other political leaders, leadership is demonstrated mainly by leaders' "ability to make difficult decisions and [their] willingness to take risks when you can't be certain of the outcome."[19] He also argues that courage and political instincts are not sufficient to make a great leader. He identifies five other necessary skills: competence, the ability to communicate, charisma, perspective, and charm.

In the political arena, competence refers to the leader's ability to act like a CEO, to communicate a vision and a direction for the country, and to demonstrate political skills in moving the policy agenda along. His reference to acting like a CEO suggests that political leaders must possess a sufficient number of management skills like being able to hire employees, to evaluate performance, and to follow a strategic plan. Communication requires constant efforts to inform and to connect with the public, partisans, and colleagues in the House of Commons. It is not necessary that a leader be a great orator. We have considerable evidence in Canada that effective communications is not necessarily matched with strong speaking or writing skills. Jean Chrétien was most effective when he discarded his teleprompter and relied on his well-honed ability to communicate with individual Canadians by speaking directly to them.

In political circles there is a debate on whether political leaders can learn to be charismatic. While this is a complex issue, essentially charisma requires a level of personal charm and an ability to attract attention to oneself and to offer a personality that will attract the active participation of volunteers and garner the affection of partisans. At the very least, politicians must learn to perform in front of large audiences and they must, in the end, be able to communicate a consistent message about the future.

Powell identifies "perspective" as the fourth skill of a successful political leader. Those with this skill are able to see their work in a broader context, to provide a longer-term approach to problem solving, and to appreciate the historical context of the issue under consideration. The fifth attribute of a successful political leader is possession of interpersonal skills that enable the leader to be tough, accommodating, ruthless, and kind when the situation warrants it. Powell further describes it as a Machiavellian trait of having sufficient levels of charm or sinuousness to demonstrate the "fierceness of the lion and all the craft of the fox."[20]

At the conclusion of his analysis, Powell writes, "Great leaders are both born and bred. They need to be brave and endowed with extraordinary political instincts, but they also have to be armed with a range of skills if they want to carry people with them." Drawing on the Machiavellian theme of his book he concludes, "If they are to stay in power they have to have steel in their soul."[21]

Going through the rigours of a leadership campaign and eventually becoming the leader of a political party strengthens an individual's leadership capability. But all leaders will tell you that becoming a leader does not mean that one is ready to manage the party. The victory of winning party leadership demonstrates an ability to guide, inspire, and articulate a vision that others want to support. But managing the party requires a different set of skills and experiences. Management is the ability to move tasks forward, to ensure that teams are working effectively, and to harness the skills and capabilities of the organization to ensure your vision is executed and goals are met or exceeded.

Fortunately for most new prime ministers, they will have spent some time being the leader of the opposition before becoming leader of the country. This period will have allowed them to match their management skills with the organizational needs of their party. Instinctively, leaders implement management practices that mirror their own personalities and cognitive styles and match the characteristics of their own organizations. While few of them are able to articulate their philosophical management principles, they will all make management decisions that are eventually discernible and (hopefully) consistent. It is therefore not surprising to note that almost all recent prime ministers took advantage of their years in the Office of the Leader of the Opposition (OLO) by making substantial changes in the organization of their offices as well as in the personnel. Most observers see the turnover as a reflection of weaknesses in the staff. However, it is more likely to be a reflection of the leaders' attempt to match their management style with the skill set of the senior team.

Chrétien's and Harper's decisions to shake up their respective OLOs and bring in new teams of senior players is clear evidence that they had both come to the realization that the teams that had got them to the top of their parties did not match their needs and their styles as they moved into national campaigns.

I vividly recall Chrétien's decision to seek out Jean Pelletier as his chief of staff in the OLO. In the early years of Chrétien's time as leader of the opposition in 1990 and 1991, he was fighting off allegations from elements in his party, as well as from the media, that he was "yesterday's man." At the same time, he was struggling to build some momentum behind his leadership of the Liberal Party so that he would be ready to combat Brian Mulroney's successor.

He had a remarkably able team of policy advisors and operational people,[22] thanks to the recruiting efforts of Eddie Goldenberg, but the office was not coalescing around a particular purpose or direction. In part, this was because Chrétien was still slowly getting used to his new leadership role, and the staff were also out of sync with his needs and aspirations. Despite being an astute observer of Prime Minister Trudeau's management style around the Cabinet table, he was not totally prepared for the new responsibilities as party leader, since he did not possess any of the levers of a prime minister that he had seen Trudeau successfully use in managing his government.

His initial management style was not perfectly suited to leading a political party. Chrétien had established a well-earned reputation for making tough (and often unpopular) decisions, and prided himself on being able to make them quickly after a reasonable round of consultations. As a general rule, he relied heavily on the advice of his few advisors, whom he trusted to present all the relevant facts in order for him to make a decision. Over the years, he had developed a strong bond of trust with his staff, but he was also very mindful of their strengths and weaknesses and was always aware that the personal interests of the messenger can sometimes contaminate advice. Since biases are inherent in advisory positions, Chrétien always sought to hire people who had reputations for being "smart" and were interested in evidence as the basis for policy advice. He was not particularly interested in ideological or partisan people, since he preferred to do the politics himself, leaving the policy work to his staff.

In those critical months in early 1991, Chrétien concluded that he needed a "quarterback" for his core team. As a result, we began a systematic search for a chief of staff who would complement his management style and integrate the talents of his individual staff into a team-oriented working environment. The hiring of Jean Pelletier, a former college classmate of Chrétien's, journalist, and Quebec City mayor, rounded out the senior management team that would essentially remain in place for the ten years that Chrétien was prime minister. In Gilbert Lavoie's biography, he describes the difficult time Pelletier had in deciding to accept Chrétien's offer of joining his former classmate in Ottawa as his chief of staff. Pelletier recalls, "Il m'a téléphoné, disant qu'il voulait me voir. Il m' demandé de venir à Ottawa diriger son bureau de chef de l'opposition. J'ai pris cinq semaines avant de lui donner une réponse. Pour moi, c'était une très grosse décision."[23]

In appointing Pelletier to chief of staff, Chrétien found someone who appreciated his hands-off management style and who had sufficient experience as a manager in his own right to bring a new focus on the policy agenda to the Office of the Leader of the Opposition.[24] For someone who did not tend to shower public praise on his staff, Chrétien often pointed out the important role that Pelletier played in his own success as prime minister. Lavoie captured this sentiment very well when Chrétien was quoted as saying about the arrival of Pelletier in the Office of the Official Opposition, "C'est peut-être la journée la plus importante dans ma carrière quand il est venue, parce ce que j'avais besoin de quelqu'un d'autorité."[25]

The relationship and interaction between the leader and the chief of staff are critical, but not the only reflection of the style of government and leadership that will come together around the prime minister. Style is also reflected through choices made in the creation of the Cabinet system and through relationships between the prime minister and ministers, and with the public service. With Chrétien, we created a governing infrastructure that was tailored to his approach and style. He preferred a small Cabinet with a minimum of meetings, and a general orientation that was orderly, professionalized, and decentralized. Chrétien also reformed the Cabinet committee system, shifting the balance of power away from the public service so that it was squarely in the hands of the ministers. The committee system enabled ministers to stay on top of departmental activities and to be engaged in decision-making. Jean Carle, Chrétien's first head of operations in the PMO, recalls that Chrétien's experience as a minister influenced him in defining a decentralized system. Carle also remembers that Chrétien felt strongly that "you had to earn your way into positions of authority. There would be no witch hunts against conservative appointees. It would take awhile to implement the government's agenda, and it was crucial to build a partnership with the public service."[26]

Lawrence Martin captures the contrast between the leadership styles of recent prime ministers in his 2010 book, *Harperland*.[27] In it, he notes that the Prime Minister's Office under Chrétien could be heavy-handed on particularly sensitive or crucial issues but also gave senior ministers considerable independence to carry out their departmental mandates. He trusted his ministers to carry out their responsibilities and bothered them only if they got into trouble. Don Boudria, who served as a Cabinet minister under Chrétien, said, "He was very clear what he wanted accomplished, but that was the end of it, to the point where you were wondering sometimes, 'Am I doing this right?' He would never tell you anything. You were kind of craving some feedback."

In the case of Paul Martin, Lawrence Martin describes his management style as "flat, lacking in hierarchical discipline."[28] Cabinet meetings were chaotic, and there was no attempt to bring issues to a point where decisions were made and responsibilities allocated. Sometimes

Martin "would try to exercise some authority by pounding the gavel on the table. He sometimes pounded so hard that Emerson thought he was going to break it. But order was still slow in coming."[29]

Before Chrétien, Mulroney ultimately adopted a similar approach to managing his office after a few years of learning the ropes and replacing his chiefs of staff on a number of occasions. Reports from this era show a hands-off attitude and a trust that his ministers were capable of managing their own affairs. Lawrence Martin provides an example of this approach with regards to handling of negative press reports: "If a story broke and shit was flying in the paper, you might get a call saying [from the Prime Minister's Office], 'What the hell's going on?' So we'd give them the background and they'd say, 'Okay, you guys deal with it.'"[30] Those who had been a part of the Conservative government in the late eighties and early nineties noticed a significantly different style when Harper moved into the leadership of his newly merged party. His approach has been to centralize all policy work, especially the communications apparatus, and to limit the influence of his ministers on individual files in their own areas of responsibility.

Harper is an interesting example of how circumstances and personality define the leadership style of the leader. Before becoming prime minister, Harper learned his leadership skills as a member of Parliament, as the head of The National Citizens Coalition, a national interest group whose primary purpose is achieve "more freedom for less government," and in the mail room and computer systems department of a Canadian multinational oil company.

The interaction of personality and circumstances in defining Harper's leadership style is difficult to characterize. However, it appears that he learned a lot from his days in opposition, as a number of those interviewed for this study mentioned that during Harper's early months as prime minister he would ask how Chrétien might deal with a particular situation, since he felt that they shared similar management styles – decisiveness, a reliance on a small number of advisors, an interest in getting at the facts, and a stubbornness to stick with a decision once it is rendered.

Derek Burney, the leader of Harper's transition team in 2006, feels that Harper's majority government victory in the May 2011 election will allow Harper to shift his style of governing away from the tightly controlled management style that characterized his first five years as prime minister to a more inclusive manner that brings the public service into the policy tent:

I don't want to hear any more crap about minority government and politics every day. Now is the time for ideas. If you guys have got them, you
better stand up and express them, because this is a government that is
going to be a little more receptive to good policy ideas than it was when
it was looking over its shoulder because it didn't know whether it's got a
three-month life or a six-month life.

You don't get out of a mindset like a minority parliament overnight. It's
going to take time, and the challenge is going to be for the senior bureaucrats to stand up and come forward with some ideas. How many times
have you heard, "They don't want to listen to us – their focus is on politics"? And I'm saying, "OK, I've heard that now for five years, guys. Get
over it. Now you've got a majority government. Make it work."[31]

Evidence suggests there is no ideal leadership style. Prime ministers
need to adapt to the circumstances in which they find themselves – the
Cabinet they lead, the economic and social circumstances of their era,
and, importantly, the problems that arise through the behaviour of their
Cabinet colleagues. How prime ministers exercise these judgments and
how they use their style vis-à-vis their Cabinet colleagues affects the
fates of their governments as well as their own political futures.

In the end, prime ministers' decisions are the product of their own life
experiences and the benefits that they can derive from both their political and public service advisors. As Richard Neustadt often reminded
newly elected American administrations, "All new presidents are vulnerable to arrogance and ignorance, their own and that of their associates."[32] As a consequence, given the considerable potential for failure,
transition experts such as Wellford delivered a well-developed man-
tra for new transition teams: "Good planning, organization, focus, and
discipline, taking their cues from the best practices of past transitions,
strongly supported by the nominee/president-elect, blessed with a little luck, can greatly increase the chance of success."[33]

Political Advisors during the Transition Period

The rise of political advisors (or exempt staff)[34] as permanent actors
within the machinery of government is well documented across a
broad spectrum of OECD countries. They are here to stay, representing one of the most widespread developments in governance in years.
Typically, they are young, relatively inexperienced, and not very
knowledgeable about how government works and the challenges of

working in a public bureaucracy, but they are loyal to their minister and partisan in their approach to their work. They have wide-ranging responsibilities: they prepare correspondence, write speeches, communicate with constituents and citizens, deal with legislation, advise on policy, coordinate the minister's work and activities with the PMO and, most of all, connect with the public service at all levels within the minister's portfolio.

Two features of political advisors distinguish them from public servants. First, they are hired directly into a prime minister or minister's office at the pleasure of a minister – bypassing the merit-based approach used for entry into the public service – and their jobs are terminated when the prime minister or minister leaves office or when their services are no longer required. They owe their position in the government to the minister and to the political party in power, without whose support they cannot function in their job and cannot hope to progress in their career as political advisor. Before the passage of the Federal Accountability Act (FAA) in 2006, political staffers were entitled to join the permanent, nonpartisan public service on a priority basis once their partisan days were over and they had worked for three years in a minister's office. Since the passage of the FAA, that route has been effectively closed off, as has moving into private sector government-relations work, which is no longer allowed under the act.[35]

The second defining feature of political advisors is that they also provide their minister with political, partisan, and policy advice on issues of the day. As a result of their closeness to the minister and the important role they play in advising him or her on a wide range of issues, it is easy to recognize that they are a vital part of modern government. As Tony Blair pointed out in defending the important role of advisors in his ten-year tenure as U.K. prime minister, "They bring political commitment, which is not necessarily a bad thing; they can bring expertise; and properly deployed, they interact with and are strengthened by the professional career civil servants, who likewise are improved by interaction with them."[36]

According to Peter Aucoin, the growth of the modern political advisor in Canada began in the 1950s:

> Until that point, ministers functioned with a modest personal office in which almost all exempt staff were clerical. Incremental growth occurred in both ministers' offices and the Prime Minister's Office (PMO) through the next two decades. The total number of political or exempt staff for the

government grew with an expansion in the number of ministers in the 1960s, and in the 1970s the number of authorized staff in ministers' offices went from five to 12. By 1990–91 there were 490 exempt staff, of which 99 were in PMO. Following the election of a new government in 1993, the total number of political staff diminished to 427 (with 76 in PMO) in keeping with the working environment of the day. But by the end of the decade, the numbers had grown again up to 525, with 80 inside PMO and an increase of almost 100 across ministers' offices. The number of political advisors has stayed relatively steady over the past eight years but with a notable increase of advisors in PMO – 93 as of 2007.[37]

The nature of the relationship between a minister and political advisor is unique, with the result that there is no universal definition of responsibilities. In each case, the job's parameters are developed at the discretion of individual ministers. In practice, however, the functions of political advisors tend to fall into well-defined areas: advise on political issues, develop or comment on policy options, maintain relationships with other political actors, and assist in communications and media strategy.

With increases in the number of political advisors have come increased concerns about their role, the nature of their accountability, and their impact on the relationship between the public service and political leaders. At the heart of this concern is the recognition that political advisors can exert significant influence over political leaders. As their numbers grow, political observers and citizens alike need to understand how this paradigm shift affects good governance.

When they operate with transparency and in a cooperative manner with the public service, political advisors have the potential to strengthen the functioning of government. Under the right circumstances they can assist policy development by viewing the policy proposals coming from the public service through a political lens. They can also shield the public service from being pressured to undertake political functions on behalf of ministers and they can strengthen a minister's ability to manage complex political dynamics. All of these benefits build on a model of good governance if there is a respectful relationship between the advisors and the public service.[38]

But with advantages come the potential for weaknesses. The challenge is to embrace the benefits that political advisors bring to the table while minimizing possible vulnerabilities. In reality, there are concerns that political advisors have contributed to a growing separation between the public service and political leaders by seeing the public service as non-supportive of the government's agenda and defining their role as implementers as opposed to policy generators. This unease is heightened in the case of minority or unstable coalition governments or where political advisors act as gatekeepers, controlling access to a minister.[39]

The fact that the OECD has recently noted the growing importance of political advisors underscores the magnitude of the relentless changes taking place in most Western democratic countries, towards a larger role for political advisors at the expense of the public service.[40] In his 2010 memoir, Tony Blair often refers to the important role played by his staff: "They were an unusually talented group of people. The thing I liked most about them? They defied category. They were one-offs. Very normal but not very conventional. Very human; and with that touch of a magic potion that distinguishes those who strive from those who merely toil; those who take life as it comes and goes to live life like an adventure."[41]

Cabinet Secretaries

The second set of players that will have a tremendous impact on the success of a prime minister is the senior public service, particularly the secretary to the Cabinet, who is traditionally a career public servant chosen by the prime minister to serve as the focal point of his dealings with the vast public service. For a new prime minister, previous experiences with the public service and an overall appreciation of its traditional role in Canada will help to define the nature of the relationship.

For example, Jean Chrétien's acknowledged respect for the public service was forged early in his career as a young parliamentary secretary to the minister of finance, Mitchell Sharp. Chrétien acknowledges this in his first book: "I got to know such great public servants as Bob Bryce, Louis Rasminsky, Simon Reisman, and Edgar Gallant. They were men of long experience, with brilliant minds and great integrity, who shunned intrigues and the cocktail circuit in order to dedicate themselves to the public good. They always made me feel welcome among them, they were extremely patient and helpful, and I felt that the education was better than in a university."[42]

It is an understatement to say that the relationship between the prime minister and the cabinet Secretary is complex. Traditionally the secretary to the Cabinet aspires to become the prime minister's most trusted advisor, especially in policy matters. However, for a number of reasons, the prime minister does not always reciprocate this level of personal intimacy. First, while the secretary to the Cabinet is focused on serving only the prime minister, the prime minister has multiple sources of influence, especially the chief of staff and party apparatus, with which he or she interacts regularly. It is therefore important that the prime minister establish early on in their working relationship how he intends them to interact, so there is no room for misunderstanding.[43]

Kevin Lynch has summarized succinctly the role of the secretary to the Cabinet / clerk of the Privy Council Office:

As a starting point, the clerk's job is to support the prime minister as the most senior advisor to the prime minister from the public service side, and to provide input on the machinery of government issues, where the machinery options should always be viewed as the means to achieve an end and not the end itself.

Part of the job of the clerk is to understand, from both the platform and early meetings with the prime minister, what he or she wants to achieve at the end of their mandate. It is then the task of the clerk to use the public service to assist the prime minister in achieving this end in a non-partisan way.

In terms of the transition needs, the first common-sense step is to help set up the government according to the wishes of the prime minister by providing an interface between the public service and the political side – machinery, cabinet, cabinet committees, etc. It is crucial to have a clear understanding at the beginning about how deputy ministers and ministers should intersect, how the PCO and PMO should intersect, and how the clerk and the prime minister should operate together.

If you don't get these relationships right at the beginning, it will make running the government very difficult in the future.

It is especially important that ministers know that their public servants are there to give them their best advice, but that the decisions are still made by elected officials.

An important further point to raise with the prime minister is that he must be assured (and he must believe) that public servants will implement any decision the government makes, even if it is contrary to the advice they have given. To encourage a worthwhile dialogue between the politicians and the public service, it is important to establish early on that it is not disloyal to disagree with a minister or to advise against a preferred course of action. The government should welcome diverse and sometimes contrary views in exchange for loyal implementation. This process needs to be clear. If it starts to muddy, there will be confusion on everyone's roles and responsibilities.

In addition to providing policy advice, the public service is responsible for managing a broad range of programs. What managerial issues does the prime minister want to address while in government? How can the government become more efficient and effective? What administrative changes would you like to make?[44]

The Media

In any democratic environment, the media play a critical role in enabling citizens to access information. The media can help them make informed choices and can serve as a form of check and balance to elected representatives. At times, an antagonistic relationship between the media and government can support a healthy, well-functioning democracy. In other times, tension between the media and politicians or public servants can be detrimental. In both cases, the media can and should ensure the government is held to account for statements that are made, claims that may prove to be false, and promises that need to be kept. Without a doubt, the media have acquired the status of political actors or institutions. The government of the day is now required to make a continuous and systematic effort to win the attention of the media. This is not pursued as an end in itself but as a necessary step in gaining the attention and support of the wider public.

While the media do not have a direct role in transition planning, it is obvious that any media attention paid to transitions will have some impact on the work of the transition team. As any casual observer of social change will know, the media are undergoing a dramatic transformation in the way they report the news and the way in which the industry is structured.

This is not the place to muse on the future of the news media in Canada. But a few observations about political reporting might provide some insights into the work of transition teams.

The media as an expression of the public interest has been a topic of considerable discussion in the United Kingdom. It has been concern of politicians and policymakers that the media, collectively, threaten the public good. In 2010, the Institute for Government convened a series of roundtable discussions about the impact of the media on political institutions. They concluded, "There is an uneasy stalemate between policymakers and the media, with the public serving largely as spectators."[45]

They also noted that the media can set the parameters of how the public perceives the competence of a newly elected government. In 2004, Paul Martin's transition team decided to use the media to communicate to Canadians that the Martin team was well prepared to govern. Unfortunately for them, the media chose to highlight the connections that the transition-team members had with the lobbying community. So instead of communicating professionalism and preparedness, media reports highlighted Martin's close association with lobbyists and large corporations.

Research also shows an increasing tendency towards personalization in politics, focused on the popular appeal of the leaders of each party. The media have contributed to this trend by adopting a personality-centric approach to the coverage of politics and electoral campaigns. This has led to an assumption that leaders with engaging media personalities have a direct effect on voting behaviours. However, studies continually show that elections are decided only rarely on the performance and electoral appeal of an individual leader.[46] Although the prevailing view is that the media enhance the standing of the prime minister, in reality the media have typically the opposite impact by diminishing the standing of political leaders over time. Moreover, the current media landscape with the multiplicity of news sources and hundreds of distribution channels that are mediated through an entertainment lens has reduced politicians' ability to influence the public.[47]

Traditionally, transition teams have avoided the media and have done most of their work behind closed doors, both in preparation for their transition work and in the post-election period. In 1993, Jean Chrétien convened a press conference immediately after the election on 25 October to introduce the head of his transition team and to answer questions about his immediate plans to reconvene Parliament. This brief exposure to the media is more typical of the way in which transition teams interact with the media in Canada.

All players within the transition scenario need to be mindful of the role of the media within the democratic system. While managing the media will continue to be difficult as more journalists learn to appreciate the importance of transitions, leaders will need to carefully consider and build a media strategy to support transition activities rather than hide behind a wall of silence that has normally accompanied federal transitions. The sequencing of events, particularly between the election results and the swearing-in of a new Cabinet, is a period of intense activity where anonymity and secrecy facilitates the whole process. The ideal time for establishing a solid working relationship with the media occurs during the days immediately following the swearing-in, where the leader and the key players within the political party have the opportunity to provide some insight into the style and characteristics of the newly elected government.

Conclusion

Since 1957, at the federal level in Canada, there have been eight minority governments and eleven majority governments, many of them the result of a change in government. Given the unpredictability of election results and their relatively close outcomes, there is no good reason to plan a transition based on a specific outcome. Given the tenuous hold that parties have over the electorate, the first two phases of the transition planning cycle should be completed without too much attention paid to the likely outcome and whether the election will result in a minority or majority government.

Obviously, the post-election phase is centred on the election results, including a minority or majority situation where the basic consideration is whether the government will try to govern as if it has the support of Parliament or will orchestrate its own defeat in the House of Commons and appeal to the electorate to reward it with a majority government to overcome the dysfunctional effect of a minority government. One certain result of the relative frequency of minority governments is that there are more transitions to prepare for and there is more uncertainty and tension within the transition teams during the planning phases and the execution of transition phases.

Related to the frequency of minority governments has been the emergence of the "permanent election" campaign in which political parties have adopted campaign strategies and techniques continuously to gain political advantage over their opponents. This is particularly true during periods of minority government when the government and opposition parties are in a constant election mode in the event of a sudden election call. To support the permanent campaign are "professional" political managers, who are increasingly evident in Canada as the political parties, and especially the Conservative Party, are hiring more staff on a permanent basis to prepare for elections.

This chapter started with a description of the three types of transitions in Canada followed by an overview of the four phases that to a degree accompany all transitions. Much of the remainder of the chapter discussed the elements of political leadership and management style to sensitize the reader to the wide variation in style and the obvious impact that it has on political advisors, on the public service through the clerk of the Privy Council, and on the media, who have the responsibility to report on the transition activities of an incoming government. To this point, the key political advisors to the incumbent government and the opposition parties are doing all the thinking about the transition. The public service has not yet been engaged, and the membership of the transition team takes on life as the decision point to create the transition team draws closer. The remaining chapters in this book elaborate on the four phases and detail how transition planning is typically undertaken at the national level in Canada by transitions teams, regardless of political persuasion.

3 Pre-Election Phase:
Kick-Starting the Transition

By failing to prepare, you are preparing to fail.

– Benjamin Franklin

Make the best use of what is in your power, and take the rest as it happens.

– Epictetus, Greek philosopher (55–135)

Leadership is getting the right people to do the right thing for the right reason in the right way at the right time with the right use of resources.

– Anonymous

Introduction

The pre-election planning phase begins with the politicians and the public service building two parallel processes to support the transition. Ultimately, the politicians or party officials of the transition team lead, but the secondary role of the public service is pivotal to ensuring a smooth and effective transition following an electoral victory.

As previously discussed, there are four phases to a transition: pre-election, election period, post-election, and consolidation. In the pre-election period, there is limited contact between the transition exercise being undertaken by politicians and that being developed by the public service. But as time progresses, the two sets of players merge their agendas and begin to work together, overcoming obstacles, and, if all goes well, developing a mutually trusting relationship.

The purpose of the pre-election phase is to develop a plan that maximizes the opportunities presented to a newly elected government while seeking ways to reduce the hazards that inevitably lie in wait.[1] The risk of making serious mistakes that might undermine a new government's effectiveness increases for parties that have been in opposition for many years and have had little experience as governing parties.

This is the time for creativity, the time to grasp the opportunity to cast the net as widely as possible – to look at new ways of managing government and to enlist a diverse range of knowledgeable people to explore innovative ideas. This is a particularly good time to examine developments in some of the OECD countries, but especially in countries comparable to Canada: the United Kingdom, Australia, and the United States.

This phase also provides the transition team with an opportunity to do some "head-hunting" for possible staff for the Prime Minister's Office and for ministers' offices. Depending on the size of the Cabinet, the staffing requirements for exempt staff are in the range of five hundred people, so it is never too early to identify talent.

This phase is, of course, particular to each transition, whether to a returning government or a newly elected one. Each transition is affected by intersecting events and situations that require attention. However, whatever the circumstances, each involves a number of steps and actions, dictated largely by the requirements of our Westminster system.

Transition Team

There is no hard and fast rule for when transition planning should start. Some political parties have begun the transition process more than eighteen months before the general election. Others, especially in provincial politics, only after a surprise win on election-day. The right timing is dictated by the likelihood of winning the election, the level of interest in new directions, and the confidence that the key players around the leader have in the value of the transition exercise.

Most newcomers to the transition game discover they are busier than they had anticipated. As mentioned earlier, I began the work on the Chrétien transition almost a year before the general election, and I had organized our first transition meeting more than nine months before the actual election. Given that the transition work involved a good deal more than Cabinet formation and the swearing-in ceremony, there was sufficient work to keep the core team very busy all this time.

The pace of work and the degree of enthusiasm for the exercise will depend to a large extent on external factors. In particular, the public opinion polls will dictate the rhythm of the work. When the polls are favourable and predict a majority government, the leader is usually keen on thinking about post-election issues. When they are discouraging, it is very difficult for the transition team to advance its work with much enthusiasm, although political veterans will always point to examples of fickle public opinion and counsel that a good election campaign can change voting intentions.

As mentioned earlier, Chrétien built a transition team over the course of a year in advance of the anticipated 1993 general election. Paul Martin did so six months in advance of the Liberal leadership convention. Mike Robinson, who headed up Martin's transition planning team, remembers responding quickly to Martin's impatience to be ready by organizing a series of meetings at his farm in the summer of 2003, with Jack Austin and Arthur Kroeger in attendance.[2] According to Robinson, "This core team met fairly early on with Paul, who had some strong ideas about what he did and didn't want to do once he became prime minister. Among his convictions was his strong desire to create a larger Cabinet, to give a more substantial role to parliamentary secretaries, and to keep as many people happy as possible."[3]

The first evidence that I have on preparations for a Chrétien's 1993 transition is a series of memoranda between August and October 1992 that circulated among John Rae, Eddie Goldenberg, and Jean Pelletier. In October 1992, I met with the three of them to set the transition work in motion by settling a number of planning issues. The agenda for the meeting was:

- To discuss a framework for a transition plan;
- To identify activities along a critical path for an election in 1993;
- To identify people to interview who could inform the transition exercise;
- To create the transition team

  - Structure
  - Frequency of meetings
  - Membership

- To discuss deliverables;
- To develop a budget to facilitate the delivery of a transition document, of approximately 200–300 pages, by March 1993.

Later in the fall of 1992, I met with Tom Axworthy, former principal secretary to Prime Minister Trudeau, who emphatically argued that "transition should be part of the prudent planning to take over." He also provided some transition advice by arguing that "the undue power of chiefs of staff and lobbyists should end. We must lower the partisan element in government and special efforts must be in government to distinguish between lobbying which is ok and influence which is not." He also initiated the important discussion about the appropriate relationship of the public service with politicians by arguing that "the PMO is not to serve as a parallel bureaucracy but as a coordinating function." As a result, he suggested that the transition team "make contact with PCO right away" in order to establish a good working relationship.[4]

Over the past twenty years, each prime minister has reached out to a select group of individuals to take on the responsibility of planning the transition. The planning period allows a party to thoughtfully discuss and debate issues they will face upon assuming leadership of the nation. A disciplined and strategic approach to the planning period will ensure that the hectic days following an election victory will run smoothly and to maximum benefit for a new leader, according to more than forty people who were interviewed for this study.

The transition team meetings are discreet and held behind closed doors, leading one to wonder how these people come to be asked to serve in such a capacity. A look back to the Mulroney era and through to our current prime minister reveals that most individuals who are chosen to lead the transition exercise already know the leader well and, as former public servants, academics, or lobbyists, have a good knowledge of how government works.[5] It may come as a surprise to know that these people are not particularly partisan, but they do bring to the position political instincts that allow them to appreciate the full ramifications of their work.

Chrétien was a case in point. He was never particularly interested in hiring hyper-partisans to work directly for him, although he did recognize the need for people who understood politics. Since his cognitive style was attuned to interpreting every policy issue from a political perspective, as a general rule he preferred to do the political triaging himself, without staff filtering the issues for him. As a result, he hired staff who had had a strong interest in policy in addition to politics.

Carle remembers having conversations with Chrétien in 1992 about his expectations of the work of his transition team. He recalls Chrétien saying, "The transition team must be very credible to the party and to the public service. In the early days of a new government they have to act like ambassadors so their integrity cannot be questioned. They also must be experts, act in a statesman-like manner, have diplomatic skills and exercise good judgment." The transition is not a partisan exercise. If you are too partisan, it will bite you. As a result, the transition team needs to have some distance from the campaign, since the objectives are so different.[6]

When asked how he came to be the leader of Mulroney's transition team preparing for the 1984 election, Bill Neville, who had been at the Canadian Imperial Bank of Commerce at the time, and already known Mulroney, recalled, "I had been Clark's chief of staff, so I'd been through a transition, if you will, and there weren't many Tories around who had been. We hadn't been in government very often in that generation. And early on – even before the campaign started, anyway – I wrote the odd speech for Mulroney when I was at the bank, just as a favour. And he asked me if I would help take a look at the transition thing and get something organized quietly."[7]

Interestingly, Neville remembers that Mulroney also gave a similar assignment to Eric Nielsen. "Typical Mulroney, eh? He loved to give two people the same job and usually not even tell the other person so that he could get different points of view. Nielsen had this thing going as well as I did, but in the end I continued on with transition planning until after the 1993 election."[8]

When it came time for Harper to find a transition team leader in 2005, he chose Derek Burney, who at the time was teaching at Carleton University. Harper's chief of staff called to ask him to head up the transition team, but unfortunately, also notified Burney that Harper had already appointed two people to the team. Burney knew one of the nominees, so he immediately refused the offer.

Undeterred, Burney recalls Harper, to his credit, trundling all the way to Carleton from Parliament Hill to meet with him in his tiny library cubicle of an office. Burney explained to him, "Well, I'm a bit like you – if I have a team, I want to pick the members of my team!" Harper assured him he could pick anyone he wanted to join the team. "But," as Harper reminded Burney, "you have to understand I'm trying to satisfy the factions of the party. It's still a new party and I need as many people inside the tent as possible." Eventually the two came to a mutually satisfactory agreement and Burney began the process of building his team.[9]

Once a transition leader is chosen, it is up to him or her to build a cohesive team that can serve the leader through to an eventual victory at the polls or at a leadership convention. The team members are most often engaged because of their specific skills, including the ability to develop and formulate public policy, an understanding of the public service and the machinery of government, political strategy and communications, as well as experience at the centre of government.

One recruit targeted by Burney for Harper's transition team was Elizabeth Roscoe. She had served on Mulroney's transition team in 1984 and at the time had helped implement the newly designed chief of staff positions in ministers' offices. With this background, in addition to serving as a chief of staff for four years in the Mulroney government, Roscoe was asked by Burney to join the team. Accompanying her were Bruce Carson, Ian Brodie (Harper's chief of staff in the opposition leader's office), Ray Speaker, Peter Burn, and Maurice Archdeacon.

In the wake of the Commission on the Sponsorship Program, Harper was preoccupied with developing a regime that would make government more accountable and less influenced by lobbyists. As a result, the composition of the first Harper transition team, as it had for Martin, attracted some unwelcome attention from the media once it was known who was serving on the team. Unfortunately, Roscoe's status as a registered lobbyist made her a target for those who were looking for more distance between the incoming government and the interest group and lobbying community. While the issue had the potential to undermine the credibility of the transition work, Roscoe's reputation for professionalism diffused a difficult situation that could have derailed the whole operation.

In 1993, Jean Chrétien decided to use a two-group approach for his transition planning. The first group was assembled to prepare the groundwork for a government transition by helping him learn about the changes that had taken place in government during the almost ten years of Conservative government (Mulroney and Campbell) and preparing him for the fiscal reality that his government would face if he won the general election.

The mandate for this group was:

- To make recommendations to the leader of the opposition on the organization and structure of the federal government, should he become prime minister after a general election, which would be held sometime in 1993;
- To make recommendations about all other matters normally associated with the transition from serving in the role of opposition to that of governing;

- To discuss with the leader of the opposition the strengths and weaknesses of major transition issues;
- To prepare a transition book.[10]

The group comprised Shelley Ehrenworth, president of the Public Policy Forum; Judith Maxwell, president of the Canadian Policy Research Network and former president of the Economic Council of Canada (which had been disbanded by the Mulroney government in an earlier budget); Dan Gagnier, former senior executive in the federal government with special expertise in federal-provincial affairs and then vice-president at Alcan (and later chief of staff to Jean Charest); and Donald Savoie, professor of public management at the Université de Moncton and frequently published author on the evolving role of central agencies at the federal level. Simone Philogène, who was working with me at the time in my consulting work, served as a most capable note-taker for the meetings.

None of the members, at the time, had ties to the Liberal Party but they all had a passion for good government, and they were willing to provide their expertise. Because of their long-standing interest in these crucial policy issues, they accepted my offer to become part of the planning group for a Chrétien government.

We met regularly during 1992 as a "no-profile" group to prepare for a couple of face-to-face meetings with Chrétien.[11] Knowing his strong preference for short briefing materials, we sent two-page notes to him every few weeks, covering the key economic and social changes taking place in Canada at that time. We had seen how the 1991 Aylmer Conference had challenged Chrétien to provide solutions to looming deficit and debt problems and to rethink the role of government in an increasingly competitive and global economy.

The agendas for the nine meetings of the transition team that first met on 11 November and completed their work in October of 1993 indicate that each of the meetings lasted two hours and Chrétien attended twice, although he received the minutes from each meeting. In the end, more than a hundred people were interviewed for the transition book, including former Liberal and Conservative federal and provincial politicians, former political staff from the three major parties, Liberal and Conservative senators, and retired public servants. In addition, we conducted an extensive review of the published transition literature in Canada, the United Kingdom, and the United States.

Chrétien created the second transition group the night before the general election on 25 October 1993. I had travelled to Lac des Piles near Shawinigan for a meeting with him, to discuss final plans for the transition. At that point, after almost a year of planning, he had decided on the structure and size of his Cabinet, the Cabinet committee system, the Cabinet selection process, and the content of the orientation program for the Cabinet, and he confirmed how he planned to work with the public service and the secretary to the Cabinet, and finalized plans for his move to 24 Sussex Drive.

That evening, he informed me of the people he wanted on his second transition team. As usual, he had given it a lot of thought, seeking to balance the interests around the table so that no single person or set of interests would skew the advice. Being particularly sensitive about seeking the advice of people who had substantive knowledge about an issue, but who did not have a personal stake in the outcome or stood to gain by it, he chose eight people drawn from two different lists of potential members. The first group was chosen from a list of individuals who were not interested, for a variety of reasons, in moving into the PMO after the election, but had a strong interest in Chrétien's success as a prime minister. These included Gordon Ashworth, Joyce Fairburn, Ross Fitzpatrick, John Rae, and myself as the chair of the committee. The second group, most of whom had worked in the Office of the Leader of the Opposition, would form the nucleus of the PMO and would have to live with the consequences of the decisions taken during the post-election and consolidation phase of the transition. This group included Jean Pelletier, Peter Donolo, Chaviva Hosek, Penny Collenette, and Eddie Goldenberg.

Chrétien asked me to invite this group to his opposition office on Tuesday morning after the Monday evening election results had been counted, to begin the transition process.

Elizabeth Roscoe remembers that each team member brought a different skill set and a very different political orientation to the task. She describes the transition team as "small and without ego. It was a real 'doing' team. Everyone just dug in and away we went."[12]

Tim Murphy, who was a member of the 2004 Martin transition team, recalls the strategic decision to bring Arthur Kroeger, with his experience as deputy minister in the federal public service, into the team. "Obviously, Arthur Kroeger was meant to bring credibility to the Martin government. There was a perception that the barbarians were at the gates, with a new set of people coming to the table. So our intention was to communicate to the public service that we were not a bunch of people coming to whack away everything that is sacred to them and cut them off at the knees. And part of the reason you reach out to people like that is to send the message to the public service and the system that there are people who know what you do around the table as well. So you don't need to panic, but also you want access to their expertise and experience. And Arthur was there for both of those reasons."[13]

Even though Harper had led the lobbying efforts of the National Citizens Coalition from 1998 to 2002, as leader of the opposition he came to believe that the lobby industry was too powerful. When given the opportunity, he set his sights on severely crippling the connections between the lobbying firms and the government. Ironically, while his first piece of legislation as prime minister disallowed public office holders from moving into lobbying jobs for a period of five years, he has made little effort to stop the flow of former PMO staffers to lobby firms, private sector companies, and industry associations that lobby government regularly.

Being a member of a transition team has obvious consequences – notably some public profile and the reputation for having "inside" and confidential knowledge about a newly elected government. For some transition team members the experience can enhance their careers, but none of those interviewed felt that it had changed the trajectory of their careers. This response is not surprising, given the efforts that are made to recruit transition members who have no direct interest in the outcome and who have direct experience in government. To include those with experience is vital to anchoring the work around viable options and realistic expectations.

With transition teams weighted in favour of experience, the more likely direct outcome of serving on one is that it is sometimes difficult to maintain personal and professional friendships in light of the secretive and confidential nature of the work. The secrecy barrier is "high" and it can create unease among those who are not on the transition team but are close to the centre of power and those who are on the team. As a result, the strength of personal friendships and political alliances is tested when transition teams are assembled.

Simone Philogène recalls those early days after the 1993 election where the value of experience and being able to separate friendship from working relationships were critical:

One of the things I found interesting when I was working on the 1993 transition was how the behaviour of those people that had been around for a long time, who had lived through other government transitions, and seen the beginning, the middle, and the end of a government differed from those of the less-experienced staff. The experienced staffers appeared to know the limits of their participation and, at the outset, acknowledged that their involvement would end inevitably at some point. They conveyed the impression that they had a job to accomplish, while the less-experienced

---

Behind the Scenes: Getting on a Transition Team

As is the case with most positions in Ottawa, getting on a transition team is about relationships and experience. In 1984 I was lucky enough to be on Prime Minister Mulroney's transition team, where I was responsible for advising and preparing the new government's political staffing approach. That work led to a structural change in how ministers' offices were set up. That work also brought experienced individuals to the newly designed chief of staff position that helped to assist new ministers. What was learned from the 1979–80 Clark government was that the new millennium government needed experienced political advisors on the ground in order to be adequately prepared.

This experience, as well as my background in having served as a chief of staff for a few years with the Mulroney government, led me to have a number of working relationships and friendships with a number of former PMO staff. Two of them, Hugh Segal and Derek Burney, were asked to begin work on the 2006 transition. Given my previous experiences with organizing ministers' offices, I was asked to put some transition material together.

Being on a transition team taps into your political knowledge, your knowledge of government, and your knowledge of what needs to be done right away. Like with most things in life, you only get one chance to get it done right. You get one chance to participate in a change of government, and people will recall how well the transition is done. How many times in the country's history do you actually get to see a change in government close up? Not often. There are not going to be many opportunities in one's lifetime.

Elizabeth Roscoe, member of the Harper transition team, 2006

staffers seemed to be jockeying for attention, sensing that there were future rewards at stake.

This distinction was useful to me when one of the experienced staffers from the Trudeau era approached me the day after the election and asked, "Do you know who your friends were before the election?" "Of course," I said. And then she retorted, "Well, make sure you remember who they are, because the day you're no longer part of this, those people will be the only friends you have left." I never forgot that – ever, ever.[14]

Making the choice of the person to head the transition team could logically be seen as the start of the transition process. Reflecting back on the experience and having interviewed all those who headed transitions since 1984, I conclude that there is no single job description for this task. As is so often the case with personnel issues, the choice is situational, depending to a large degree on the needs and skill set of the leader, the availability of people who might be available and have the necessary abilities, and the optics of the choice within the political party. At a minimum, the leader of a transition team needs to have or likely will develop a close relationship with the leader, to understand how government "really" works, to communicate well, to be the public face of the transition after the election, and to be trusted by the campaign team and those who will move into the PMO.

Once a transition team leader is selected and the team is in place, many people make one of two false assumptions about the initial work being undertaken behind closed doors. They either believe that the team is engaged in developing policy options and campaign strategy, or they envision the team immediately digging into the secretive business of forming a Cabinet.

First Principles

As a starting point, transitions do not include policy development. Policy development is critical to the party and to the leadership of the country, but it is not the role of the transition team to take the lead on developing the policy platform of the party. This is best left to the campaign team and the leader's office. While there is some obvious linkage between the policy agenda and the transition plan, its relationship is sequential. The development of the platform comes first. Then the transition plan lays the groundwork for a smooth transition of power, to ensure that all pieces of government come together to implement the vision and initiatives laid out in the platform.

It is true that some of the most important decisions made by a leader revolve around the Cabinet and its structure. But I would argue that the transition team should set this discussion aside for a later time, in order to focus on three key issues: gaining an appreciation of the leader's general philosophy about the role of government in society, understanding the cognitive style of the leader, and zeroing in on the leader's priorities for the short term and long term.

Before planning for the transition, the team must have a clear understanding of these three issues. Leaders are commonly unable to clearly articulate their philosophy or cognitive style, so the role of the transition team is to encourage leaders to take the time to think through these issues and to help translate the leader's approach, style, and vision into concrete outcomes. A preliminary series of questions can be used to guide this conversation. What role should government play in society? What do you believe about the relative importance of Canada's key governance institutions – Parliament compared to Cabinet compared to prime minister? Do you prefer a decision-making model that is top-down or collaborative? What do you want to accomplish as prime minister?

It is necessary that there be a crystal-clear understanding between the team and the leader, and sometimes this means being willing to ask tough or awkward questions of a potential prime minister. They need to answer basic questions about how hard they want to work and how much energy they have. They should also articulate their thoughts about the relative strengths and weaknesses of their colleagues and the caucus. Who is seen as a possible successor? Who are the leaders within the party? Who are the gifted communicators?

The transition team must also play the role of realist at times, and it should be made up of people who have an appetite for change but who can stay away from impossible dreams. The team must be firmly grounded in the possible and ensure that the leader appreciates the realities to be faced in office.

The transition team must also be able to translate the approach and philosophy of the leader into a responsive machinery-of-government environment. They must also understand the role and importance of the public service. Few political leaders have an appreciation for the complexities of managing a relationship with the public service, or know how to maximize the benefits that a positive and productive relationship can bring to the government of the day. As a result, the transition team must bring to the task an ability to gauge the pulse of the public service. They need to have a keen understanding of staffing trends, including motivations and skill sets, and whether the public service continues to be able to attract the best and brightest into government service.

Opportunities for decentralization can be considered, as well as new public management and alternative service-delivery opportunities. As in other industries, technology and social media can transform services to the public, improve productivity across departments and agencies, and engage citizens in Canadian democracy.

The more substantive the transition team's thinking is on the role of government and the levers available to the incoming government, the more complex and substantive the transition can be. There is an ongoing debate within government circles about whether a "big" transition is a good idea. Undertaking a wide-ranging transition can be risky and complex. Much can go wrong, especially if the incoming party is inexperienced. But the transition period is the best time to make major changes away from strong vested interests and established power bases.

An example of the importance of setting priorities for the 1993 transition team was the work that the group did to restore trust in government. A central theme of the election campaign and, as a consequence, the transition planning was to find ways to restore integrity in public life. My notes of our transition meetings show that we spent considerable time looking for ways to restore public confidence in government by having the prime minister take the lead "in establishing integrity for his government from its inception." We were very aware that integrity in government is a complex issue that could quickly become symbolic without any substance. I noted in my records of the meeting that integrity in government is a "two-edged sword," because "while integrity is essential to restoring confidence in government, great care must be taken to avoid establishing unrealistic standards and raising unreasonable expectations since failure to deliver will further erode public confidence." Specifically, the transition book included plans to rebuild integrity in government by:

• Reducing the size of ministers' offices;
• Adjusting the level of benefits to ministers, members of Parliament, and public servants;

- Limiting the activities of lobbyists;
- Making the appointment process more merit based;
- Developing conflict of interest rules for ministers and their staff;
- Revising the contracting and procurement rules;
- Examining the pension plan for members of Parliament;
- Monitoring election spending;
- Revamping political party financing;
- Creating an office for ethics.

Important Working Relationships

Election Team

Even though the election is not yet underway during this phase, it is important that at least one part of the campaign preparedness team is in sync with the transition team. At a minimum, there needs to be close collaboration between the policy (platform) drafters and the transition team, since the transition must be able to effect campaign commitments, especially those the leader promised would be implemented immediately after the election campaign.

A failure to establish a good working relationship can have serious consequences for an incoming government. In the United States, Harrison Wellford has highlighted this issue on a number of occasions: "Suspicion between campaign and pre-election transition planners in both the Jimmy Carter and Bill Clinton transitions embarrassed the President-elect, amused the press corps, and delayed key transition decisions."[15]

On reflecting back on the 1993 transition, Carle recalls his surprise at the almost instantaneous change from electioneering to governing mode. On the shock of becoming part of the government he recalled, "No one in government is ready for the monster of government. We spent the past eighteen months concentrating on winning an election and have not thought too much time about the practicality of governing. It is a big surprise when it happens. Things unravel so fast that you have to be prepared. The day after the election you are the government and the old government is gone.'"[16]

A good example of a successful linkage between electioneering and transition planning took place in 1993 when, in Welland, Ontario, and three weeks before the general election, Jean Chrétien articulated what his first three decisions would be once his government was sworn in. He would approve the $6 billion infrastructure program, cancel the

EH-101 helicopter contract that had been negotiated by the previous government, and halt privatization of Pearson Airport in Toronto. The timing was not accidental – it served an election purpose but also gave the transition team time to work out the details and to signal to the PCO that these issues would be among the first items to be dealt with at the first Cabinet meeting. In this way, Chrétien was able to demonstrate that he was a "man of action" and "as good as his word" by following up quickly on his promises. As a general rule, knowing as many of these policy commitments as possible in advance of the election gives the transition team sufficient time to consider the implementation challenges embedded in the policy decisions, such as machinery-of-government and personnel options.

Wellford captures the essence of a successful relationship between the election team and the transition group when he writes, "To borrow Isaiah Berlin's simile, successful transitions are more like hedgehogs than foxes: they focus on one or two big things – a compelling thematic message – rather than skip nimbly among many small ones. The greatest gift the campaign can give to the transition is to clearly articulate the themes that will become its mandate."[17]

Readying the Leader to Govern

Some leaders respond well to evidence-based argumentation grounded in statistics, data, and facts. Some become engaged through anecdotes, stories, and humour, while others prefer tightly scripted logic. The cognitive style of the leader also has an important impact on their choice of Cabinet structure and their decision-making system. Some leaders like collaborative decision-making by engaging colleagues in conversation and debate. Other leaders prefer to formulate policy on their own and might prefer to use Cabinet as a forum for testing, adjusting, and validating their ideas. Still others use Cabinet as a method to communicate their decisions. Understanding these dynamics allows the transition team to outline appropriate options for prime ministers as they decide how best to manage their Cabinet.

Even the issue of how to manage the leader's time needs to be considered carefully by the team, based on the leader's personal style and approach. In opposition, leaders have time for many activities that are no longer possible as prime minister. Learning how to manage one's time is a cardinal rule of being a successful prime minister. As Tony Blair noted in his memoirs, "Show me an ineffective leader and I will show you a badly managed schedule. This has nothing to do with the number of hours worked – I came across leaders who worked the most ridiculous hours, 18 hours a day for frequent stretches of time – but whether time is used properly."[18]

The planning phase is the ideal time to prepare the leader of the party to govern, especially if the leader is a member of an opposition party with no government experience. As I discovered through working with Jean Chrétien on his 1993 transition, even a leader with considerable government experience needs to spend time becoming acquainted with the levers of power and, more importantly, getting up to speed with what has happened in government over the time that the party was in opposition.

As a general rule, it is best to assume that the potential prime minister knows very little about government and governing. Stephen Harper and Tony Blair had never been in a Cabinet room before they became prime ministers, so their understanding of the importance and functioning of the institutions they were about to lead would have been learned in rather informally.

A typical day in the life of a prime minister will be very different from any time before. It is filled with meetings, written and oral briefings, conflict, and decisions. It is not a world for those who cannot make tough decisions relatively quickly. It is also not a job for people who want to be liked by everyone they meet. As a consequence, the first phase of the transition is an ideal time to confront both the substantive policy issues that await a new government and some of the personality characteristics that might prove difficult for a politician who has just become prime minister.

In Chrétien's case, the consensus was that he would have little difficulty dealing with the volume of work, with the decision-making process, or with having to make unpopular or difficult decisions. He had already spent more than thirty years in federal politics as a Quebec MP and had been the target of many personal attacks on his integrity, values, and policies. However, it was decided that he would benefit from reacquainting himself with some of the key policy issues that had developed during his years out of politics.

Despite personal interest in public affairs and public policy, no one is properly prepared for policymaking at the prime ministerial level. In our Westminster system, the buck really does stop at the desk of the prime minister, so there is an obligation for the prime minister to master the key files in order lead Cabinet. In Chrétien's case, even before the transition work began, the Aylmer Conference had been organized for the Liberal Party leadership to wrap their heads around some of the most complex issues facing the nation. As Brooke Jeffrey noted in her definitive book about the Liberal Party, "It was still up to Chrétien and his team to construct an alternative policy agenda Canadians would find appealing. Without this, the Liberal Party could not hope to return to power."[19]

In addition to providing the Liberals with the beginning of a policy agenda, Chrétien personally found the conference very stimulating and admitted that it was an effective way to engage him in policy. As a result, we decided during the transition-planning phase to introduce him to a wide range of economic, social, and foreign policy experts in an informal setting, to bring him up to speed on a number of policy issues.

Role of Spouses

Brian Mulroney set a precedent in 1984 when he arranged to provide an office for his wife, Mila. Initially, many political commentators questioned this decision, seeing it as unnecessary and expensive for a non-elected person. Shortly, however, the need for such support became obvious and was accepted as a legitimate cost of government. At minimum, the spouse of the prime minister needs an executive assistant as well as a person from the correspondence unit of the PMO designated to deal with the correspondence she receives. (In Canada, thus far, all spouses have been wives.) As well, it is not uncommon for the spouse to have her own working agenda that supports good causes or, more often, attends events in the prime minister's place. These activities need to be supported in the same professional way as those of the prime minister, since the spouses are, de facto, representing the government in these duties.

In general, it is up to the prime minister and the spouse to carve out an appropriate role. Some spouses have obvious leadership capabilities and interests, while others prefer to stay behind the scenes. In any case, all play a very significant role in supporting their prime ministerial spouse. Even those who remain in the background are major players in terms of advising their own spouses on a wide range of government decisions, including Cabinet appointments, policy options, and staff hiring.

Geoff Norquay remembers the first time he met Mila Mulroney. "At the time, they had three young children around the ages of six, four, and two. And one of them made the mistake of saying, 'Mommy, I'm bored.' And there was this stream of Serbian that erupted, that ended in English. The last thing she said was, 'In politics, you are never allowed to be bored!' And she's saying this to a six-year-old, a four-year-old, and a two-year-old, very seriously. I vowed at that point never to cross Mila Mulroney! It scared the shit out of me!"[20]

A transition team can't ignore the relationship between leader and spouse. In some cases, the spouse will bring very clear ideas into certain areas within the prime minister's authority. Mike Robinson remembers working with Paul and Sheila Martin. "There were a couple of Cabinet posts where Paul had no choice, because Sheila had a very strong view about what was going to happen to certain people because of her relationships with their spouses. In the cases of some appointments, you could tell that a certain degree of Cabinet making had taken place in the bedroom. That is to say, she had some views about the personnel but she didn't either ask for a role or intrude. It was just the nature of their relationship."[21]

As closely as the transition team works with the leader, it is important that the spouse also has confidence in the team. Because of Norquay's previous experiences working for the Clarks and the Mulroneys, he already knew a lot about the influence of political family members. Not only is spousal advice important, but the spouse's opinions of potential employees, who will be spending a lot of time with the leader and be close to the family, are extremely important in hiring decisions. So when discussing the possibility of playing a leading role on his transition team, Norquay ended the conversation by specifically asking Harper what his wife would think about his being on the team. As he recalls,

At the time I had spent the last three or four years going on TV, carving Harper up whenever I could. Remember, this was a period of time when Progressive Conservatives thought they could come back and take the Alliance Party out, and they thought they could take us out. Eventually, we finally agreed that neither could take out the other, so we had to get back together again. But I did not want Harper going home at night and his wife, Laureen, saying, "What did that jerk Norquay say to you today?" You know, based on my earlier experience, that's the way I thought of it. And Harper kind of chuckled and he said, "Well, actually, it was kind of her idea that I hire you"![22]

A spouse can also play another important function. She can be the consistent and long-standing "Rock of Gibraltar," the prime minister's most trusted advisor, and the person who best understands the values and principles that drove the prime minister to seek the party leadership and contest the general election. There are few data on this particular spousal role, but Derek Burney recalls two interesting incidents that reinforce this concept:

> I remember a funny event before the first Gulf War. [George H.W.] Bush wanted to chat with Mulroney, so I arranged for him to travel to Washington for a very small dinner in the White House. The Canadians included the prime minister and his then chief of staff, Stanley Hartt. And on the American side it was Baker, Dick Cheney, Colin Powell, Brent Scowcroft, and Mrs Bush. When I realized that Mrs Bush was attending, I quickly apologized to Mulroney. I said, "Well, Prime Minister, if I had known Mrs Bush was going to be here, I would have told you to bring Mila." He said, "That's all right. But do you know why Mrs Bush was invited?" I said, "No. What was she doing there?" He said, "Derek, she's the keeper of the flame." I said, "What do you mean by that?" "Well," he said, "You know, when it really comes down to it, she's the only one in that room that he can really trust!" So, don't ever underestimate the influence that the spouse has on these guys."[23]
>
> If Mila had seen something negative on television that Brian hadn't seen, did I ever hear about it the next morning! It wasn't unusual for me to start the morning with a phone call from 24 Sussex from a very persistent prime ministerial spouse. "Did you know what was going on in my husband's government last night?" "No, I didn't see that CNN special at 2 a.m.! Please tell the prime minister that I was asleep!"[24]

Public Service

The bulk of responsibility at the early stages of the transition preparation period within the public service falls to the clerk of the Privy Council, whose department takes the lead on coordinating briefing materials across government. Traditionally, and when the transition will follow a general election, the clerks participate in early meetings with the transition teams of the governing party and of the opposition parties so that they can develop an overall sense of their governing priorities, should they win the election. This is a difficult role for clerks, since it places them in the delicate position of preparing for a potential change in government while still serving the government of the day. The fine balancing act is possible only when all players acknowledge the independence and professionalism of the public service in its role to provide the government of the day with "fearless advice and loyal implementation" while simultaneously preparing to welcome a new prime minister.[25]

In the early stages, the secretary will also name a senior public servant to take the lead on the transition process. At the federal level, this person is often the deputy secretary of plans in the PCO, but at the provincial level an appropriate person is sometimes seconded from another department. In either case, whoever is chosen must bring stature and a sense of service ethic to the exercise, since both the opposition and the government of the day must be confident that things will get done when the election is over and the formal transition begins. This individual will join the clerk in meetings with the opposition if they meet before the election, and from that point will become the main contact and will provide a sense of consistency throughout the process.

In the view of Nicholas D'Ombrain,[26] "Transitions must be approached with care and delicacy, especially those that involve a newly elected government."[27] In the early stages the pressure is mostly on the central agencies but especially on the Cabinet clerks and their staff in the PCO. D'Ombrain emphatically underlines the importance of this work, since so much is at stake in the early days of a new government: "PCO must do first-class work, since this is all they have to offer to the new government. If the work is done poorly, they will quickly lose the confidence of the new government."[28] He also cautions about trying to impress a new government by overwhelming it with oral briefings and a high volume of materials. His advice is succinct and clear. "The higher the mountain of material, the less useful it will be. Moreover, the transition team will want to focus on few areas, so don't try to shove your priorities down their throats. It won't work."[29]

As a general rule, the Privy Council Office will cover a wide range of activities in their transition planning – from the most broad and general to narrow and precise ones. Here are some of the activities described by Nicholas D'Ombrain that the PCO would undertake in preparation of a newly elected government:

- Monitor broad platform promises
- Care for the "nuts and bolts" of the transition team's needs

- ○ Where they sit and work
- ○ Security clearances

- Issues of a personal nature to the PM

  - ○ Security around PM
  - ○ Move to 24 Sussex
  - ○ Budget and salaries of ministers and staff
  - ○ Nature of the relationship with ministers and deputy ministers

- Figuring out the PM's style of managing

  - ○ How much material will be useful?

As the transition exercise becomes more intense and moves into the electoral period, a larger group of PCO staff becomes involved. These are the people who develop the briefing books that the PCO will hand over to the incoming prime minister and the PMO the day after the election. This team will also coordinate logistical support for the incoming prime minister's transition team and help to coordinate the parallel development of briefing books across government.

In the preparatory phase, each deputy minister begins to coordinate the development of briefing books for the benefit of incoming ministers. It should be remembered, however, that since the public service is not privy to party platforms until the election is called, deputy ministers must remain cautious about anticipating policy ideas and solutions coming from political parties. To prepare for potential policy issues, the clerk will often organize a group of deputy ministers with policy expertise to engage in an initial discussion on key policy files in play at the time. This enables the public service to prepare for a wide range of policy options without attributing potential ideas to any single political party.

Beyond policy, however, the preparatory phase will be used by individual departments to ensure that the remaining components of the briefing materials are ready. Judith LaRocque, the current ambassador to the OECD and former deputy minister of Canadian heritage, describes how she and her team prepared for the transition when she was a deputy minister:

In our department we prepared three different types of briefing material. First, we had what we called "The Department," which included everything you wanted to know about the department, including its mandate and programs. The second document contained everything you wanted to know about the portfolio, including all the agencies. Both of these documents were kept "evergreen" because we never knew how often we were going to change ministers, since, in fact, we had more than twenty ministers in ten years. And then the third book – and probably the most important one – was what we called the "Hundred and Fifty Day Book," which described all the obligations and ministerial time requirements for the next 150 days.[30]

Many departments have a similar system, albeit with different names and configurations. The "Hundred and Fifty Day Book" is prepared to help ministers survive the first months in government, and a deputy minister tries to ensure that this book is comprehensive and up to date. It will include such things as appointments that need to be filled, Supreme Court decisions that will affect a minister and the department, court cases in which the department is involved across the country, and legislative issues. Everything that can hit a new minister in that first 150 days of office is included in the book. If the transition book is well prepared and comprehensive, it will become one of the most useful tools for a new minister. It provides a glimpse of the breadth and depth of the portfolio and can make the difference between a minister sinking or swimming early in the government's mandate.

In general, the volume of briefing material produced by the public service is so overwhelming that a minister can scarcely be expected to absorb it all. As a result, the briefing material, in practice, often becomes reference material that is used by ministers and their staff throughout their terms in office. Like many aspects of transition planning, there are no templates to develop briefing books, either at the departmental level or within the PCO. Sometimes the clerk develops multiple, parallel sets of briefing books tailored to each political party and the policy platform that each has proposed. In recent years this practice has been abandoned in favour of a single set of materials that are consistent across all parties, with opportunities to tailor material to the policy platform of the party that wins the election. When deciding to move forward with one set of briefing books, Alex Himelfarb, a former clerk of the Privy Council, notes, "Our advice obviously has to be politically sensitive, and you have to make some modifications in your advice, depending on which political party you are talking to – but public service advice is public service advice."[31]

That being said, as the public service prepares for a transition, it is important that the clerk and PCO invest time in preparing the deputy minister community not only for the mechanics of a transition, but also for a potential shift in attitudes and ideology. There is a learning curve for the public service on the ideology of a new, incoming political party, especially if that party has been out of power for many years. To adjust to the new government, the public service must also adjust its assumptions, language, and approach in order to maximize its ability to support the new leadership.

"Ideology" is often considered a purely political term, but the public service is not above developing one of its own. According to one former deputy minister, the transition of the Harper government into power in 2006 exposed the fact that the public service had developed its own ideology:

> Moving into the briefings, we at PCO felt that we had done a good job in preparation. We were taught to give fearless advice and we had prepared one set of books that captured what we considered was non-partisan, independent public service advice. When Harper's team arrived they thought we were totally nuts and negative. They had a different world view, a different language and a different approach to governing, compared to how we had been operating for the past decade. It was very difficult for us to realize that we needed to change our tone, because our advice to the incoming government was coming across as pessimistic and unbalanced. They felt that we hadn't understood the meaning of their policy platform, while we felt we were being really helpful. Harper's team came in well prepared but we, as public servants, had a hard time making the shift to understand their viewpoint. It took us time to realize that although we saw ourselves as neutral, we had, in fact, developed a vocabulary that was perceived by the new government as unsupportive of their views.[32]

Political parties in Canada now universally publish policy platforms while on the campaign trail. If and when a party comes into power, it is expected to follow through on the commitments outlined in its platform. Establishing trust between the political leaders and the public service means first understanding what the government wants to achieve. According to the same source, "We can't establish trust if they don't think we're on their page."[33] In the weeks leading up to an election call, the clerk needs to ensure that the deputy minister community is prepared to make any necessary adjustments in approach, tone, language, and ideology to support an incoming government.

Without a doubt, the performance of the public service during and after a transition sets the stage for its relationship with the government

---

Behind the Scenes: The Early Phases of the Transition Work

The transition unfolds in a number of ways. In the public service it begins when there are rumours of change in leadership or an election. We would first organize a meeting of policy deputy ministers in order to develop strategies about policy issues. However, this would have to be done with some caution, as you do not want to presume anything.

We would then develop a core transition book that is about making the government, making the Cabinet, making the committees, making appointments, and the general process of transition that a new government will endure. In that book there will be some strong political views, so you are providing the government with the frame in which they will put their political agenda. Third, we guide the government through the hot political issues that come with the transition.

We then make any structural or machinery changes that will be necessary for the transition. Finally, there are strategic briefings and policy files. These are all typical steps in making a transition work.

Alex Himelfarb, secretary to the federal Cabinet, 2002–6

---

of the day. Tony Dean, a former secretary to the Cabinet in the Ontario government, believes that the transition exercise is one of the highest callings for public servants. During transitions he told his deputies that how they conduct themselves, the materials they produce, and the advice they give during the transition, and the six months after it must be at the highest level of performance that can be attained. Alex Himelfarb agrees, saying emphatically, "You've got to give them the best of what you've got."[34]

The hallmark of the Canadian public service is the ability to support the government of the day in a non-partisan, loyal, and independent manner. These attributes must remain "front and centre" during the transition to ensure that the parties vying for power can remain confident that the public service will serve them loyally, should the task of leadership fall to them.

Sir Robert Armstrong, a former secretary of the Cabinet in the United Kingdom, summed up the characteristics that a public servant must embody: "You need to be dispassionate, you need to be fair-minded, you need to be thorough, you need to be able to subordinate your personal and political view to the work of your department and to the service of the government of the day. And you need to be discreet."[35] On this issue, the last word goes to Nicholas D'Ombrain who describes the duties of the public servant: "Officials must offer advice, and ministers must listen to it and then decide whether to accept it; and officials must not be intimidated from doing their duty."[36]

In many ways, the preparations of a transition team supporting a political party and those teams put into place within the public service are similar. Each side recognizes the need to address three types of issues: (1) implementation of policy issues, which focus on what the incoming government wants to do; (2) machinery-of-government issues, which address how to govern in order to achieve the policy objectives; and (3) procedural issues, which deal with the many activities that need to take place for an orderly transfer of power to occur before and after the swearing-in ceremony.

The two parallel processes diverge, however, on one key principle: the public service must not presume the outcome of an election. According to Kevin Lynch, a former clerk, "Your role as a non-partisan public servant is to start the process with a clean, non-presumptuous slate."[37] This begins with the clerk and must permeate the entire deputy minister community. In practical matters, it means that the public service must study and treat each political platform equally, and it must anticipate and prepare for every feasible eventuality following the electoral result.[38] Unlike a transition team that focuses solely on the best interests of its own party, the transition process undertaken by the public service is government-wide, and the complexities of a smooth change require large-scale coordination and individual attention to detail.

Within Canada, the transition exercise is not entrenched in a prescriptive system. Rather, Kevin Lynch describes it as a principles-based system anchored in the necessity of the public service to loyally serve both the current and future government. "The same way the government is both campaigning for their next mandate and still operating as the current government, the public service is both serving the government of the day as well as getting ready to serve a new government. You have to understand that principle. And then you have to give effect to the principle on various specifics that you can't prescribe, because every transition is different."[39] It is because of this complex reality that Lynch considers the transition exercise "one of the highest callings of the public service."[40]

This challenge is placed front and centre when the time comes for the first meeting between the Official Opposition Party and the clerk. Within political and public service circles across Canada, there is some debate if this critical first meeting should take place before an election or a new leader has won a leadership contest with their party. Routinely, these first meetings happen during the election period, but it has also been known to occur during the transition planning phase or before the election writ has been dropped.

Giving permission for the secretary to meet with opposition parties is at the sole discretion of the incumbent prime minister, who may grant or deny permission outright. The advantage of an early preliminary meeting between the clerk and the opposition is that it allows the public service to get a sense of the priorities and approach of a potential incoming government and to prepare accordingly. And the briefing goes both ways. This meeting will give the opposition party a sense of the current state of the public service and the machinery of government. It allows the transition process to adopt an iterative approach, with two-way dialogue informing the briefing materials on each side of the transition equation.

As already mentioned, this convention has been set aside in recent years by prime ministers Martin and Harper. As a result, the opposition parties have resorted to gathering information for transition purposes by posing questions in the House of Commons, through participation on parliamentary committees, and through other channels made available as a result of the regular cycle of government.

The delicate issue of if, and when, the clerk can meet with the opposition has been formally addressed in other jurisdictions, including Australia, New Zealand, and the United Kingdom. In Australia, for example, the government first tabled guidelines in 1976 that provide for pre-election consultation with the opposition. The guidelines ensure a smooth transition if an election results in a change of government, and prescribe the system within which the opposition is entitled to behave vis-à-vis consultations with the public service.[41] In the Australian system, the pre-election period begins three months prior to the expiry of the House of Representatives or of the date of the election announcement, whichever occurs first. During this period, shadow ministers may be given approval to have discussions with appropriate public servants in government departments.

The procedure is initiated by the relevant opposition spokesperson making a request of the minister concerned, who then notifies the prime minister of the request and asks if the prime minister agrees to it. These discussions occur at the initiative of the non-government parties, not at the discretion of public servants. It is the responsibility of public servants to inform their ministers when the discussions are taking place; however, the detailed substance of the discussions is confidential. Ministers are entitled to seek general information from public servants only as to whether the discussions have been kept within the agreed purposes.

During these meetings, public servants are not authorized to discuss government policies or to give opinions on political matters. The subject matter of the discussions relates only to the machinery of government and administration (this can include the administrative and technical practicalities and procedures that would be involved in the implementation of policies proposed by the non-government parties). If the opposition representatives raise matters that, in the judgment of the public servants, seek information on government policies or expressions of opinion on alternative policies, the public servants are required to suggest that the matter be raised with the minister.

In the United Kingdom, a similar practice has been in place for some time. "Prior to the 1964 election, any formal contact between the opposition and Whitehall was strictly forbidden. But, with Labour out of power for 13 years, new conventions, subsequently labeled the 'Douglas Home rules,' were drawn up permitting contact between the opposition and Whitehall in the lead up to an election. They allowed for pre-election discussions between the opposition and civil servants on 'machinery of government issues' to ensure better preparation for a potential change of government."[42]

Most observers of the Cabinet system in the United Kingdom consider meetings between the opposition party and the public service an important element in good governance, since it guarantees a seamless transition in the wake of a change in government. In his published memoirs, David Blunkett (former secretary for education in Blair's 1997 government) commented very favourably about the behaviour of one of the new permanent secretaries whom Blair had hired from outside the public service. What impressed Blunkett was the practical approach that Michael Bichard adopted in dealing with Labour when they were in opposition. He remembers Bichard saying, "If you're able to tell us the direction you're going and what policies you are developing, we won't waste our officials' time in doing something that is entirely contrary to what you want and therefore they will feel that they're doing something meaningful and will be able to carry it forward after the election. So, let's all have a very sensible view of this, and it doesn't mean that we're presuming they're going to implement it; or presuming that if you win we will have to."[43]

Canada has not adopted any formal conventions or guidelines to govern the transition period. In their place, the operative approach is based on principles. As a result, the public service and their counterparts serving on political transition teams must adjust to the realities of the day and the preferences of the prime minister in preparing for a potential change in leadership.

When the meeting between the secretary to the Cabinet and the political transition team does take place, each side has its own agenda, although it is not a meeting of equals, since the transition team will be placing its aspirations and needs before the public service. Clerks arrive at the meeting with a well-established idea of what issues need to be addressed, but will especially take the opportunity to demonstrate that the public service will be responsive to the needs of the government. When in 2003, Cabinet Secretary Tony Dean first met with the Ontario transition team of the then leader of the opposition, Dalton McGuinty, he wanted to set the right tone, within the conventional boundaries of what a clerk can and cannot say to the opposition:

> We walked into the first meeting with a table of contents that showed what we were thinking about for transition materials. We also had a couple of actual products that showed the style, the font, and the length of the briefing materials. But, more importantly, we asked the transition team if they felt there was anything missing from our table of contents. Was there anything that they didn't see that they were hoping to see? And so they were able to walk through our product and help us make adjustments, based on what they felt would be useful, should their party win the election. I wanted them to have a sense that we're on top of things, that we're planning ahead of the game, and that we're bringing a customer-service ethic to the transition exercise. I was saying, Listen, this is our agenda for today's meeting, but you've probably got one, too, and we want to hear what your expectations will be. We're not assuming that we get to define what transition is.[44]

The clerk will also pose a number of questions during this meeting that will help the public service prepare for various electoral outcomes.

He or she will want to know what the political team thinks about the structure of government and whether there is an appetite to create, merge, or break up departments. These questions will provide clear signals about the intentions of the leader of the opposition, and they allow the clerk and the PCO team to begin thinking about how to plan appropriately. The more open and forthright the dialogue is at this first meeting, the more confident each party will be in the other's capabilities.

One area in which the public service can expect to be kept at a distance is in the deliberations surrounding the Cabinet. The clerk will be able to make some suggestions about the size of Cabinet and the related challenges and opportunities, and offer ideas on where an incoming party might want to double up on some portfolios and how Cabinet committees might work. This type of institutional experience can provide a political transition team with valuable insight and advice, as

---

Behind the Scenes: Briefing the Opposition Parties

My experience has been that only the main opposition party wants to be briefed. You want them to have a sense that you're on top of the issues, that you're planning ahead of the game, and that you've got a strong sense of service ethic. We asked them to listen to our public service agenda, but we were also there to hear what their expectations were. We were not assuming that we would define what their transition should be.

In reviewing our materials, it gave them a chance to ask important questions. They asked about the structure of the government, if we wanted to change the number of ministries, if we wanted to merge or de-merge some ministries, and they were curious about the decision-making machinery of the government. We didn't actually give them any of our materials, but we walked them through it so they would get a flavour for issues.

Right away there were clear signals about the big changes they were thinking about making. They were very forthright and as a result we had an open discussion. Nonetheless, I still felt like I was a caretaker secretary at that point; I had no expectation of carrying on. Interestingly, the NDP didn't ask for a meeting, even though we offered to provide one in the interest of being non-partisan and even-handed.

Tony Dean, secretary to the Ontario Cabinet, 2002–8, interview,
17 November 2010

it deliberates on the process of making a Cabinet. But in the end, the PCO team will likely keep its remarks circumspect. And, like all other aspects of the dialogue during this meeting, the clerk must always be cautious about how ideas are presented. Himelfarb recalls, "I never got specific about anything that would criticize the government. Our advice on the Cabinet and the machinery of government draws from our experience but is never linked to specific examples from previous governments."[45]

As one can imagine, this first meeting can have wide-ranging implications. A successful outcome requires both sides to be frank and open, but remain respectful of the current governing party and recognize that the outcome of the election is in question. Coming out of this first meeting, the clerk may receive clear signals on the intentions of the opposition about machinery of government. As the clerk, PCO, and deputy minister community prepare for a transition, significant thought should go into the preparation of machinery-of-government options. The transition period is one of the few opportunities to put forward these ideas, and the opportunity should not be taken for granted or missed altogether.

Preparing for the Personal Side of Transitions

All secretaries to the Cabinet are aware that the transition they are preparing for could signal the end of their tenure in that position. The Canadian data suggest that most clerks leave their position with the arrival of a new government. Despite the professionalism displayed by all individuals who have served as clerk, it is a position that requires a close and trusting relationship with the prime minister. It is therefore not surprising that many prime ministers have preferred to appoint a new clerk early in their mandate, partly as a result of a perception that the current clerk was too closely associated with the outgoing government, but also as a personal decision about leadership styles and working relationships.

Despite the fact that the odds are against clerks keeping their job, they are aware that their performance during the transition exercise is a continual job interview. Working in a very high-risk environment, the clerk is given a very short time to impress an incoming prime minister and build relationships with the new government. As a political transition team prepares for an election and then for the assumption of power, they will be closely observing the clerk and his or her deputy minister colleagues, considering the best candidates to fill the position. The transition team will be asking themselves whether the current clerk will support their policies, how well they know him or her, and whether the clerk will be a good fit to work with the prime minister and the PMO. As important, they will assess whether the clerk is considered a "friend" of the previous government.

Given the strength of the traditions surrounding the role of the federal Cabinet secretaries in Canada, they consider themselves professional public servants without party affiliation. However, the lens used by the political transition team will be drastically different from that used by the public service on itself. For example, the incoming Harper government had a strong assumption that the then clerk, Alex Himelfarb, had "liberal leanings." This was based largely on the fact that he had been perceived as central in developing many of the Chrétien and Martin government's key policies, many of which were seen as particularly progressive. Following their intelligence gathering from among their operatives, the Harper people had worries that his activist thinking might be at odds with their own conservative, small-government philosophy.[46]

In a similar manner, the relationship between a minister and deputy minister, and also with the minister's chief of staff, can hinge on interpersonal considerations. Public service leaders need to be prepared to analyse the leadership style of the key players across each political party and adapt accordingly. On the basis of experience, deputy ministers should assume the incoming minister knows very little about government and public administration, although they can always hope that their minister may have served in an earlier Cabinet in a federal or provincial government.[47] The public service must understand that it is natural for an incoming government to be suspicious of public servants and to question their loyalty to the new government. As deputy ministers move through a transition exercise, their ability to build trust, provide honest advice, and support the minister in the first months of office is of primary concern.

The public service must also prepare for a new team of people taking over the Prime Minister's Office. Without fail, these individuals tend to be highly motivated, career-oriented, partisan, and ambitious, but unfortunately, they are often perceived as arrogant and lacking in experience – which is a combination of characteristics that can make life difficult for public servants. The ground rules need to be established as quickly as possible, in order to build a good working relationship with the PMO team, and each public service leader needs to assess the interpersonal dynamic across key members of the team. Deputy ministers need to learn how to partner with the PMO on causes of common concern, but also be able to employ co-optation or coercion tactics when necessary.

Principles into Practice

Transition teams tend to work below the sightlines of the caucus and its leadership but are making recommendations that will have an immediate impact on the whole caucus, should they win the election. Possible machinery changes, implementation strategies for primary policy decisions, and the relationship of the public service and its unions to decentralization or privatization initiatives – these are all examples of key decisions taken by the leader that will have a significant impact on the caucus in the event of an electoral victory.

Traditionally, the caucus is not closely involved in these discussions, but during this phase of the transition, prime ministers such as Chrétien liked to engage key caucus players who had a depth of experience or were particularly politically savvy, to act as a sounding board for such issues. Political veteran MPs like Herb Gray, David Collenette, and Brian Tobin, and former ministers like Mitchell Sharp and Ed Lumley, fell into this category of valuable counsellors. Chrétien was also naturally predisposed to involve people on a "need to know" basis. He was, and still is, very dismissive of ongoing planning committees with long shelf lives but short agendas. As a consequence, he preferred to send out the transition team to meet with people who had the expertise (read: experience) and sufficient "skin in the game" to make a worthwhile contribution to our deliberations.

To ensure that the decisions are wrapped into future planning, someone among the senior staff should be kept informed about the planning work during this phase so that there is a record of the decisions. If it is clear who will assume the role of chief of staff after the election, this is the right person to be informed of all key decisions. In 1993, because Jean Pelletier was standing as a Liberal candidate, his success at the polls would mean he could no longer continue as the chief of staff to the leader of the opposition. Despite his candidacy, however, he was kept informed of all key decisions, and he played an important role in the planning phase of the transition. As it turned out, Pelletier lost to a Bloc Québécois candidate and he reclaimed his old job the day after the election.

One of the most important ways of developing a transition plan (especially for the neophytes) and kick-starting the process is to prepare a critical path model (or Gantt chart) for the whole exercise – starting from the preplanning period until the end of the consolidation period. In the 1993 Chrétien transition, at the end of the exercise there were forty-one separate elements on the Gantt chart that were part of the transition plan. These included obvious items such as Cabinet formation and the decision-making process, but also logistics for the move into 24 Sussex, a list of staff who would need security clearances, the agenda for a two-day Cabinet orientation session, and assistance to the outgoing government – especially to Kim Campbell, who we expected would lose her seat.

Some incoming governments have developed and publicized a plan for 100 days of action, while others have preferred to wait until the Cabinet is sworn in before moving forward with an explicit plan, but as we will learn later, many parts of the public service will have developed 100-day plans of their own.

Another component in the planning process is finding an effective way to communicate information to the leader and to record decisions in order to avoid any possible misunderstanding later. As described earlier, each leader has a particular preference for the way in which information is transmitted to him or her. Some prefer to be verbally briefed, others like to engage in debate, while others prefer short or long memoranda – each style requires a different way of packaging information, and it is during this phase of the work that different writing styles, option formats, and records of decisions are developed. This and many other non-trivial tasks consume large amounts of time and are best completed during this phase, before the "heavy lifting" of the election and post-election periods. This is the best time to try out innovative ways of transmitting information and testing the leader's learning styles.

In Chrétien's case, he had a strong preference for briefing notes of two pages, even for relatively important files, although he was quick to agree to face-to-face meetings when he felt that different points of view would give him a more rounded perspective on the issue. Further discussions of the practical elements in implementing a transition will be found in later chapters.

Conclusion

This chapter described the pre-election phase of the transition exercise. It started with the crucial and complex selection of a transition team and the critical appointment of the person who would head the transition exercise and guide the process through all four stages. It also took an early look into the important and crucial relationship between the transition team and the election campaign team, and revealed the complexity of the changing dynamics between the transition team and the public service.

At this point in the storyline, an argument has been made that a transition exercise needs to find an efficient way to understand the leader's general philosophy of the role of government in society and the policy instruments that are perceived by the leader to be most effective. Second, appreciating that each leader arrives at position as the chief of their political party with a particular cognitive style, the transition team must look for ways to take advantage of the leader's style. While most people involved in transition planning are not necessarily familiar with the extensive literature on cognitive style, they all recognize how important, for example, it is that the decision making processes lines up with style of the prime minister.[48] Finally, knowing in advance the incoming government's short and medium term policy priorities helps the transition team focus its work and find congruence between policy and process.

The chapter also highlighted that the pre-election phase is the best opportunity to ready leaders for their new job. Most political leaders in Canada have very little management experience and some have equally meagre political management experience. This is the time for the transition team to identify the strengths and weaknesses of the leader and the fill the gap in their skill set. While most leaders are reluctant to admit to weaknesses, they soon learn to appreciate the need for upgrading their rusty management skills and learning new ones. At a minimum, the readying stage is a valuable opportunity to demonstrate the importance of time management and self-discipline. It also gives the transition team the chance to match policy priorities and the leaders knowledge in those areas.

The chapter also highlighted the preparatory work done by the secretary to the Cabinet, the PCO and the many policy and operational departments and agencies in the public service. In particular, the material in this chapter underscored how the political side and the public service operate independently and along parallel lines in advance of an election or before the selection of a new leader within a political party.

Since one of the themes of this book is about the importance of relationships, the chapter concludes with a brief reference to the important but almost always overlooked role of the prime minister's spouse who often plays a very important role in the formation of the government.

All of this preparatory work leads to the development of a transition plan that is described in detail in the next chapter.

4 The Transition Plan

A ruler's intelligence is based on the quality of the men he has around him.
– Niccolo Machiavelli

No one was ever lost on a straight road.

– Indian proverb

Introduction

This chapter unpacks the parameters that define a transition exercise. While the core of the transition revolves around matching the right people to key positions of government, it ensures that the machinery of government reflects the needs of the incoming government. This chapter therefore provides insights into the key elements, including the structure of the Prime Minister's Office, the considerations that go into governor-in-council appointments, the structure of Cabinet, the appointment of Cabinet ministers, and the decision-making process. The chapter concludes with the first of a number of references to the role of the secretary to the Cabinet and the Privy Council Office during preparations for a transition.

Key Elements

The transition plan dictates the speed, rhythm, and style of the transition. It is a direct reflection of the leader of the party and should be developed, almost in its entirety, during the planning phase. While decisions specific to some positions may need to wait until election results have been tallied, the transition plan necessarily compels a leader to engage in the difficult process of moving forward with the government's policy priorities and balancing the need for machinery-of-government changes.

Derek Burney remembers the task of preparing the transition plan for Harper: "We met regularly and prepared a detailed transition briefing book," he recalls. "What little reference material on transitions in Canada there might be is not readily shared. So we basically started from scratch, with emphasis on practical need and our own best instincts, drawing heavily on our personal experiences in government. The primary focus was on what a new government needs to know, and above all, what it needs to do initially to get organized as a government."[1]

When Mulroney was presented with his transition plan in 1984, the first page artfully captured the delicate balancing act that encapsulates a transition plan: "This briefing book generally provides two types of information – things you have to do and choices you can make. Where choices exist, we have tried to include reasonable options for your decision, accompanied in most cases by our own advice on which seems preferable. You, of course, are free to choose as you wish."[2]

While there are myriad decisions to be addressed in the planning phase, prime ministers must take into consideration four critical elements that will have direct bearing on their success and that of their government. First is the prime minister's choice of personal staff, but especially the chief of staff, since this person will serve as the "eyes and ears" of the prime minister in countless meetings and interactions with others. The chief of staff plays the position of quarterback for the government, and a great deal of thought needs to go into who might be the best choice for this critical position.

The second set of decisions revolves around the size, structure, and membership of Cabinet. While there has been some criticism in recent years about the steady weakening of Cabinet and Cabinet ministers as a collective decision-making body, the Cabinet still can have considerable impact on the direction of a government. Without any formal constitutional anchors, Cabinet is still the ultimate decision-making body in the land. For those who go into politics (or government, for that matter) and want to influence policymaking, the Cabinet table is the only place to be.

The third key element in the transition plan is the relationship that the government wants to establish with the public service. This decision will be determined by a large number of factors, but it will be crucial in setting the direction of the government, defining its policy agenda, and in implementing its election promises.

The final element in the plan is development of a media strategy for the transition, since anticipation of the swearing-in ceremony will engender much speculation and comment from the national media.

The success of a government, like that of any organization, depends on the quality of its people. Election success depends on the quality of the campaign team. The effectiveness of the transition plan depends on having the right people on the team, and newly elected governments can implement their agenda if they have recruited and promoted the right kind of people for the key jobs. It is therefore not surprising that dealing with staffing decisions and the hundreds of key appointments that must be approved by the prime minister can be daunting.

Staffing decisions generally fall into two categories: exempt staff,[3] which includes staff in the prime minister's and ministers' offices, such as political advisors, policy and communications experts, and support staff; and governor-in-council appointments, such as senior public servants, ambassadors, judges, and CEOs and board members of Crown corporations and agencies. As noted earlier, over the last forty years the number of exempt staff has increased steadily, as the importance of the role has expanded and taken on more meaning.

It would be difficult to argue that all these staffing decisions are crucial or vital to the government or to Canadians in general, but a discrete number of extremely important appointments are made by the prime minister that will define the "personality" of the government. As a result, the transition team needs to take a close look at identifying the key jobs to be immediately staffed by the prime minister. Experience shows that in addition to the exempt staff appointments, and the usual round of diplomatic ambassadorships, there can be as many as twenty governor-in-council appointments in the first six months after an election.[4]

Prime Minister's Office

The list of exempt staff positions requiring the prime minister's attention can be long, but the key staffing decisions focus on the recruitment of skilled individuals for the Prime Minister's Office. The PMO is composed of the prime minister's own political staff. The role of the office and its organization is developed in its entirety according to the preference of the prime minister, subject to parliamentary scrutiny of proposed estimates. The transition team can and should guide a prime minister-to-be in thinking through the most appropriate role, structure, and staffing for the PMO that will fit with his or her personal leadership style and the needs of the government.

The PMO is concerned chiefly with the coordination of policy development and the guidance of partisan interests. The principal support functions of the PMO have been to budget the prime minister's time, schedule and arrange travel and engagements, process the prime minister's correspondence, and handle all constituency matters. Over the years, the PMO has been organized to give political advice to the prime minister and to perform political analyses of policy options. It has been the political liaison with caucus, ministers, and their chiefs of staff. PMO staff have drafted the Throne Speech, other speeches, and public statements delivered by the prime minister; managed media relations and briefings in advance of question period and other meetings; advised on senior appointments outside the public service proper; and coordinated GIC appointments made on the recommendation of ministers.

One of the more difficult issues facing the operations of the PMO is in the demarcation between its role and that of the Privy Council Office. Successive clerks of the PCO and PMO chiefs of staff have sought to distinguish their roles and those of their respective groups by drawing distinctions between substantive advice that is "politically sensitive" and political advice that shows "administrative sensitivity." Whatever merit that might have as a theoretical model, it provides only a minimal practical basis for role definition. But not addressing the distinction between these two offices can lead to confusion and potential antipathy between two groups that are both critical to the leader's success. The question of role distinction might be better served by focusing on the principles that are most germane and upon which roles can be built. For example:

- Defining the government's agenda and its priorities is essentially a political issue, for which the PMO is primarily responsible; realizing the agenda by processing the necessary policies through Cabinet is essentially an operational issue, for which the PCO is responsible.
- The appointments of senior full-time personnel, especially deputy ministers, are fundamentally a management issue for which the clerk should be the prime minister's principal advisor and agent. Other GIC appointments are essentially political and should be controlled and directed through the PMO, although a more merit-based system would improve the quality of the appointments.

- Whether a particular policy will work or whether it is administratively sound is a matter for PCO advice and resolution; whether a policy will be acceptable to the government's various external publics, such as its *political* soundness, is a matter for PMO advice and resolution.

In its leadership role, the PMO is the main driver of the government and is ultimately responsible for ensuring implementation of major elements of the government's program by other ministers and the public service, and ensuring their acceptance by the country at large. In its communication role, the PMO should be an open channel, a two-way link between the prime minister and the multitude of constituencies that must be dealt with. The marketing and public-relations aspects of this function are obviously important. In its political role, the overriding concern of the PMO must always be what is best for the government, for the party, and for the prime minister.[5]

In light of the importance of a well-functioning PMO to the success of the government and the prime minister, the first appointments made by the prime minister into this office are critical and have to be done early in the mandate, preferably before the Cabinet is sworn in. The key jobs include chief of staff, executive assistant, senior policy advisor, caucus liaison, legislative and house planning, and communications director. The true challenge in managing the staffing process for the PMO is in recognizing that politics is about rewarding the party faithful, while remaining realistic about which candidates can truly add value and expertise for the prime minister within the office. It is useful to remember that loyalty without talent is a recipe for disaster.

In its first two years the Mulroney PMO suffered crisis after crisis, primarily because the prime minister had chosen partisans, who offered more loyalty than expertise. While loyalty and partisanship are important, a leader will need to choose partisans who also have identifiable skills in given areas. Appointments into the PMO generally do not allow time for on-the-job training – the pace can be brutal and the stakes are high. A new prime minister needs to choose people who are talented and will serve and promote the interests of the leader first and foremost, not their own. The PMO should not be filled with individuals who relish seeing their names in the newspaper every week. Rather, being comfortable with and even preferring anonymity and discretion should be ingrained characteristics of the people appointed into the PMO. With these criteria in mind, the key responsibilities associated with each key position are enumerated below.

There is no ideal size for the PMO although recent developments suggest that successive governments since Chrétien have become larger, as has the privy council office.

Chief of Staff

The chief of staff (or "principal secretary," during the Trudeau era) is the senior political advisor to the prime minister and has overall responsibility for the management of the PMO. He or she is the most senior staff liaison on political matters between the prime minister, the office and ministers, the caucus, the party, and the campaign strategy team. It is up to this individual to ensure that the prime minister is adequately informed and advised on matters in these areas, and that the leader's needs and views are adequately conveyed and represented to the other relevant parties. The chief of staff also serves as a spokesperson/representative for the prime minister in meetings and in communicating with important outside interest groups and individuals. Finally, the chief of staff represents the prime minister's interest in the appointments, ensuring that the administrative process for formalizing GIC appointments being managed in the PCO conforms with the prime minister's overall approach to governing.

As a former chief of staff, Powell observes, "The main skill needed for the job is the ability to keep a very large number of balls in the air at the same time and not to allow even one of them to fall to the ground."[6] While juggling many issues at the same time is a desirable skill, ultimately the key attribute of the chief of staff is the ability to say no to the prime minister when he or she wants to make a decision that is not in the public interest or in the interest of the government. At that moment, the job becomes a very lonely one, where the chief of staff's values and ethical fibre are tested to the limit.

As a consequence, the chief of staff should never be perceived or act as a personal friend. There is a fine line to be drawn between friendship and the offering of objective advice. Few effective chiefs of staff have crossed the line by becoming a close personal friend of the prime minister.

Maintaining some distance is a very important element in the chief of staff's ability to do the job well. It is therefore not surprising that leaders of the opposition or prime ministers in Canada have reached outside their inner circle for their chief of staff. It is their way of balancing the need for independent and frank advice and ensuring some continuity among senior staff.

Jean Pelletier once said to me that having an undated letter of resignation tucked away in an easily accessible place is perhaps the most effective device to remind the chief of staff of the obligation to provide honest advice.

Executive Assistant

The executive assistant is assigned the complex responsibility of managing the prime minister's time – not an easy task, in light of the constant demands made on the leader. The executive assistant leads day-to-day management of the prime minister's personal schedule and appointments, and the management of the paper that flows directly to and from the prime minister. This individual also acts as the PMO liaison and provides input into the tour groups and programs, liaises with the RCMP on security, oversees the senior staff at 24 Sussex, and accommodates the needs of the prime minister's spouse.

Senior Policy Advisor

The senior policy advisor provides political input to the government's legislative and policy program. This individual is responsible for monitoring the government program (as it comes into the PCO/Cabinet secretariat process), identifying significant political problems within the program, advising the prime minister of their implications, and, where necessary, instituting remedial action on the leader's behalf. The senior policy advisor liaises with ministers and key officials on the political aspects of major policy questions and represents the prime minister and PMO on special subcommittees or task forces set up to deal with substantial policy questions. This person retains senior staff responsibility for ensuring the prime minister is adequately briefed and prepared for his or her parliamentary role, and serves as the prime minister's representative by liaising with important outside opinion-makers and interest groups on policy.

Head of Communications

The communications director manages the PMO communications and media-relations program and contributes to the coordination of overall government communications. This individual manages the prime minister's day-to-day relations with the national news media, including organizing interviews and press conferences, and issuing releases, speech texts, and statements. The director conceives, develops, and executes special communications projects such as prime ministerial "addresses to the nation," and serves as the PMO link to a central government group mandated to coordinate overall government communications. The director is also responsible for the management of government advertising contracts and acts as a liaison to senior party and campaign communications personnel, coordinating PMO programs with their needs and activities.

Caucus and Party Liaison

This most critical position is sometimes treated as an afterthought by the transition team. As the title suggests, the key role of the caucus and party liaison person is to provide a strong bridge between the PM and the key members of the caucus and the party, whose ongoing support is crucial to the prime minister. The incumbent provides an invaluable service by constantly "feeling the pulse" of the party, in the House of Commons, in the Senate, and around the country. The person in this position should have an excellent network of relationships and be able not only to assess the mood of the party but also to gather information on the opposition and be able to predict how they will react to government policy initiatives. The Mulroney PMO was remarkably successful in this respect. As a result, Mulroney was able to manage his caucus adroitly through many political crises by taking advantage of his wide-ranging and well-developed network of relationships, sustained by an impressive information-gathering system in the PMO that identified those who supported him and those who were inclining to remove him from his job.

Ministers' Offices

Ministers have the authority to staff their offices with advisors and assistants who are not departmental public servants, who share the minister's political commitment, and who can supplement the professional, expert, and non-partisan advice and support provided by the public service. Ministers are accountable to the prime minister for their offices' exempt staff personally hired by them. In the same way that the PMO supports the prime minister, the office of a minister is vital to his or her own effectiveness. The political staff ensure that their minister's partisan political work in the constituency or within the caucus is kept separate and distinct from the minister's official departmental responsibilities.

Like the prime minister, a minister benefits from a dual stream of advice coming from both political staff and the public service. As a result, it is critical that the staff minister staff are fully informed of the limits of their responsibilities and authority. The prime minister expects ministers to establish productive and professional working relationships between their political staff, their deputy minister, and departmental officials. The appointment of political staff ensures that the public service is not used for partisan purposes, so that it can continue to serve successive governments as a politically neutral institution.

Embedded within a minister's office are a limited number of departmental assistants employed by the public service. The deputy minister, in accordance with conditions set by the Treasury Board, assigns these individuals from departmental resources. Their role is to liaise with the department and provide the minister with administrative support and general assistance on departmental or other government matters. While the transition team would not have any involvement in the selection of departmental staff, it would be interested in making sure that these important "connecting" positions are filled.

In general, the exempt staff help to manage the minister's time and provide partisan political support and advice. Their responsibilities include liaison with the party, Parliament, and interest groups, constituency work, travel and correspondence, media relations, and policy advice. Departmental officials, through the deputy minister, or exempt staff provide separate channels of advice and different kinds of operational support for the minister. Exempt staff do not have the authority to instruct departmental officials, but they are often in contact with each other and the department, and can be called upon for information through channels provided by the deputy minister.

Governor-in-Council Appointments

There are approximately 600 full-time and 2,300 part-time positions in agencies, boards, commissions, departments, and tribunals filled by governor-in-council (GIC) appointees. Also appointed through the GIC system are lieutenant governors, judges, and certain ambassadors and high commissioners named from the ranks of career public servants.

Technically, these appointments are made by the governor general, but convention dictates that he or she follow the advice of the prime minister. Upon gaining office, the prime minister is provided with a list of vacancies in key positions that need to be filled. These appointees can be broken down into four major groups:

- Deputy ministers and associate deputy ministers: approximately seventy-five in number, they manage the departments and agencies that characterize the core public service and are usually appointed from within the permanent public service.
- Heads and members of agencies, boards, commissions, and tribunals: they are recruited from all sectors, this group of approximately five hundred varies widely in background, responsibility, and remuneration.
- Heads of Crown corporations: these individuals are mostly presidents, chief executive officers, and a few full-time chairs of Crown corporations. For these approximately fifty people, the compensation and terms and conditions of employment vary as widely as they would for private-sector counterparts.
- Part-time GICs: These 2,300 positions include most chairpersons, directors, and members of Crown corporations, federal agencies, boards, commissions, and tribunals.

In addition to such factors as gender, regional, cultural, and linguistic considerations, the prime minister's choice is often circumscribed by legislation. In many cases, appointees must possess specific qualifications, while in other cases boards must maintain a certain profile. The management of the GIC appointment process is no small feat, as there can be as many as four thousand appointments made in the course of a four- to five-year parliamentary cycle.

In the past, prime ministers, key ministers, some officials in the Prime Minister's Office, and a select number of officials in the Privy Council Office handled the appointment process, discreetly and without particular reference to stakeholders outside this tight circle of key players. But by the time the Chrétien team arrived on the political scene in 1993 there had already been calls from the public, key stakeholder groups, senior personnel secretariat in the Privy Council Office, and some political quarters for a permanent change to an excessively partisan appointment system. It is hard to identify the point at which it became apparent that a serious overhaul in the Canadian patronage system was needed, but the uproar that followed Brian Mulroney's decision to appoint his wife's hairdresser to the National Capital Commission is a good example of how irresponsible the system had become.

As a consequence of the attention directed at the appointment process during the Mulroney years, Penny Collenette was recruited 1993 to assume responsibility for governor-in-council appointments in the prime minister's office. She quickly found common cause with senior officials in the Privy Council Office, and they worked together to radically reform the appointment process by advertising upcoming openings for appointments and publicizing the qualifications for each of the then more than three thousand appointments.

John Manley, a former minister and deputy prime minister under Chrétien, recalls the groundbreaking work done by Penny Collenette. With Prime Minister Chrétien's strong support, she insisted that all nominees for GIC appointments be competent for the job. Since so many government appointments are not necessarily meritorious, but are based instead on partisanship defined in the broadest terms, in the mid-1990s her emphasis on demonstrated competency was a new concept. Collenette was also committed to rebalancing the gender mix among GIC appointees. She was very insistent that for every vacancy there was at least one female candidate. While she wasn't always successful in appointing a woman to the position, she was "fearless" in providing advice, according to Manley, and ultimately she did change some of the attitudes of ministers and the prime minister when it came to making government appointments. Her persistence and willingness to "push back" were important elements in improving the quality of appointments in the 1990s.

Chrétien fully recognized the enormous power that the prime minister has in being able to make recommendations to the governor general on these many federal government appointments. Some appointments can be made only by the prime minister, but even in cases where ministers have the legal obligation to make them, Canadian tradition dictates that the prime minister has the final say. Given the pivotal role that appointments play in tipping the distribution of power in favour of the prime minister (and by extension, his office), Chrétien was prepared to make changes in the process but was reluctant to transfer his powers to an unelected independent body that he felt was unaccountable to Canadians and to Parliament.

John Manley, who served as minister of industry and later as finance, also recalls the challenges he had in managing the appointment process as a minister. Given the breadth of his portfolio, he estimated that as minister of industry he would be responsible for hundreds of appointments if he served a full four-year term. One of his major responsibilities as minister would be to ensure that qualified people were identified for the jobs and that all appointments were made in a timely manner and on a schedule that was developed by the Prime Minister's Office.

Before liaising with the PMO, Manley had to consult with the appropriate regional caucuses when he was considering making any GIC appointment. The process used by the chairs of the regional caucuses varied considerably, depending on the personalities involved. When Herb Gray was the regional minister for Ontario, he would spend at least one hour each week with the Ontario caucus to discuss appointments slated for approval in upcoming Cabinet meetings. This time-consuming process was streamlined considerably when Manley took over as chair of the Ontario caucus. He felt that their time would be better spent looking at policy issues than in examining the qualifications of potential appointees. Consequently, he distributed the names of nominated appointees to caucus members for their comments, and they were invited to provide input to him on an exceptional basis. In Manley's view, this simplified process was as effective as the earlier one and it freed the minister to do other things.

It is always important to acknowledge that, in the end, the prime minister has the final say in all GIC appointments. While it is very difficult to document good examples of instances when a prime minister made an appointment without consultation with the director of appointments or the responsible minister, there are anecdotal data on specific appointments. The individuals interviewed for this book agree unanimously that when a prime minister intervened or failed to consult, it usually turned out to be a poor appointment.

Judicial appointments are especially important in Canada, since our justice system is so important in balancing the work of the legislature and of the executive. The importance of the appointment of the governor for the Bank of Canada is similarly an extremely important one, given the centrality of the work of the Bank in defining Canada's economic environment. Despite the growing importance of the courts, the Bank of Canada, and many other government agencies, the current system operates in much the same way as it did thirty years ago. In John Manley's view, "We suffer from a lack of transparency, established job criteria, and a lack of respect for competence."[7]

Cabinet-Making

Unless one has worked within the small circle of government that has access to Cabinet meetings, few people really understand how the Cabinet functions. This is partly because each prime minister has complete authority over building his or her own Cabinet. According to Bill Neville, "Of all the prime ministerial prerogatives, none is more powerful – nor more personal – than the leader's right to name those who will serve as ministers in the government."[8] The prime minister must manage within broad legal requirements, but is essentially unfettered when deciding the number of ministers serving in Cabinet, the assignment of portfolios, and the people who will hold them.

Because Cabinet-making brings with it vast personal prerogative, there is no right way to tackle this activity. The road map begins with a decision on the size of the Cabinet. Some prime ministers prefer an inclusive approach that allows for as many Cabinet positions as is reasonably possible. Others try to minimize the size of Cabinet in an effort to make it more manageable. Neither approach is wrong. The transition team must carefully consider the strengths and weaknesses of multiple approaches to the size of Cabinet and recommend a formation that best meets the needs of the leader for the time. As always, the final decision will rest with the prime minister.

As discussed in chapter 2, prime ministers have chosen different-sized Cabinets in order to respond to a wide range of considerations. This includes the size of the elected caucus, the need for broad regional representation, and the range of the government's policy agenda. The two operational maxims in determining the size of the Cabinet are first, each successive addition to the Cabinet is chosen from among a less-suitable and less-competent cadre of potential ministers, and second, with each additional Cabinet member, the quality of the discussion around the Cabinet table decreases proportionally.

When Paul Martin became prime minister in 2003, he brought a leadership style intended to develop his Cabinet into an inclusive and collaborative decision-making body. Mike Robinson, the head of his transition team, remembers having a number of conversations with Martin sketching out Cabinet positions and potential people to fill the various jobs: "First of all, the advice to Paul was to have a smaller Cabinet. He rejected that advice and wanted to have the largest Cabinet he thought he could justify, in order to achieve a collaborative decision-making model. Furthermore, he also made the decision that he was going to swear in the parliamentary secretaries as privy councillors, to broaden the inclusiveness."[9]

Ian Clark, currently a professor of public management and a former secretary to the Treasury Board noted, "The smallest Cabinet in recent history was formed by Kim Campbell bringing only 23 ministers to the table. That is considered small by Cabinet standards, but anyone with leadership experience can attest to the difficulty of discussing anything substantively across a group of over 20 people."[10]

In this regard, Derek Burney is critical of the size of the Stephen Harper's 2011 Cabinet. "I think it's egregious. I think it's obscene. It's not even helpful. I had the conversation about Cabinet size with the Prime Minister in 2006 and as a result we cut it down to twenty-six from Martin's too-large Cabinet. At the time I said, 'Prime Minister, once you cut it down, it's only going to go up! It's not going to go down anymore, so let's get it as slim and trim as we can.' I reminded him that you have all of these egos in the Cabinet room. Instead of having to manage twenty-six, you've got thirty-nine. Well, it doesn't make your job easier!"[11]

Once the size of Cabinet has been established, its structure and organization need to be addressed. The transition team will often begin with the structure established by the former regime. The starting point is to determine whether or not it is necessary to change the structure, and if so, to what advantage. For example, how should Canada be organized for dealing with foreign policy? Over the years, the prime minister has become the central player in developing foreign policy, and most federal government departments and agencies have staff dedicated to international issues. At the same time, Canada has maintained a portfolio of departments with mandates focused on foreign affairs, international trade, aid and development, and defence and security. How should these organizations be coordinated, and what implications does this have for the structure of Cabinet? Where does the role of foreign policy advisor fit into this mix? These decisions should be made within the context of the government's priorities and based on the approach of the leader.

Over the years, prime ministers have structured one-, two-, or three-tier ministries, depending how "equally" they want their ministers to be treated and whether they prefer working with a relatively large or small Cabinet. The tradition in Canada is to build a one-tier ministry in which all ministers are members of the Cabinet. A two-tier ministry is one in which all ministers are members of the Cabinet and others are members of a smaller executive committee, normally referred to at the federal level as Priorities and Planning.

The three-tier model has the same features as the two-tier, with the addition of a group of ministers who are not members of the Cabinet but are a part of the ministry. The three-tier model has been a fixture of British government for many years and has been used in Australia as well. Regardless of how many tiers the prime minister creates, the ministers are members of the Crown, sworn to office, and bound by Cabinet secrecy and collective responsibility. Most important, "when the Prime Minister appoints a minister to head an organization, the House of Commons may be assured that the minister will be fully accountable for its activities."[12]

In a three-tier ministry, those who are in the Cabinet are without a doubt the "senior" ministers in the government, and those who are members of the Priorities and Planning Committee are similarly more "senior" to the others. There is not necessarily a strict correlation, however, between membership in the Cabinet and, say, heading a department. Some departmental ministers may be outside Cabinet and some ministers without departments may be in it. For both practical and political reasons, however, it makes sense to have the portfolio ministers in the Cabinet and ministers of state outside it, each reporting to a portfolio minister. But all of this is the prerogative of the prime minister.

The three-tier system has a number of advantages. It enables a prime minister to develop ministerial talent by assigning people to progressively more senior and demanding positions. It also assigns each non-Cabinet minister to a Cabinet minister to whom they report politically and administratively. This makes the junior jobs genuine training positions, with Cabinet ministers as the trainers. It establishes a clear hierarchy within the ministry and allows for a better division of work within each portfolio. The entire burden of travel, public speaking, parliamentary and committee work, and liaison with interest groups does not fall on the shoulders of a single minister.

The move to a three-tier ministry almost always involves an increase in the overall size of the ministry, which means more ministerial jobs for aspiring members of caucus. In theory, it can allow government to exercise greater political control over the administration through the presence of more ministers than would be possible in a single-tier system. Also in theory, it can allow the government to be more closely attuned and responsive to the population with more ministerial "eyes and ears."

Notwithstanding these considerations, there are a number of reasons why the three-tier system has never really caught on in Canada.
Experience shows that Canadians do not appreciate the difference
between Cabinet ministers and junior ministers. They tend to think
that every minister heads a ministry, with all of the attendant bureaucracy and cost. Similarly, ministers themselves do not always accept the
senior/junior distinction. Achieving adequate regional representation
is always a challenge in Canadian Cabinet-making and can also be a
problem in a three-tier ministry. In practical terms, no province, region,
or interest group would be satisfied if its minister were not a *real Cabinet*
minister. Finally, the creation of a Priorities and Planning Committee
(P&P) or inner Cabinet in a two-tier system effectively differentiates
among ministers without excluding anyone from Cabinet.

Canadian leaders have chosen to steer clear of a full-scale three-tier
model for a variety of reasons. Nevertheless, history does not need to
continue to repeat itself. The transition team should present the leader
with as many options as logically align with his or her leadership style
and approach.

Following considerations of size, structure, and organization comes
the difficult task of deciding how best to populate the Cabinet positions.
As mentioned earlier, it can be very difficult to reorganize the size and
structure of Cabinet in the midst of a mandate. These decisions should
be made with long-term stability in mind, although with a minority
government the considerations might be different. Selection of members of the Cabinet should come as the final phase, once the structural
elements have been solidified. As a prime minister continues to lead the
government in the years to come, change can come by moving people
in and out of Cabinet based on the needs of the government of the day.

When selecting members to a Cabinet, a prime minister will take into
consideration characteristics such as experience in government, loyalty,
professional knowledge, and regional, ethnic, and age representation.
There are no hard-and-fast rules that need to be followed – the prime
minister has complete authority over who is selected, and, over time,
who stays in Cabinet. The tradition is to fill the Cabinet with members
of Parliament, but there have been instances where a prime minister
has also appointed a senator into it. Perhaps one of the more controversial decisions of a prime minister in recent years was Harper's appointment of Michael Fortier to a Cabinet position, despite the fact that he
was not an elected MP at the time. Three weeks after the appointment,

he was formally summoned to the Senate and took on the role of minister of public works and government services.

The starting point for selecting the Cabinet is the core positions, and then less-important ones are filled. One of the first decisions to be made is whether to appoint a deputy prime minister, followed by the choice of possible candidates to lead the finance, treasury board, and external affairs portfolios. Other key positions will depend on the priorities of the government and the personal perspective of the leader. When Mulroney was selecting Cabinet ministers in 1984, his transition plan provided advice, which continues to hold true today:

> You will feel that some of your supporters deserve to be rewarded and that you have an obligation to so reward them. Both feelings undoubtedly have merit in several cases. But the point to be emphasized – and I do so with all my strength – is that cabinet appointments should not be considered rewards for past service. They are simply too critical to your present and future to be assigned on any basis other than choosing the best or most talented people you have available to you. There are a multitude of other "reward" prerogatives at your disposal and I urge you to use them, as you deem appropriate. But, subject only to the broadest requirements of representing regions et al., you truly should choose the best and the brightest for your cabinet.[13]

Those who have been involved in transition exercises know that this is easier said than done. In an ideal world, talent, experience, and capability should always win out over other considerations.[14] Gerald Kaufman, a former minister in Britain's Labour government, captured this dynamic in his irreverent reflections on how to be a minister: "Some prime ministers do indeed seek to create an administration consisting entirely of political clones of themselves. In addition, though, prime ministers face the need to provide representation for the various ideological strands in their parties, partly in order to achieve an equitable balance, partly to keep certain troublesome nuisances quiet. Anyone who wishes to qualify for the latter category should manage a nice compromise between being troublesome enough but not too troublesome."[15]

One challenge that a prime minister faces in comparison with his presidential counterparts is that he is typically obliged to select a Cabinet from among fellow elected members of Parliament. While there is no requirement for prime ministers to limit themselves to elected officials, Canadian convention speaks to the expectation that the Cabinet will be representative of the country through our elected officials. It is therefore interesting to note that only 20 per cent of current members of Parliament have had some political experience before being elected. Compare this to the United States, for example, where more than 70 per cent of those in Congress worked in politics before being elected, either as unelected officials, political advisors, or staff members to an elected official.

While most of our MPs pursued a professional career before being first elected, the vast majority of them had only limited experience in governing in any political arena.

It appears that Tony Blair had a particular view of "best fit" in Cabinet appointments. He saw ministerial appointments as fundamentally satisfying a political need. Unlike Bill Neville, he considered competency and expertise to be secondary attributes. To ensure the primacy of political considerations, Blair sought the advice of the chief whip on the performance of the members of Parliament in the House of Commons so that he could choose those who had been particularly supportive of the government's policy preferences (and probably his leadership).

In addition, Blair received confidential briefings from public servants about the performance of his current ministers in order to have an independent assessment when considering a Cabinet shuffle. However, to ensure that the public service did not inflate their influence on Cabinet-making, Jonathan Powell observes, with tongue firmly in cheek, that the opinion of a minister's driver should be valued more than the opinion of a permanent secretary, since, unlike the permanent secretary, the chauffeur, being an observer of the minister's unvarnished behaviour, would be a better judge of ministerial performance.[16]

It might be expected that the prime minister would use the experience gained by members of Parliament as "shadow ministers" in making Cabinet choices, but there is no guarantee that having been a shadow critic will increase the likelihood that the appointee will be a good minister. In fact, Powell makes an observation about the value of shadow Cabinet members on the basis of his experience with the Blair government: "A new prime minister should not worry about continuity with shadow cabinet positions. Whatever experience has been gained in opposition is of little use in government, and in any case some politicians are better in opposition than they are in government."[17]

Key Cabinet Positions

While not the most important position in the Cabinet, the decision to appoint a deputy prime minister (DPM) is one of the most anticipated appointments made by a new prime minister. No rules determine whether there is a need for a DPM except that Canadian prime ministers have sometimes used the appointment to shore up political support or to benefit from the skills of a particularly gifted administrator. In the United Kingdom, the DPM position has often buttressed the political weight of the prime minister. Jonathan Powell saw the DPM role exclusively in a political context by stating, "The leader needs a Deputy [Prime Minister] who can reach parts of the party that he cannot and who can help ensure loyalty in the cabinet and more widely."[18]

While there is some debate about the importance or value of the DPM position, one indisputable and crucial relationship in the Canadian political system is that between the prime minister and the minister of finance. In essence, the prime minister controls the Cabinet decision-making system and the appointment process, while the minister of finance is responsible for government spending, the broad economic management of the country, and its fiscal and tax policy. Given the allocation of responsibilities between these two key positions, it is not surprising that the prime minister will spend an inordinate amount of time in choosing a minister of finance.

The prime minister needs to find an individual who will give comfort to the business community and will project an image of confidence to the general public. At a minimum, the prime minister is looking for a "sound," dependable, and honest relationship with the minister of finance, one that produces an annual budget accepted by the key stakeholder groups around the country.

Unfortunately, for many prime ministers, these attributes often belong to politicians with their own aspirations to become the leader of their party. As a consequence, given the experiences of recent prime ministers in Australia, the United Kingdom, and Canada, the appointment of the minister of finance is increasingly problematic.

Parenthetically, when the minister of finance is underperforming, the prime minister and his office will quickly move to fill the policy vacuum. This is one crucial Cabinet position that cannot suffer from a weak appointment, and there are always people in the PMO and within the public service ready to deal with tax and spending decisions, should the opportunity present itself.

There are, of course, other important positions in the Cabinet; one of the most challenging in terms of its appointment concerns foreign policy. Heading the Ministry of Foreign Affairs, Trade and Development gives the minister high visibility by providing many opportunities to perform on the international stage. As a consequence, it is a highly valued Cabinet position and eagerly sought out by senior ministers. However, over the years as a result of the increased role of the prime minister in foreign policy through the G8, G20, APEC, the UN, and others, the minister of foreign affairs must be willing to cede the ministerial space when the prime minister takes centre stage. Despite the sharing role inherent in this Cabinet position, as Tony Blair points out, based on his own experiences in dealing with a number of foreign ministers, one distinctive characteristic of this ministerial portfolio is that "no one ever wants to stop being foreign secretary."[19] He continues: "Of all the jobs, that's the one they get to thinking is theirs and should jolly well continue being theirs until the end of time, or at least the end of the government, and even then some harbour the thought that they had done it so well, shouldn't it be elevated above the squalor of party politics?"[20]

Once the decision of "who goes where" is made, prime ministers owe ministers their direct and personal leadership, support, and ear when they need it. Because the making of Cabinet is the personal prerogative of prime ministers, they are solely responsible and accountable for its composition and performance.

Mandate Letters

One example of the value of being well prepared for a transition is the need to develop mandate letters for each minister. These letters form the accountability accord for ministers, outlining the overall government priorities, the minister's portfolio responsibilities, and specific personal goals for the minister. The substance of these mandate letters is developed by the transition team during Phase One and then later written by the PCO in Phase Three under the close watchful eye of the transition team. "Mandate letters are critical because, after all of the picture-taking and celebration, they capture the to-do list right off the top."[21] They are developed using the tentative Cabinet structure chosen by the leader and will reflect the leadership approach of the prime minister.

For example, Chrétien distributed mandate letters that were to the point and strategic, leaving the operational and tactical approach for implementation to the minister and his or her team. Alternatively, the mandate letters developed by Harper and his transition team are more detailed and prescriptive, in keeping with his approach to managing the government.[22] Following the 2006 election, Harper also insisted that the mandate letters be handed out the day of the swearing-in. With so many inexperienced ministers moving into key positions, there was a need to give them either a script or the mandate letters so they had specific speaking points for the inevitable media scrums.[23]

Cabinet Decision-Making

Chaired by the prime minister, Cabinet provides the forum in which ministers reach a consensus and decide on issues where political and strategic considerations come to bear on proposed ministerial actions. Consequently, the decision-making process that sets the rules and protocols for the operation of Cabinet is another crucial decision for prime ministers. Obviously, it should reflect their own style of governing, including how hard they want to work, whom they trust within Cabinet, the degree to which they are willing to share power, and their preoccupation with administrative efficiency.

Ground rules for the conduct of Cabinet business are few but essential for maintaining Cabinet solidarity and practical effectiveness.[24] The prime minister leads all aspects of the Cabinet decision-making process, organizes Cabinet and Cabinet committee decision-making, determines the agenda for Cabinet business, and chooses committee chairpersons to act on his behalf. The bulk of collective ministerial deliberations take place in Cabinet committees. Committee chairpersons act for the prime minister and with his or her authority. The basic goal of this system is to settle as many questions as possible at the committee stage to increase the efficiency of Cabinet, allowing it to concentrate on priority issues and broad political concerns.

Within this structure, Cabinet government works through compromise and consensus, culminating in Cabinet itself. Cabinet and Cabinet committees do not vote on questions before them. Instead, the prime minister "calls" for the consensus after ministers have expressed their views. Before taking over the reins of power, a leader should have a well thought-out strategy for how to structure the Cabinet committee system and how decision-making will unfold. This is an enormous responsibility and source of power for prime ministers, and will directly reflect their leadership style.

Both the business and deliberations of Cabinet are secret. The Cabinet's collective decision-making process is protected by the rule of confidentiality that ultimately protects Cabinet solidarity and collective ministerial responsibility. Confidentiality also ensures that ministers can frankly express their views before making a final decision. Once a decision is made, ministers are expected to collectively support the decisions of Cabinet in Parliament and in public.[25]

Many prime ministers choose to use a Priorities and Planning Committee as an executive committee of Cabinet, one establishes the goals and objectives of the government, monitors the political health of the party and government, and ensures that the bureaucracy is broadly responsive to the priorities and plans of the committee.

Cabinet committees are a part of the Cabinet system and can vary in number, size, and mandate. Some prime ministers have enjoyed managing a large number of committees that all feed into the Cabinet process, while others have preferred a simpler decision-making process. Chrétien has written about the Cabinet committees and noted that the committee reforms that were initiated under Trudeau were intended "to take the preponderance of power from the bureaucratic mandarins and give it back to the ministers. The committees were to enable the ministers to know what was going on in all the departments, to take part in all the decisions, and to make their political decisions predominate over the bureaucratic decisions. In the old days most ministers had no idea what the government as a whole was doing. Under the new system they could know if they took the trouble to find out, and they could take part in the discussions."[26]

Machinery-of-Government Considerations

One of the most important responsibilities of the prime minister is to allocate functions between ministers to ensure that the Cabinet and the government are structured in the best way. The general activity of allocating responsibilities and organizational design is referred to as machinery-of-government issues. "The key objective is to structure government in a way that responds to current challenges, thereby ensuring a constant focus on the key issues. To achieve this, the Prime Minister has to be able to act quickly to change the structure of the government."[27]

Some of the key principles that define the work of machinery-of-government experts are:

- Changes to the organization of government are a matter for the prime minister, on the advice of the Cabinet secretary.

- Machinery-of-government change is disruptive and costly for the organizations involved and can distract them from delivery of programs for some time afterwards, so there needs to be a clear explanation of why change is required.
- Decisions need to be taken on the basis of the best possible analysis of the pros and cons to a machinery change.
- For the implementation of larger changes, a dedicated transition team should be established to support the permanent secretary and the board.
- Effective communication is crucial to a successful change in the machinery of government.
- Resources transferred to a new or important department should be sufficient to support the functions transferred.
- Staff generally transfer with a function when it moves from one department to another, subject to the receiving permanent secretaries' judgment about the most appropriate fit of people to roles at the most senior level.

Each prime minister has faced the daunting decision of whether or not to reorganize the machinery of government. This is a responsibility that every successful prime minister has taken seriously and is one area in which the transition team must excel. According to Jim Mitchell, "A prime minister needs to surround himself with people with intellectual maturity, who can think conceptually and express themselves well, and who understand enough about government that the advice they can give about how government can be structured and organized is useful advice."[28] Leaders need to have confidence in the advice given and in the wide-ranging repercussions of their decisions.

Most important, the time to make changes to the structure of government is at the beginning of a mandate, when the reins of power are being taken over and a Cabinet is being built. And unless a transition team thoughtfully prepares options in advance of an election, changes to the structure will be almost impossible to accomplish. The complexities and costs involved with these types of initiatives are too important to be done quickly in the wake of an election victory and without the professional advice of machinery experts.

Those who have been involved in transition planning can attest to the challenge of taking on the restructuring task. Ian Brodie, who was chief of staff and a member of Harper's transition team in 2006, has lived through this experience. "If I had known then what I know now, I would have asked PCO to come up with a list of machinery changes of its own. You could fix some of these jurisdictional issues between departments when you are first sworn into Cabinet that are later lost when you start governing."[29]

A transition team always starts with the structure that has been implemented by the former government. The question then becomes, is it necessary and beneficial to make changes? The team that supported Chrétien through the 1993 transition reviewed the vast changes that had recently been made by Kim Campbell and decided that the benefit of restructuring would not outweigh the costs. As a result, Chrétien chose to maintain the structure that he inherited and made only minor adjustments – the most significant being a scaling back of the public security department that Campbell created. At the time Chrétien strongly felt that it was far too intrusive for Canadians, and he took the opportunity at the beginning of his first mandate to reorganize the portfolio.

As previously discussed, intra-party transitions have produced the most extensive machinery changes. For example, major reorganizations were implemented when Turner took over from Trudeau, Campbell from Mulroney, and Martin from Chrétien. Specifically, Turner dismantled the two Cabinet-level policy-coordinating agencies[30] that Trudeau had created by abolishing the two coordinating secretary of state development departments in an effort to show his disdain for the elaborate planning apparatus that had grown up while Trudeau was prime minister. In 1993, Campbell led a wide-ranging reorganization, decreasing the number of departments from thirty-two to twenty-three, and dramatically shifting deputy ministers from one portfolio to another without warning or apparent rationale. Although these changes had been planned for some time, Campbell took the opportunity immediately after her swearing-in to reinforce the symbolism of a new regime by merging departments and creating some super-ministries to improve program delivery.[31]

Under Paul Martin, the downsizing of Cabinet was reversed and instead was increased dramatically, because he needed to reward the members of his caucus who had supported him in his quest for the party leadership. As well, his personal preference for roundtable discussions convinced him to widen the circle by creating a large Cabinet and then including ministers of state in his Cabinet meetings.

In every transition scenario, a prime minister must weigh the benefits of changes to the machinery of government against the significant costs that are incurred. Changes should be made to reinforce good management principles and not solely for leadership optics. In undertaking an assessment of potential shifts to the structure of government, a transition team should clearly lay out the rationale, benefit, and costs of any restructuring proposals. Restructuring should be considered in order to reduce duplication, to vacate an area that does not fall under federal jurisdiction, to discontinue programs that are not meeting the intended goals, or to end programs that are no longer necessary. When assessing the costs, leaders need to be cognizant that machinery changes can be disruptive to labour management relations, controversial with stakeholders, and distracting for ministers and officials. A recent study in the United Kingdom estimated that hasty decisions resulting in structural changes to government are typically disruptive for up to two years.[32]

Key Public Service Appointments

A transition team must also put considerable thought and deliberation into how an incoming government will work with the public service. Unfortunately, many incoming governments know little about the public service and do not appreciate the importance of the relationship. The transition team must prepare the leader to send clear messages about the nature of collaboration between the public service and the incoming government and set the stage for a productive working relationship as soon as possible.

First and foremost, a productive working relationship between the incoming government and the public service begins with the relationship between the prime minister and secretary to the Cabinet. The secretary to the Cabinet (clerk of the Privy Council) is the head of the public service and is the deputy minister to the prime minister. As a result, the secretary wields considerable traditional power as a gatekeeper to the leader and as the individual who exercises enormous control over the process of accessing the prime minister and Cabinet. The relationship between the prime minister and the clerk is crucial. Prime ministers cannot delegate this relationship to someone else without substantial loss to their authority and indeed to their ability to manage government. The clerk is the prime minister's representative in dealing with deputy ministers and agency heads and must be seen by them to carry the authority of the government.

To be successful, a clerk must be dispassionate, fair minded, discreet, thorough, and able to subordinate personal and political views to serve the prime minister and the government of the day.[33] An effective, comfortable relationship between the prime minister and the clerk allows the prime minister to have a simple and direct line of authority into the public service.

Early in their mandate, prime ministers often appoint a new secretary to the Cabinet. The decision to replace the secretary is not a negative reflection on the skills and abilities of the incumbent but simply reflects the reality that the secretary must be someone with whom the prime minister is personally comfortable and who shares or complements the prime minister's leadership style. That being said, the appointment of a new secretary rarely happens immediately following an election. The Cabinet secretary plays too pivotal a role during the transition period, especially during the lead-up to the swearing-in of the Cabinet, to be replaced by someone without the experience and understanding of the transition issues. However, once the transition has moved to the consolidation phase and the machinery is functioning well, the prime minister may begin putting a personal stamp on senior ranks of the public service.

In order to solidify the relationship between the political and public service leadership when a new government is formed, the transition plan should allow for a meeting between the prime minister and the deputy minister community as soon as possible after assuming office. This is important, not only to establish in the minds of the public service the importance the prime minister attaches to their support role, but also to establish clear expectations. This meeting should include a generic outline of the government's game plan so they know there are changes coming that will affect them and they can situate the changes in a context consistent with the leader's goals and objectives, and their value to the government. Prime ministers should also share their views of their relationship to their ministers and to the principal public servant, the clerk of the Privy Council.

Without a doubt, a party that comes to office after being in opposition for many years will bring some degree of scepticism about the loyalty, or more accurately the neutrality, of the public service. Politicians often bring a "them/us" mentality into government, where the public

service is perceived as being particularly loyal to the outgoing government. The issue of loyalty is an especially difficult concept to quan-
tify because it is probably more of a perceptual issue than one related
to actual behaviour, although close friendships between the outgoing
government and the senior public servants are not unusual.

Regardless of the posture of the new government towards the public
service, our Westminster conventions are based on the proposition that
the public service will be totally loyal to the government in power. The
Values and Ethics Code for the federal public service requires that public servants "give honest and impartial advice" and "loyally implement
ministerial decisions, lawfully taken." Moreover, they are expected to
"maintain the tradition of the political neutrality of the Public Service."
During the transition period, the public service is particularly sensitive
to maintaining its non-partisan profile in order to avoid accusations
that it favours an electoral outcome.

Despite the existence of codes of behaviour and the admonitions ema-
nating from central agencies, it is impossible to ensure that public servants are value-neutral, because all senior officials are forever "actively
involved in politics in the broad sense of the authoritative allocation of
values for society."[34] Barker goes on to point out that "public servants
(at all levels) have never been value-neutral, and they have become less
so as their discretionary powers have increased. Many of the decisions
they make oblige them, or give them the opportunity to inject their own
views as to which values should take priority."[35]

As a consequence, new governments learn early in their mandates
that they can count on the loyalty of the public service from the moment
the election results are known. Despite the deep-rooted inclination to
be distrustful of the public service, one of the true tests of a new government's ability to demonstrate leadership is how it behaves in its
efforts to make "them" into "us," by carefully using prime ministerial
prerogatives and by nurturing and earning the loyalty and support of
the senior ranks of the public service.

In advising Mulroney on making senior personnel changes to the public service, Bill Neville wrote, "Contrary to the impressions of some, you
will find that the majority of these individuals are bright, competent and
hardworking and offer skills and experience which you would be hard-
pressed to replace and without which your government simply cannot
function. The other basic comment I would offer under this heading is
similar to the caution I entered in regard to changes in the machinery of

government: in approaching senior personnel issues, please make haste carefully. Again, the process is more complex than some seem to understand and the risk of serious mistakes is very much there."[36]

The prime minister has authority to appoint the deputy ministers and associate deputy ministers. A critical advisor to this process must be the clerk of the Privy Council, who is most familiar with the complexities of the system and the individuals involved. Nevertheless, it is the prerogative of the prime minister to seek advice from a variety of sources. Derek Burney remembers that he provided an assessment of the senior ranks of the public service based on "80 per cent of what I knew and 20 per cent based on canvassing people like Arthur Kroeger," who had recently completed an assessment of the deputies on behalf of PCO just prior to the election. According to Burney, "The conclusions that Kroeger reported were profound for those who were familiar with the Canadian system of government. I thought his findings were important, so I arranged for Kroeger to brief Harper to familiarize him with the deputy minister community."[37]

The Media

Transition teams need to give some consideration to the degree to which they want to interact with the media. There are many pros and cons to whether a public transition is advisable, but the key elements in deciding to go public would be if the incoming government wants to give a profile to the transition exercise, if it wants to develop a close relationship with the national media, and if there are any policy issues that the prime minister wants to highlight in advance of the swearing-in ceremony.

Traditionally, the transition period after an election is a quiet one for the national media, so the media agenda is traditionally driven by the government-in-waiting instead of the press corps that is hungry for news. Despite this quiet time, the transition team in most circumstances will be developing a media strategy that includes preparing a narrative for the newly elected government that will roll out at the swearing-in ceremony and beyond.

Two examples of communications strategies are presented below to demonstrate the full range of communications that a transition team develops in the course of its deliberations. The key messages for the government after the 1997 election reveals a simple series of messages building on the track record of the first-term Chrétien government. The communications strategy in 1997 was:

Key messages:

- To convey decisiveness and commitment to action (as was the case in 1993);
- To provide Canadians with good government during the summer months;
- To implement the policy agenda as outlined in "Securing Our Future Together";
- Low key – the government is back to work;
- Announce the dates of the

  o Swearing-in
  o First Cabinet meeting
  o Cabinet retreat
  o PM's summer schedule;

- Vetting of new ministers;
- Expression of thanks to the Canadian people for their support.

In 2000, the political and economic ground had shifted significantly from three years earlier, and the communications plan after the 2000 election reveals a different set of priorities for the third-term Chrétien government:

Key messages:

- Rejuvenated government, ready to meet challenges of the new economy;
- New team with new players;
- Government is prepared to be creative in solving policy challenges;
- In a hurry to deal with the issues raised during the campaign;
- Integrity in government;
- Prepared to renew the public service.

Challenges arising from 2000 election:

- Addressing the attacks on the integrity of the PM;
- Managing the mandate during a leadership campaign;

- Looking at ways to address the need for Western representation in Cabinet;
- Modernizing the role of Parliament and of the member of Parliament;
- Securing the prime minister's legacy in two years.

Interestingly, while governments in recent years have invested heavily in building a more aggressive communications capacity in order to better target their messaging to the public, there is no indication, at the present time, that either media relations or communications are as core an activity to transition planning as they are in governing.

Conclusion

This chapter begins the task of developing the building blocks for a transition, regardless of its type. The key elements that were described in this chapter for inclusion in the transition book for a new prime minister include sections on staffing, Cabinet-making, and the relationship between the incoming government and the public service.

With regards to staffing of the PMO and ministers offices, it is important to underscore the importance of hiring the right people for the key jobs in the PMO and in ministers' offices. All jobs in these organizations are important, since any weak link in the organizational structure will put the government or a minister at risk.

This section also emphasized the centrality of Cabinet-making in the transition. The size of the Cabinet, its structure, and appointments are all pivotal decisions for a new prime minister. Given that so few ministers have enough relevant work-related experience before their appointment, it is especially important that the suitability of ministers is fully explored before the swearing-in of the government. While all positions in a single-tier or multi-tiered Cabinet are important, prime ministers must give special consideration to the appointment of their deputy prime minister, the minister of finance, and the minister of foreign affairs. To buttress the smooth functioning of the Cabinet system, prime ministers have to give careful consideration to the decision-making process, including the use of Cabinet committees, and to the content of the mandate letters that will define the agenda for ministers at the early stage of the administration.

This chapter also continues the complex discussion of the important role played by the public service in the transition planning and the way in which the political and public service agendas will merge at a later phase in the transition. Finally, the chapter concludes with a short discussion of the role of the media in transition planning.

The stage is now set to move to the election phase. This is an exciting and, at times, surreal period as the transition team ramps up its work with the goal line clearly in view. While most of the media attention will be focused on the election, the policy priorities of the various parties, the performance of the leaders, and the daily polling results, the transition will work off-site and will take advantage of this "quiet" period to bring all the transition strands together into a coherent and seamless plan.

5 Election Phase: Putting the Building Blocks in Place

Prime ministers require the hide of a rhinoceros, the morals of St Francis, the patience of Job, the wisdom of Solomon, the strength of Hercules, the leadership of Napoleon, the magnetism of a Beatle, and the subtlety of Machiavelli.

– Lester B. Pearson

Introduction

The political side and the public service continue their activities in parallel without much interaction over the course of the thirty-five-day election period. At this point, the transition work has entered Phase Two of transition planning, with both sides accelerating the pace of their work. As well, as depicted in the figure 5.1, both sets of players are adding additional resources to the transition "funnel" as the scope of work expands and more detailed information is added to the transition mix.

On the political side, the level of effort is determined by the probability of winning the election and forming the government. For those who feel they have a very good chance on election day, the work is also expanding and becomes more serious. For those parties with low expectations about winning, only a few elements of a complete transition plan will be completed in the unlikely chance that the fortunes of the party will change dramatically during the election.

For partisans working in ministers' offices and the PMO, the transition has an added complexity, since they still have to provide a level of professional support to the sitting government. The prime minister

Figure 5.1. The Evolution of a Transition

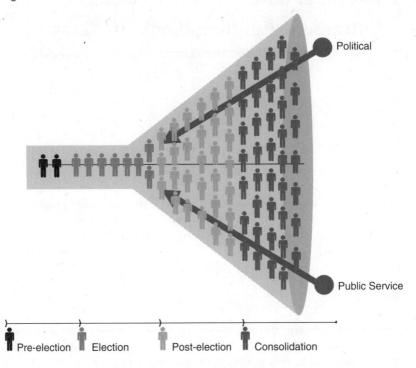

and ministers are still in power and must always be in a position to govern throughout the election campaign. The opposition parties' level of effort will be dictated largely by the election polls and the degree to which they feel they have a good chance of winning. For example, in the May 2011 election, the New Democratic Party spent almost no time preparing for a transition, since they did not see themselves as having any real chance of forming a government. However, there were moments during the last days of the campaign when everything seemed possible, and emails started flying back and forth as the NDP looked for experts on government transitions.

The Liberals, who entered the campaign as the Official Opposition, prepared for a number of possible scenarios. They concentrated mostly on minority-government combinations and the way in which they would comport themselves in the event of another minority government. At all times, and regardless of the polling data, the opposition parties are forced to make a choice in an election campaign between spending resources that will garner more votes or investing in planning for a transition that may never be implemented.

By far the most active planning during the five-week election campaign takes place within the departments and agencies of the federal government. The transition exercise now takes on the look of a major government initiative, engaging hundreds of policy analysts and coordinators. Over the course of the campaign, each and every department and agency will initiate some form of transition planning.

The way Phase Two plays out very much depends on the expected outcome of the election. As a result, the daily tracking polls affect the rhythm of the work. When the governing party appears to be on the verge of re-election, the PCO and departments prepare for continuity and the resumption of the previous government's agenda. When it looks likely that one of the opposition parties will triumph, attention turns to the fundamentals of governing. The briefing books get larger, and the scope of the work takes a broader perspective, to accommodate a new minister from an opposition party.

A number of conventions are generally accepted and followed during elections in Canada. First, there is an overall prohibition on announcements regarding new policy decisions during election campaigns. Similarly, no major spending decisions will be made during the election. Third, it is expected that the government will not make significant appointments to key positions within the public service or in any of its agencies, unless there is an urgent need to do so. In those cases that require a governor-in-council signature, consultations with the leaders of the opposition parties are expected to take place. That being said, the prime minister has the right to proceed alone unless legislation dictates the support of the other parties (e.g., the appointment of heads of parliamentary agencies).

Of particular note has been the practice initiated by the Harper government to limit the activities of public servants during the election campaign. Arguing that public appearances of public servants during an election campaign might undermine their non-partisanship, the Harper government has completely curtailed any activity of the public service during a campaign. These rules apply to all areas of federal activity, including speeches by ambassadors in faraway countries, presentations at conferences, or explanations of current government policies to an inquiring public. This is despite the fact that there are already established practices associated with the caretaker conventions

**Behind the Scenes: Pressures to Make Governor-in-Council
Appointments during a General Election**

We wanted to appoint a lieutenant governor in British Columbia. That
was the one time Glen Shortliffe (clerk of the Privy Council at the time)
had to say no, because it was not appropriate for the prime minister to
make such a high-profile appointment in the midst of an election. In
essence, we were cautioned not to make any appointments during the
election, regardless of the rationale.

In fact there was considerable pressure on Prime Minister Kim Campbell to make policy decisions regarding a couple of pet projects right up
until the day of the election. I was the one who resisted the relentless
pressure by not allowing it to happen. Repeatedly, we were both shocked
at the access that lobbyists had had under Mulroney, and the results they
were expecting from Campbell as a result of their earlier success with the
previous government. At one point, I told her, "You know, I'm not going
to bring it all to you and tell you all about it. But just so you know, I'm
going to say no to everything." She said that was fine.

There were definitely also some interests out there, including former
members of Parliament. They had some pet projects that they wanted
done, and they expected us to do it. I tried to keep these issues as far
away from her as possible, because she had way too much to do, but
these contracts and appointments had a way of finding their way to her.
In fact, from the day she became leader we were constantly being pressured by individuals and groups who expected us to complete their pet
projects. Kim wanted to do things differently as a new prime minister,
but I don't think she had a very firm view in her mind about how to do
it differently. It was too early in her mandate, and the demands never
allowed her to define her style and her new approach to governing.

As a result, when the party abandoned her after the 1993 election, Mr
Chrétien did a very classy thing by reaching out and offering her a number of government appointments in order to soften the impact of the electoral defeat. Losing elections are devastating things for parties to have
to go through, and it is especially the case for the leaders who are held
accountable for the loss.

Jodi White, head of transition team to Kim Campbell, 1993,
interview, 5 April 2001

that protect the apolitical nature of the public service and avoid the use of resources in a manner that would be to the advantage of a particular party. The conventions and practices also aim to prevent controversies about the role of the public service distracting attention from the sub-stantive issues in the election campaign.

Because it is impossible to predict when elections will take place in Canada, in recent years many public servants have had to cancel public appearances or meetings they had committed to before an election was called. In the absence of any explicit protocols on the behaviour of pub-lic servants, these restrictions have created confusion in the ranks and some embarrassment for Canada in international forums. This current practice provides further evidence that protocols and procedures are needed to define the appropriate role of public servants during election campaigns, aside from undermining Canada's credibility around the world. These issues will be addressed in the concluding chapter.

Of greater importance than the limiting of senior public servants' activities is the dispersion of Cabinet ministers and their staff to their respective ridings across the county. In essence, the governance of the country is placed on hold during the election period, and a caretaker system kicks in that minimizes the obligations of ministers and lim-its the scope of their activities. In most cases, ministers are quickly followed by their political staff who, on the day the election writ is dropped, resign or take a leave of absence from their government jobs and begin their partisan activities on the election trail while a skeleton staff is left behind to provide an ongoing link between the minister, the department, and the PMO.

For those familiar with the rhythm of work in Ottawa, the election period is particularly quiet for the public service, since the decision-making apparatus no longer functions regularly or predictably. The usual activities of lobbyists and government relations firms crawl to a halt. The business of governing essentially shuts down for the five-week election campaign and the following two-week transition period, and in addition there are weeks of inactivity until Parliament is called back for the Speech from the Throne. As a result, this is a good oppor-tunity for the government relations firms to provide clients with an analysis of the latest public opinion research on the likely outcome of the election, and it gives them the chance to recruit talented staff who become available after an election.

During an election campaign, the pace of work increases for those who are involved in the transition planning. Because the national media are covering the activities of the leaders of the major political parties as they crisscross the nation, transition teams that are operating at the political and public-service levels are free to carry out their work with little public scrutiny or media interest.

We will now look at this fascinating period in the transition process from three perspectives – political, central agency, and departmental.

Political Perspective

On the political side there are actually two approaches to transition planning taking place in the course of the election. The governing party is often reluctant to formalize a transition team and to move ahead with formal planning, since they are the incumbents and may feel there is little need for any formal planning. Unfortunately, we know from experience that too few incumbent governments spend much time planning for their next mandate. Instead, they prefer to spend most of their time and resources finding ways to ensure electoral success. A good case in point is the 2011 election, when virtually no transition planning was done by Stephen Harper or his senior officials in the PMO. Given the rather modest announcements coming out of that election, it appears that little thought was given to reviewing its past practices or to looking forward to governing in a majority government.

However, during the election campaign there is considerable work to be done by the incumbent government's transition team. As a starting point, there is an excellent opportunity to meet with the clerk of the Privy Council to discuss possible changes to the machinery of government, the organization of the Prime Minister's Office, and the viability of platform commitments made during the campaign.

This is also a very good time to review the effectiveness of the Cabinet system, including the committees. Regardless of whom the prime minister appoints to the Cabinet, much can be accomplished by reviewing the effectiveness of the Cabinet decision-making system that was used by the previous government.

Upcoming governor-in-council appointments are worth reviewing during this period as well, since it gives the PMO and the senior PCO personnel an opportunity to plan for the post-election period. As noted earlier, governments are under pressure to make appointments during election campaigns, especially in instances when it appears they may not be re-elected and therefore will lose the opportunity to appoint their own people to various government jobs after the election. However, such pressures are extremely distracting during an election, since they consume valuable energy and time of the prime minister. In our conversation about her role as the head of the Campbell transition in 1993, Jodi White recalls having to fend off many attempts by those wanting the prime minister to make a large number of appointments during the 1993 general election, reminiscent of the appointments Trudeau made in 1984 as Turner took over in an intraparty transition.

For the opposition parties, the time between the dropping of the writ and election day is largely, if not entirely, taken up with activities that will result in winning as many seats as possible. Almost all of the leaders' time is taken up with meeting candidates, dealing with the media, and, of course, trying to persuade citizens to vote for the party and its candidates. As anyone who has been involved in the sprint to the finish line will know, it is a gruelling and exhausting experience.

However, on the basis of interviews I conducted with political staff, it is increasingly being recognized by the leaders of the opposition parties that good transition planning will ease the move from electioneering to governing. As a consequence, the leaders of most opposition parties will continue the work of their transition teams during the election campaign. Since most transition teams are made up of people not normally involved in the day-to-day campaign, this work can continue in parallel with that of the election team.

As a general rule, opposition parties are at a distinct disadvantage when preparing for the possible transition to power. They generally have little previous experience with governing at a senior level of government and, more important, they do not have access to the expertise of the public service. Since the mid-1960s, prime ministers have traditionally given the Cabinet secretary permission to meet with the major opposition parties before the election to discuss transition issues and to provide a sense of continuity if the opposition eventually won the general election. However, for reasons not readily apparent, both Prime Ministers Harper and Martin have refused to permit their Cabinet secretaries' requests to continue this long-standing tradition. By disallowing any contacts, they have redefined the nature of transition planning in Canada and placed the opposition parties at a severe disadvantage in their work.

For the opposition party transition team, the daily public opinion polls have a significant psychological impact, as well as a real impact on the pace of the work. When the polls show that an opposition party might win the election, the pace of transition planning accelerates.

Conversely, when the numbers show little hope in this direction, the level of their activity matches their declining trend lines.

At a point in the not-too-distant past, governments-in-waiting would be accused of being arrogant or presumptuous if it became known that they were preparing a transition plan. While there is no explicit policy about transition planning either within a political party in Canada or as part of the protocols that govern the behaviour of public servants, it seems no longer newsworthy to report that an opposition party has been preparing a transition plan.

An example of how a transition book is organized can be found in the outline that the Chrétien team used in 1997 in preparing for the federal election. The bullet points represent the outline for the briefing materials that were presented to the prime minister one day before the election on 2 June 1997.

- Size of the Cabinet
- Cabinet and Cabinet committee structure
- Structure of PMO
- PMO personnel
- Vetting of new ministers
- Orientation session for ministers and exempt staff
- Agenda for meeting with deputy ministers
- Communications plan
- Deputy prime minister appointment
- List of key thank-you calls to be made

Two further examples of how transition books are prepared are found in Appendix 4, which contains the outlines of the transition books used by Chrétien in 1993 and by the Harper team in 2006. While many Canadians may have been concerned about the Conservatives' readiness to govern the country, given their relative lack of experience in government, a quick glance at the table of contents reveals that Derek Burney, who led the team, had developed a very complete transition plan for Harper in the event that he won the election.

Notably, the section on "ethics and accountability" demonstrates the priority that the new government gave to this issue. In addition, the section on the public service is a reminder to readers that incoming governments no longer see the public service as a benign presence. This section contains summary biographies of the most senior public servants and a discussion paper on a strategy to deal with the public service.

Public Service Perspective

Privy Council Office

No rules or protocols govern the behaviour of the Privy Council Office and the other central agencies during an election. However, the central agencies monitor the parties' progress during the election and adjust their briefing materials to account for every reasonable election outcome.

The Privy Council Office transition team usually takes advantage of the election campaign to compile its wish list of machinery changes that it feels a newly elected government may want to implement in the interest of efficient government. Ever since the major machinery changes that were introduced by Kim Campbell in 1993, new governments have been reluctant to make wholesale changes at the beginning of their mandates, although Paul Martin's 2003 government is a notable exception.

Most important, the election time gives the central agencies an opportunity to coordinate their own activities and to ensure that each department and agency is preparing a transition plan for a possible new minister. In this regard, the agencies work individually with departments and provide templates to deputy ministers who have had limited experience with government transitions. They also tap into the expertise of departmental experts so that the transition materials being prepared by the PCO are current and accurate. While all central agencies have a well-choreographed transition planning cycle, in the United Kingdom, Sir Gus O'Donnell broke from tradition during the last election. Recognizing that there was a real possibility of a "hung" Parliament outcome, he organized a series of scenario planning exercises with senior public officials who played the roles of key political players in order to anticipate the consequences that might unfold. Although none of the scenarios produced the actual results of the election, it did encourage officials to look at the full range of electoral outcomes. The lesson from the U.K. experience is "Expect the unexpected."[1]

Given the central role played by the Department of Finance, it is not surprising that it has a particularly important role in transition planning. In particular, during the election campaign the department is preparing its most up-to-date fiscal and economic outlook for the nation. These materials are crucial for the newly elected government, regardless of whether a prime minister is returning to office or there is a new one.

Departments and Agencies

From a departmental perspective, the deputy ministers of each of the federal departments prepare their own individual transition plans. Of course, they are also responsible for all of the agencies, boards, and commissions that report to their ministers. For example, the deputy minister of industry has three ministers and eight entities reporting through him or her to the minister. In transition planning the deputy minister is responsible for ensuring that ministers have the appropriate transition materials for their use.

The deputy ministers operate under one of three possible scenarios: a new government will be elected that will, by definition, result in a new minister being appointed; the same government will be re-elected, but a new minister will be appointed to head the department; or the same government will be re-elected and the prime minister will choose to reappoint the same minister to his or her former portfolio. In any of these cases, deputy ministers know they will be moving from the planning stage to governing as soon as the swearing-in of the new Cabinet is complete. They also know that ministers will rely heavily on departmental resources until they have completed their own office staffing.

Experience dictates that the average transition of a new minister after the election takes about six weeks to be fully achieved (including initial meetings with major stakeholder groups). As a result, many deputy ministers develop a six-week timeline for activities, although in certain circumstances the transition planning may be shorter or longer. In any case, deputy ministers must be very flexible in their planning and be prepared to adjust their timing of the different transition elements, depending on changing circumstances.

In general, deputy ministers and their senior associates begin their portfolio transition work in earnest three to four weeks before election day (about one to two weeks after the writ has been dropped), with the assumption that the deputy minister will have two weeks between election day and the swearing-in to adjust the transition materials in light of the election results. They also adjust their level of effort, according to Himelfarb, who notes that "departments do things differently if they think that they are an integral part of the government's agenda."[2]

From the departmental perspective, the time during a general election is precious for the deputy minister. As one veteran federal deputy minister with extensive experience in the Ontario government commented, "You have three weeks to make it work with a new minister.

If you don't hit it off with the minister, it can be a very frustrating experience for all."[3] As a consequence, the preparation time is critical to ensuring that all key elements in a transition plan are prepared in advance so that a trustful working relationship is established early on.

Richard Dicerni, the former deputy minister of industry Canada, described the essence of a successful transition as one where the relationship between the minister and the deputy minister evolves from a "passionate affair" into one more similar to a loveless, but workable, marriage.[4] An experienced deputy minister will try to frame the eventual relationship as one of some dependency, in which the minister will "passionately" seek the deputy's advice and counsel because it is trusted and fair-minded, while also creating the circumstances that will allow the minister to work independently of the deputy and the department, in a way that preserves their mutual respect and appreciation for each other's value to the success of the government.

It is always important to remember that new ministers generally know very little about the role they are about to assume, either as ministers of a particular department or as members of the ministry of the governing party. After leaving politics, many former ministers will recall how anxious they had been about their new roles and the concerns they had about their ability to master the material and to play the required leadership role as the head of a government organization.

In two of the three types of transitions, it is possible for a minister to be returned to his or her former department, but the wisest approach is for deputy ministers and their senior management team to prepare for a new minister. At the same time, they contribute to the briefing materials being prepared under the direction of the clerk for the prime minister, in which the departmental officials attempt to bring a "broad-brush overview of reality to the attention of central agencies," according to Michael Wernick, currently deputy minister of aboriginal affairs and northern development, who characterizes this as being part of an ongoing "hub-and-spoke" process where the departments serve as spokes around the Privy Council Office hub.[5]

A transition exercise has several purposes for a departmental deputy minister. Some departmental transition planners believe that departmental transition work is designed primarily to increase the knowledge base of the relevant ministers, but experienced deputies believe that their primary responsibility in preparing the transition to a new minister is to establish a trusting relationship. On the subject of achieving these two objectives, what emerges from the interviews with deputy ministers is that there are many different approaches to achieving these goals. They depend as much on the style of individual deputy ministers and the context of the first meetings as they do on the departmental transition templates that have been passed on from one transition to the next. The contextual element is more important if the minister is new to the portfolio or to elected office. In that sense, the knowledge-transfer element in the transition work is simply a means to an end. While enhancing the minister's knowledge is a worthwhile objective, the primary intent is to develop a strong bond between the minister and the department that serves him or her.

While all deputy ministers have their own style and approach to relationship building, it will be based on demonstrating the nonpartisan expertise of the federal public service. "You want the minister to see the department through the prism of the deputy minister."[6]

At the federal level, deputy ministers typically prepare a single set of transition materials, regardless of which political party is predicted to win the election. Experience has taught most veteran deputies that it is impossible to predict an election outcome, particularly during its early stages when the transition work is being allocated to departmental officials, so there is no need to prepare materials tailored to specific outcomes.

By the time election night arrives, each deputy minister will have a complete set of transition materials ready for each of the three scenario outcomes. They can use the time between the election results and the swearing-in ceremony to finalize the briefing books and to hone them for their expected recipients.

The success or failure of a departmental transition is determined early on in the process – sometimes only hours after the initial meeting between the minister and the deputy minister. Given that there is so little room either for error or for time to remedy things if they go wrong, deputy ministers who have worked on previous transitions have a significant advantage over deputies with no prior experience. This is simply not the time to learn a new craft.

There are two "bookend" laws that bracket transition planning within federal departments. The first is the Access to Information Act, which gives citizens full access to all government information not exempted for particular reasons. Given the nature of transition planning, all work done in preparation for a transition is accessible, except for those sections of the work that include advice to the minister. As a consequence, it is a challenge for deputy ministers to be as candid as possible in the briefing notes when they also recognize that an enterprising journalist or opposition-party activist can access all materials. In the end, what constitutes "advice" and whether it has to be released is a judgment call.

The second bookend legislation, the Official Languages Act, requires that all federal government documents be available in both official languages, and refers to the provision of transition materials in the language of the incoming minister. For newly appointed ministers, it is imperative that they have access to documents in the language of their choice, not because it is the law, but to ease the learning process and to establish a good working relationship with the deputy minister and senior staff. Since it is impossible to predict the language preferences of ministers during an election campaign, deputy ministers are very mindful of the obligation to have materials available in both English and French.

More important, it puts great pressure on deputy ministers to speak to the ministers in their chosen language. If there is ever a time when the bilingualism policy is put to the test, it is during the first few weeks of a newly elected government. Over the years, there have been instances of deputy ministers being replaced because of significant language issues arising between the minister and the department, especially during the early months of a new government. Because deputy ministers and associate deputy ministers are not always fully bilingual before being appointed (although it is expected that they are), there are many instances where the language skills of the senior mandarinate are inadequate during this critical period.

When preparing to brief a new or a returning minister, all deputy ministers and their departmental colleagues recognize that they do not have a monopoly over the minister's time or the information that will form the basis for the transition. Increasingly, ministers come into their portfolios with access to diverse sources of advice, drawn largely from the partisan community that helped to elect them and from a sophisticated stakeholder community.

Fully appreciating the importance of access to information, bilingualism, and the influence of third-party sources on a newly appointed minister, deputy ministers usually kick-start the transition by appointing a small team to support their efforts. As a general rule, the person in charge is an assistant deputy minister (or in Ottawa parlance, a senior director-general-level executive) who has an extensive knowledge of the department's portfolio and knows many of the key individuals who are dispersed throughout the department. It goes without saying that the designated transition leader should have the full confidence of the deputy and of the senior staff around the executive table. Great writing skills, a penchant for working long hours, and the ability to manage small teams are an especially valuable set of additional attributes.

Information

Since the primary purpose of a departmental transition plan is to establish a good working relationship with the minister, the short-term objective is to provide information to the minister so compelling that he or she is excited enough to ask for more. This relationship should be built around "honest, neutral, and politically sensitive bureaucratic advice."[7] Stated in a less formal way, deputy ministers want their ministers to tell their friends and family that "I have a cool job" or "I am an important person in my government." They would especially like their ministers to say "I like my department – and there is really good chemistry between me and the deputy minister."

To achieve that, the deputy minister needs to parcel out the information in "tapas-sized bites" so that the minister's knowledge base will be acquired slowly, over time. It is important to remember that most incoming ministers are exhausted from their recent election victory, they have very little knowledge about the subject matter that defines their portfolio, and they do not want to look ignorant or foolish in front of the public service. Most experienced deputy ministers report that the new ministers have limited absorptive capacity. One former official who knew Ray Hnatyshyn as one of the most able ministers in Mulroney's government made a very insightful observation that colourfully describes how to deal with inexperienced ministers, "They should be sent on the ice as quickly as possible. In the worst case, they can only fall on their ass, and it is well-padded so there is no reason to be shy about it."[8]

Within this framework, the deputy minister organizes the portfolio to meet the minister's objectives. As a starting point, the departmental transition team may look for issues that have emerged during the election campaign and may have a short-term bearing on the minister's work. Any issues related to the portfolio that were discussed during one of the televised national debates will draw special attention from the transition team. Obviously, the election platform will also receive close scrutiny to determine whether policies related to the portfolio are a high priority for the newly elected government.

Today, many federal departments have more than one minister. At the federal level it has become very fashionable for the prime minister to appoint a number of secretaries of state or ministers of state to support the work of Cabinet ministers. Given the differing mandates of the ministers and the ministers of state, departmental transition teams prepare a separate set of briefing materials for each of the ministers within their portfolio. For example, Industry Canada has one minister and two ministers of state. The Department of Foreign Affairs, Trade and Development has four ministers, including the minister of foreign affairs, minister of international development and La Francophonie, the minister of international trade, and the minister of state (foreign affairs and consular). This department has been further bolstered by the addition of five parliamentary secretaries in support of the minister in the House of Commons.

As a general rule, deputy ministers prepare only one set of briefing materials during the election period. They know that they have two weeks on average after the election to adjust the briefings to match the ideology or orientation of the incoming government.

Some transition-team leaders try to anticipate who their ministers might be after the election, by reviewing the biographies of the leading contenders and trying to "get to know them" through published CVs and other materials. Finally, the teams also monitor national and regional media to identify any portfolio-related issues that might ultimately affect a new minister's first few weeks in office.

Transition Documents

While it is difficult to describe the complete range of transition briefing materials provided to ministers, they do follow a template. In some ways, a transition book is like a playbook used in professional sports. It contains the equivalent of the first twenty plays in a football game – laying out in precise detail the first three weeks in the life of a new minister, but also including a 100-day (or three-month) horizon.

In the transition world, the term *briefing notes* is an oxymoron – the materials are neither brief nor in note form, and PowerPoint presentations rather than written briefing materials have also become more common during recent transitions. Some deputy ministers feel that the PowerPoint "deck" is an effective way of providing bite-sized information to ministers, despite considerable evidence that it is less informative than the equivalent written text. In any case, the PowerPoint slide presentation has become ubiquitous within the federal government as a major communications tool, and it now sets the format standard for transition materials.

Typically, the first transition book describes the functions and the possibilities of the department. It also includes financial data and the statutory roles and levels of accountability, drawn largely from the departmental performance reviews or the department's plans and priorities. It may also describe in some detail the delegated authorities that the minister will have to agree to after being sworn into Cabinet. Ideally, the first volume should have the minister asking for more information.

The second volume may describe what the minister will be expected to do during the first 100 or 150 days in office and allows the minister the opportunity to open the door into the department. It may also include a section on urgent matters that need the minister's immediate attention, such as important phone calls that must be made or people who should be visited in the early days of the minister's mandate.[9] As well, the second briefing book may also include a list of travel commitments and meeting obligations that are anticipated to take place in the first three months, a draft of the upcoming parliamentary agenda, including proposed legislation, reports that need to be tabled early in the government's mandate, major contracts that have to be tendered, an overview of any legal issues being raised in the department, any outstanding issues with the parliamentary agencies, such as the auditor general, and upcoming appointments that are the responsibility of the minister.

A third volume may describe all key individuals, organizations, and stakeholders that touch on the minister's portfolio and provide "deep dives" into the issues that are going to be important. In this volume the deputy minister may include the biographies of major players in the sector. Also included will be the messages coming from stakeholder groups and an analysis of the issues that each of these may be expected to present to the minister at their first meeting. It may also contain a detailed organizational chart of all of the agencies, boards, and commissions that are part of the ministerial portfolio. Finally, this third volume may contain detailed analyses of departmental program spending and expenditures, for the really keen members of the minister's staff or for the insomniacs.

Another briefing book may also be provided that divides the priorities of the portfolio into three sections – "must do," "should do," and "nice to do" – based on the relative urgency of the tasks to be accomplished.

Finally, during the election period, some deputy ministers prepare another kind of briefing book that looks at medium-term challenges that a new minister will have to deal with in the course of a four-year mandate. These policy briefings are very substantial and challenge the ministers to confront some of the most important issues within their portfolios. For example, in the Industry Canada briefing book the minister will find policy briefings on the aerospace, information, communications technology, and auto sectors.

At the department of aboriginal and northern affairs, Michael Wernick has added an additional binder containing a glossary of terms, including acronyms, that apply to his portfolio and to all agencies of the federal government with which the minister will have some direct contact. His department has also prepared a section of "frequently asked questions" that a new minister will find useful. Finally, given the particular nature of the portfolio, this last binder also contains information about customs and protocols that are relevant to First Nations people.

Each deputy minister is trying to balance the desire to provide as much information as possible to the minister during the early transition period while recognizing that the minister is exhausted from a gruelling election campaign, with only a limited ability to absorb new material, much of which can be complex and overwhelming.

Experienced deputy ministers use their best judgment in assembling the briefing books in terms of volume and complexity. Their hope is that the briefing materials will engage the ministers to the extent that they may ask for detailed briefings on the material that particularly interests them. Well-designed briefing materials should be able to parse a minister's particular interests so that the department can then organize and orient itself to the minister's own agenda.

During the election campaign, senior managers of individual departments also prepare special briefing materials in the event that their newly appointed minister has had no experience as a member of Cabinet. If that is the case, which is increasingly common, the department usually arranges for briefings on "how government works" and "the craft of being a good minister." These briefings have two different elements. The first attempts to cover an undergraduate political science–level program in a few hours of briefings and meetings. It might be supplemented with popular materials on how government works or with DVDs of BBC television series like *Yes, Minister* and *The Thick of It*. However, the deputy minister cannot count on the Prime Minister's Office to provide an adequate level of training or orientation for new ministers. The second element in the preparation of training for new ministers is to enlist the help of some former ministers who would be comfortable meeting with and providing insights useful to a newly sworn-in minister in a newly elected government.

If the prime minister has given the newly appointed minister further responsibilities, then the deputy minister will provide more details of the Cabinet committee system and the finer points of parliamentary procedure.

All deputies prepare their transition materials assuming that they will have a new minister to welcome into their department. As well, each department analyses the party platforms in order to ascertain the impact that the policy promises will have on the department and on agencies within the portfolio. Wernick describes the preparatory work done during the election campaign as an effort to carefully close the gap between the aspirations and expectations of elected officials and the public service.

Behind the Scenes: How Much Is Too Much Briefing Material?

A day or two after the election, Jean Pelletier came over with a couple of colleagues to meet the clerk.[10] We had a wonderful meeting and I remember Jean Pelletier being very dignified, warm, and gracious. We had, however, done a kind of "Trudeau." We had made a major mistake by preparing too much briefing material for the incoming prime minister. Lesson number one, then, is to keep it short. This is not a time to make sure you have covered yourself against any possible accusation of missing a certain topic. This is a time to present a clear, coherent package to an incoming person who has got much more on his or her mind and who needs a clear picture of what it is you're putting on the table so that they can make a decision on it. That was the one mistake we made.

Anyone who knew Chrétien would have said, "No, no, no, not for this guy. Don't do that." So we made a mistake, but it turned out OK.

Jim Mitchell, assistant secretary to the Cabinet for Machinery of Government, Privy Council Office, 1991–4

During the planning phase of the transition, the departmental transition team should also be looking for opportunities for the minister to meet interlocutors and stakeholders during the early days of his or her mandate. According to experienced deputy ministers, it is unwise to monopolize the post-election period of a newly appointed minister. It is important to remember that there are many experts and others outside the portfolio who may be helpful in providing a new minister with important information and perspectives on the work a minister must do. It is also well known that ministers become suspicious of deputy ministers who seem to be managing all of their time.

Morris Rosenberg, deputy minister in the Department of Foreign Affairs, Trade and Development, offers a number of observations about the value of documentation and sound departmental transition planning. As a general rule, the federal government public service over-prepares for an incoming government by producing too many briefing notes and "decks." To minimize the weight of the transition materials for a new minister, most seasoned deputies divide them into two piles. One set of briefing materials goes directly to the minister and the second set is sent to the minister's staff, who will have more time to read and will not initially have access to the many meetings that will take place between the departmental officials and the public service.

Rosenberg also reinforces the view of his colleagues that ministers should concentrate on addressing no more than four or five big policy issues during their first three months on the job. Since a minister should expect to stay in a given portfolio for eighteen months, on average, it is important for the deputies to establish as early as possible what priorities and aspirations ministers have for their tenure in the department and which issues should dominate their policy time. As well, during the early days ministers should also seek to establish good working relationships with stakeholder groups by travelling and meeting with key players in the sector and demonstrating a willingness to collaborate and to have two-way conversations.

Rosenberg has learned from experience that ministers should limit their plans for the policy side of the department. If the list of policy priorities is too long, the minister will not be taken seriously by his colleagues and will likely have trouble moving their agenda through the decision-making process. As a general rule, the shorter the list of priorities, the more likely it is that the minister will be successful.

In addition, most deputy ministers will remind their new ministers, during the early days of the mandate that they should remember that they are politicians first, and their accountability is to the prime minister and to Parliament. They were not elected to manage the department, and they are not expected to be accountable for the day-to-day functioning of the department. In fact, being a responsible minister requires a minister to be very cognizant of accountability to Parliament and to his or her role in Cabinet deliberations. As a consequence, early in a minister's mandate, deputy ministers typically find ways to engage ministers in a frank conversation that defines the limits of the ministers' areas of responsibilities and underscores the non-partisan and neutral role of the public service.

In this regard, one further element in establishing a professional working relationship with the minister is establishing a set of ground rules with the minister's chief of staff. It is important that the chief of staff understand the traditional advisory role of the deputy minister, the role of the chief of staff and other members of the minister's office, and the fact that the chief of staff cannot instruct the public service. It must be made very clear to the exempt staff that they must work through the deputy minister when trying to access the public service.[11]

Conclusion

This chapter covered the key elements in the second phase of the transition as the pace quickened for both the political transition team and the public service. Working in parallel with the occasional communications between the two sides, the political transition team for each party seeks to consolidate its overall plan for assuming power if they work under an election scenario or a leadership one. Similarly, the public service under the guidance of the clerk is directing the work of the central agencies and coordinating the planning being done by the deputy ministers and their teams. For those involved in the transition work, the midnight oil may be burning brighter, but for the vast majority of political aides and public servants there is only speculation that fuels their curiosity about the planning taking place around them.

In effect, the government shuts down during the election period, operating under caretaker conventions that discourage any new government spending and appointments. Many incumbent governments do not take advantage of the opportunity to refashion a re-elected government, but by now the opposition parties who sense a pending victory are hard at work developing elements of their transition plan. Experienced deputy ministers are dusting off departmental templates, bringing the briefing materials up to date, and preparing for all eventualities.

The chapter concludes with a section on the importance of documentation for transitions and the way in which notes and briefings can be critical in transition planning.

All of this preparatory work sets the stage for the next phase of the transition that brings the team out of the shadows and provides the public with their first glimpse of their newly elected government.

6 Post-Election Phase:
Electioneering to Governing

As they used to say on the Gleason Show, "And away we go ..."

– Bill Neville

Introduction

This phase is what everyone has been waiting for, and the experience is worth the wait. The post-election phase plays out in a blur of activity and excitement as all the finishing touches are put to the plan. It is also the time when a transition team first learns if all of its work is going to roll out as expected or will come apart when an unexpected event derails the exercise. During the early days of the post-election phase there are a series of first meetings with people who will play a significant role in the move from electioneering to governing – the transition team, the clerk of the Privy Council, the governor general, and potential Cabinet Ministers. But before examining these dynamics, we will first explore the practical realities for the prime minister–elect and his or her first impressions immediately after the election.

Post-Election Environment

The post-election period immediately following the campaign is by far the most intense and visible part of a government transition. Even when a government has been re-elected, emerging from the experience largely intact, there are still many opportunities for meaningful transition work. Characteristically, the politicians and the media are ready for some downtime after the physical (and psychological) effort of the previous five weeks. Most journalists who covered the election full-time basis now head for home to recover from the ordeal, while the candidates return to their ridings to celebrate, or to speculate on what went wrong. At this point, professional observers largely abandon the political scene in Ottawa, giving the transition team the opportunity to do its work in general anonymity, beyond the harsh glare of the media spotlight.

This is a quiet period for the newly elected government. It has made no decisions that can be questioned, and everyone is looking for a break from politics. All of this, of course, will change once the government is sworn into office, but for now, all is quiet and safe for the prime minister.[1] While the honeymoon period tends to be relatively short in Canada, since the return of Parliament usually signals the resumption in partisan politics, research in the United States reveals a consistent pattern of goodwill towards the leader after the swearing-in of their president.

> For a short while the President has the goodwill of the public and the Washington community. Even in politics, people do not want to attack a newcomer until there is substantial reason to do so. In the early days, there is little advantage for the President's opponents to go on the attack against the administration's people and positions. Instead, they wait to do so.
>
> The Center for Media and Public Affairs found in its charting of news coverage by ABC, CBS, and NBC that in the first 50 days of the George H.W. Bush, Bill Clinton and George W. Bush administrations, presidents got positive coverage for particular aspects of their administrations. The Center's evaluation of the press coverage for George H.W. Bush's first 50 days was 61% positive, while those numbers on the three major networks fell during President Clinton's first 50 days to 44% and rose in a similar period of George W. Bush's tenure to 48%.[2]

There is some debate in Canada over whether the transition team should have any profile at all during this period. In recent transitions, the Privy Council Office or the election campaign headquarters has issued a press release the day after the election naming the transition team members and providing short biographies. Jean Chrétien was the first prime minister to call such a press conference, in which he introduced me as the head of his transition team. As memory serves, the press conference was quite perfunctory and low-key. Probably the novelty of the situation at that time was sufficient to tame the media who attended the press conference and to limit their queries to questions about logistics and timing.

While media relations went relatively well for Prime Ministers Chrétien and Harper, Paul Martin was not so fortunate, as mentioned earlier. To demonstrate that he was well organized and ready to take over from his predecessor, he decided to invite the media to attend a meeting of his transition team. Unfortunately for Martin, the resulting photo that captured the smiling faces of his team led to some very negative publicity about the group's composition. Many of the transition team members were well-known government-relations professionals with high-profile client lists. There were others, such as Peter Nicholson, who for many years had been a close Martin advisor and that of Arthur Kroeger, a highly respected public servant who had retired in 1992 after more than thirty-five years of non-partisan federal government service, including more than ten years as a deputy minister.

Bill Neville gave considerable thought to whether the media should have access to his transition team. In his 1984 transition materials, he argued that there was a strong case to be made against doing so, that it would be to keep the prime minister and the transition team out of the spotlight while they were doing their work: "First, [because of] time itself – you face a demanding schedule to accomplish what must be accomplished in the handful of days available. Second, there is the risk factor. Remember, it was at a gratuitous (that is, unnecessary for any other purpose) news conference that Joe Clark got into new and deep difficulty over Jerusalem. And third, there are the questions of tone or image. Sure, we need to project the image of a prime minister–elect hard at work, seriously committed to the giant task of forming a new government for Canada, and not of a politician with the time or the inclination to 'play the media game.'"[3]

When the Rubber Hits the Road

While these days can be described as the honeymoon period from a media standpoint, the pace of society and of government is ongoing and ceaseless. As a consequence, the days immediately following the election campaign are filled with activity. At the core, the transition or changeover is a combination of established ritual and the first real – and absolutely critical – exercise of the prime minister's power. As Neville warned Mulroney in 1984, "The decisions you make in this period, since they centre on the key issue of who will govern with you, are probably the most important you will make. Good decisions will make everything that follows that much easier and productive for the country and the party; less wise decisions will almost inevitably cause you serious problems in the days ahead."[4] Carle describes the early days as the opportunity "to create a working environment to legitimize your actions."[5]

Paul Wells brings us the story of how Harper's team began the process of taking over the reins of power following the 2006 election. Wells notes with some admiration that only days after their minority government victory the Harper election team was already developing their strategy for the next election, without much concern about their upcoming transition to power: "The Harper team wasted no time. Six days after the election I was buying breakfast at an Ottawa café when the guy in front of me at the cash register turned to introduce himself. It was Patrick Muttart. I'd heard about him, written about him, never met him – he doesn't talk to reporters. So, I said, making small talk, 'Ready for some downtime after the election?' Nope. Muttart was already at work on a Campaign '06 post-mortem. What went right, what went wrong, and where in the rock face of public opinion could Harper plant the pitons for his climb to a majority?"[6]

The ability to change gears from intense election campaigning to governing a country is easier said than done. American expert Harrison Wellford is very clear that the time between the election and the inauguration is the key test for the transition team and its leader. He argues, "Managing this shift in campaigning to governing is the president-elect's greatest challenge and biggest opportunity. Getting him or her ready to do this is the transition team's only objective. Good pre-election planning should allow the president-elect to make a good and lasting first impression as a national, not a factional, leader."[7]

As Martha Joynt Kumar has noted regarding a number of different transitions in the United States, it is not easy for a president-elect or for the staff to come into the White House ready to govern: "Governing involves staffing the administration with people appropriate for management responsibilities, not campaign ones; developing a decision-making process designed for the work of governing and working with power centers inside and outside of government; and approaching policy from a governing perspective and timeline. The rhythms of a campaign are based on a clear electoral goal with a defined timetable and a staff appropriate for the black-and-white nature of campaigning, in which your candidate is 'right' and your opponent is 'wrong.'"[8] As

Kumar further notes, "The president needs to include staff appropriate to working in shades of gray rather than in the black-and-white election world and must enter the world in which compromise is a necessity – not the weakness it is portrayed as in presidential campaigns."[9] This often means that the skills needed to govern are distinctly different from those in use during elections.

What to do first is the crucial question, and there is no single right answer. To say that the decision is situational is simply to state the obvious. Nevertheless, first actions should have been thought through in advance of the election and agreed upon by all key players. As one might expect, even experts do not always agree. One school of transition scholars advocates that you "hit the ground running." They urge you to take advantage of the honeymoon period usually given a new leader. You'll never have all the pieces in place when you take office anyway and so should go for quick victories. Good first impressions are important.

Another school of scholars advises caution while you're still learning the ropes. You'll never have all the pieces in place when you take office, and ignorant leaders make unnecessary mistakes. It's hard to undo bad first impressions. American transition expert Stephen Hess has a piece of valuable advice: "After you have assessed your circumstances – the size of your electoral victory, makeup of Congress, state of the economy, immediate troubles in the world – it is essential to prioritize your long-term goals and then have a pocketful of doable actions ready for quick victories."[10]

The transition team begins this phase well rested and ready to start its work. However, the prime minister is exhausted physically from a five-week campaign that has included sixteen-hour days and thousands of kilometres of coast-to-coast travel. You can count on adrenaline to keep things moving up to a certain point, but the transition team needs to remember that he or she is sleep-deprived and physically drained. Some prime ministers are energized by their victory, but others are so tired that they are looking for any excuse to find time for some rest and recovery.

Regardless of the exhaustion and need for a good rest at the cottage, the tradition in Canada is to complete Phase Three of the transition in approximately two weeks. In other words, the newly elected government has approximately fourteen days to move from campaigning to governing – from winning an election to being sworn in by the governor general. This short period of time gives the prime minister–elect little time to work through the hundreds of tasks that have to be completed before taking over the reins of power.

Behind the Scenes: Learning to Get Along

During the 1984 Mulroney transition, despite the best will in the world and the good efforts of outstanding people like Bill Neville, there were some rocky times in the first few months as the new administration got used to being in government, got used to working with the public service, and got over its initial suspicions of the public service. In fact, after about a year, the prime minister changed his chief of staff. Bernard Roy, who was a fine person and a good lawyer, although not really suited to being the head of a political office, went back to Montreal and was replaced by Derek Burney. Derek was someone who had been recommended to the prime minister as a can-do, take-charge sort of guy who could bring some order to the leader's political staff.

There were a lot of strong personalities at the time. People had their own agendas and their own idea of what Mr Mulroney wanted to do or should be doing. It was difficult to bring order with all these differing agendas, but Derek did it quite well.

Derek worked very well with Paul Tellier; both of them have told me this. Derek understood the public service and wasn't coming in to try to be clerk. He was trying to be the prime minister's chief of staff by making sure that the prime minister's team was coherent and focused and that the prime minister's views were clearly expressed to the bureaucrats. Paul Tellier was there in order to ensure Derek read the signals correctly and to run the public service of Canada. They worked very well together, and we then entered into a period of excellent relations between the political level and the public service. A great deal of credit for this goes to having Derek in this position.

Jim Mitchell, assistant secretary to the Cabinet for Machinery of Government, Privy Council Office, 1991–4, interview, 17 January 2011

Lawrence Martin captures the mood of the Harper team in 2006 in *Harperland*, his insightful book on Stephen Harper. On the basis of a large number of interviews with key Harper advisors, Martin observed,

When they finally took power after so long in opposition they were a wary bunch. They knew how to oppose, how to attack, how to pull triggers. But they didn't know how to govern. They had a rookie prime minister, all rookie cabinet ministers except one, and rookie staff. Everything was new and they were in a minority situation. To say the level of anxiety was high was to underestimate the degree of tension.

"You know what it was like," recalled Bruce Carson, Harper's senior policy advisor. "It was like every day could be the last day." Carson, a sixtyish former Ottawa lawyer who had spent two decades working for federal and provincial conservatives, felt the government would be lucky to last a year. Though he was the policy man, he didn't see policy as the top priority. The top priority was discipline, not screwing up: "We had only one chance to get this thing right."[11]

When an opposition party wins an election, the primary challenge for the transition team in the early hours of the post-election period is to help the prime minister–elect to cross over psychologically from being leader of an opposition party to being the leader of a nation. The prime minister (and all key members of the PM's entourage) must make the psychological move from colleague and fellow-combatant with the party faithful to being their leader. This is a relatively easy concept to appreciate, but in practice it has proven to be very complex and difficult for many Canadian prime ministers. Those who cannot make the psychological change are likely doomed to spend their latter years contemplating what might have been and ruminating on how different it could have been if they had been able to seize the moment.

Without dwelling on the failures of some recent Canadian prime ministers, I can agree with the consensus that Paul Martin, Kim Campbell, and John Turner all had significant problems making the change when they were given the opportunity to do so. Although there are only a few instances in Canada when untested leaders became prime minister directly, it is worth speculating whether those who did would have made more successful transitions if, before moving into the "big office" in the Centre Block, they had served some time as opposition party leaders, or whether there had been other ways for them to prepare for the job.

There is little published material about this phase in the life of a prime minister, unfortunately, but Ian Brodie provides a fascinating account of the transition of Stephen Harper from opposition Leader to prime minister. Brodie vividly recalls the first staff meeting after the election in Calgary and exquisitely captures the drama of the moment when the staff realizes they can no longer address the newly elected prime minister as "Stephen." Brodie remembers how difficult it was to convince some of the staff to change the way they addressed their boss, but he was adamant that the entire staff had to do so, and at once.

It is interesting to contrast this insistence on a change in behaviour with that of the Paul Martin team, who carried on calling the newly installed prime minister by his first name. When senior staff in the prime minister's Office continued to refer to meetings with the prime minister as "a chat with Paul," the practice became a major source of merriment and confusion in the privy council office. Not only did the familiar address diminish the stature of the prime minister, it served to greatly undermine the professionalism of the staff and the prime minister's effectiveness. In fact, even today, more than eight years later, there

---

Behind the Scenes: Call Him "Mister Prime Minister"

Now that he is going to be prime minister of Canada, people are treating him differently than they had before.

Everyone on the staff called him "Stephen" before and during the election. Then, the day after the election, I insisted everybody call him "Mr Harper." Once he was sworn in, everyone, including myself, called him Prime Minister. We had to get it through our heads and, more importantly, he had to get it through his head. Therefore, I insisted that we call him Mr Harper during the transition.

I went to the staff one by one and said, "We are now the government. Tell your staff that he is to be called Mr Harper and, after the swearing-in, Prime Minister. He must be called this everywhere – in public, in private, and in all meetings." At the time I also stopped calling him Stephen.

In our first regular staff meeting following the election, the only thing that changed was that Derek Burney attended. Stephen Harper arrived from Stornoway with the new protective detail and he expected to finally get past the motorcade formalities. I would always say, "Good morning, Stephen, here's what we have," but now I said "Good morning, Mr Harper, here's what we have for you today." It jolted him back.

As we went around the table doing our normal briefings, we all called him Mr Harper instead of Stephen. You could see on his face that he was having great difficulty getting used to this. He never arranged it and I did not talk to him about it. His head would jolt back because it was contrary to our everyday process of calling him Stephen. People didn't seem to appreciate the magnitude of the change that was taking place. For us, the world was changing big time.

Ian Brodie, chief of staff to Prime Minister Harper,
interview, 6 April 2011

are still many disapproving references to this informal way of addressing the prime minister of Canada from those who worked in the central
agencies at the time.

One of the most interesting observations about how relationships
change when the election is won is provided by Robert Reich, an
academic-turned-U.S.-Cabinet-secretary, who had known Bill Clinton
for years before being asked to join his Cabinet.

Here Reich discusses the awkward issue of how to address a friend
who has suddenly become president of the United States:

> I never considered him a close friend in the sense of someone who shared
> with me, and with whom I shared, the most intimate of thoughts and
> feelings. I don't know how many close friends Bill has. I have very few.
> But I always considered him a friend in the more limited sense of some-
> one whom I respected and enjoyed being with, and who seemed to have
> the same feelings toward me. As his friend I never assumed that I was a
> member of an exclusive club. Friends of Bill must number in the tens of
> thousands.
>
> But how can I call him "Mr President" when he's still horsing around
> like Bill? I'll resolve to try, nonetheless. No more Bill, even in this journal.
> Here he's simply "B."[12]

Security Takes Over

Immediately following an election campaign, the newly elected government swings into action. The first concern of the transition team is
the matter of security, the protection of the prime minister. Again, good
planning is crucial, and it is helpful if the transition team has already
met with the head of security and worked out the logistics. Obviously,
returning prime ministers already understand the issue, and more
important, will already be comfortable with the security staff.

As a stark indication of the sudden change in status, a security bub-
ble is imposed immediately around the prime minister–elect by the
RCMP when the election results point to a winner. Within minutes of
the various TV stations declaring who will form the next government,
the transition team leader begins to implement the plan the team has
developed over the previous months.

For a newly elected prime minister with little government experience, security is the first tangible sign that things are about to change –
big time. Ian Brodie, who was responsible for the national campaign in

2006, recalls election night at Stephen Harper's Calgary headquarters. Harper seemed briefly confused to find himself suddenly separated from his supporters by a stern-looking group of RCMP officers whose job it was to keep him safe.

In contrast, in 1993, Jean Carle was able to shoo the security detail away from Chrétien's Shawinigan headquarters by simply telling the election security detail that they were getting too close for comfort. However, despite his best efforts to minimize the size of the security detail, Carle recalls, "Overnight, security moved from a group of eight relatively low-level RCMP constables to 250, officers all of whom were there to protect the new prime minister."[13] Moreover, both local and international events in the recent past, such as the break-in at 24 Sussex Drive and the 11 September attacks in the United States, have guaranteed that when it comes to assuring the prime minister's safety, security will now trump prime ministerial independence every time.

If the prime minister–elect is outside of Ottawa on election night (which is very likely, unless he or she represents an Ottawa riding), the question of the best way to return to Ottawa is the next challenge for the transition team. The RCMP will offer the use of a military or RCMP plane to ensure the flight is secure, but most prime ministers prefer to fly to Ottawa on their campaign plane along with their staff (and journalists) who have travelled with them for the past thirty-five days.

The enhanced security also extends to key positions across the government. Before being offered employment in what will become the new PMO, staff must undergo a security check. The PCO will ensure this is done as soon as possible. It normally requires a minimum of forty-eight hours, and some names informally provided will have already been cleared. Initial discussions should also take place with the ethics counsellor, who will advise potential staff on the requirements of the Conflict of Interest Code and other related issues.

First Meetings

In Canada, most prime ministers return to Ottawa immediately following election night to prepare for the transition. They are greeted by cheering crowds at the airport and a pumped-up collection of partisans ready to take on new responsibilities.

Even in the United States, where presidential transitions extend from the day of the election in November until 20 January, no time is wasted. President Obama, for example, set an early and swift pace during his post-election transition by asking his team to meet with him the day after the election. Many people have commented that this early preparation was important for him, given his relative inexperience. It was also fortuitous, according to the Partnership for Public Service in Washington, given the daunting task he faced of putting together a government and seeking to implement major policy shifts under extremely difficult circumstances. As a signal to Americans that the country was well in hand, the day after his historic election, Obama formally named the leaders of his transition team.[14]

As noted earlier, the very first day after the election and throughout the prime minister's tenure as leader of the country, advice and support will come to the PM through two distinct channels. First, through the chief of staff, who will be the key political advisor and serve as the *political* anchor. The chief of staff will normally provide support in dealing with members of Parliament, prospective ministers, the media, party workers and supporters, and for all the other demands made on the prime minister's time.

The prime minister will also be supported by the clerk of the Privy Council, who will serve as the *public service* anchor for the transition. Early on, the clerk will offer to meet with the prime minister and the chief political advisors – especially the chief of staff – to signal the need to meet frequently, if not daily, during the days of transition immediately preceding the swearing-in of the new ministry, to ensure proper coordination and communication. This early meeting is crucially important to the clerk since, as discussed earlier, it will be the first opportunity to build a good working relationship based on mutual respect and cooperation.

The long list of their areas of common interest makes evident the desirability of close cooperation between the two groups. The following is a composite list of activities that have formed the basis for a number of recent federal transitions:

- Developing a protocol for the two teams to work together on transition activities;
- Initiating discussions with the governor general;
- Reviewing the organization of the government and the ministry;
- Rethinking the structure and process of Cabinet decision-making;
- Developing a protocol to select and security-clear key personnel, including ministers and political staff;
- Identifying key appointments;
- Addressing pressing policy issues;

- Developing a plan to recall Parliament, preparing a Speech from the Throne and a strategy for the upcoming parliamentary session;
- Identifying other appointments that may be made involving government MPs (e.g., parliamentary secretaries, whips);
- Planning the swearing-in ceremony of the new ministry.[15]

The days following the election are hectic and energized by the prospect of moving ahead with the transition plan. Simone Philogène was the only staff member on the 1993 transition and has a very clear memory what happened in the Office of the Official Opposition in the days following Jean Chrétien's victory:

> I was told to come to the fourth-floor Office of the Leader of the Opposition in the Centre Block. And it was chaotic. I remember vividly Jean Carle, who had been the "wagon master" on the campaign plane, trying to deal with the waves of volunteers and staff who were streaming into the offices looking for a place to celebrate. I think that so many of the people were used to the programmed hour-by-hour campaign regimen that they just naturally went to the office not knowing what else to do. What was next on the agenda? OK, we won – now what?
>
> I have a very clear image of Jean Carle coming out of his office and telling us to sit and to wait for further direction. It was all very noisy, and this struck me as particularly out of place, since the OLO was never chaotic or noisy, because Jean Pelletier [chief of staff to Jean Chrétien] ran a very professional and organized office. So the chaos signalled something important was taking place, but we didn't appreciate how much things were going to change for all of us.[16]

Amid the chaos and bustling traffic in and out of the headquarter space, for the well-hidden transition team and the prime minister–elect, the ritual of changeover involves a number of essential components that define the hard edge of what has to be done:

- A meeting of the prime minister–elect and the outgoing prime minister is arranged (sometimes with some difficulty), so that both parties can agree upon a date for the formal handover;
- The outgoing prime minister calls on the governor general and indicates his or her intention to resign;
- The prime minister–elect calls on the governor general and accepts the invitation to form a government;

- Soon after, the prime minister–elect calls on the governor general a second time to outline (as far as possible) the contours of the new ministry;
- The outgoing prime minister formally resigns, followed almost immediately by the swearing-in of the new prime minister and ministers.

Prime Minister–Designate Meets the Transition Team

There are no fixed rules for these first meetings with the prime minister–elect but I have found that the agenda of the first meeting tends to follow a pattern, regardless of the size of the electoral victory or the style of the prime minister.

After the congratulatory "high fives" around the table and some expressions of disbelief, the meeting unfolds in a businesslike manner. The first order of business is to review the election outcome and to follow up on any unknowns, such as undeclared winners in contested ridings, and review the post-election landscape.

At this point, the prime minister might be reminded of the factors that brought the party to win the election, including the platform and the promises that were made on the election trail.

"Do what you said you were going to do." This was the message conveyed to Harper consistently by Derek Burney, Ian Brodie, and other members of the transition team. They were very aware of the criticism levelled against the Martin government that everything had been a priority to them and, therefore, they had no real priorities. Burney recalls Harper reminding his transition team, "We've got to keep it tight. I want to keep the mandates focused on the five priorities and I don't want any freelancing." In Burney's view, "The problem of governance in Ottawa is clutter, so my advice is to focus on the priorities. Now, you have to deal with the reality that things will come about that you cannot be involved in; however, at least if you have some degree of priorities that you're trying to achieve, you will be able to control the centre of your agenda, if not the periphery. My advice, then, would be: focus, keep it tight, and keep things small. We did this by recommending a much smaller Cabinet."[17]

The agenda then moves to the date of the swearing-in of the new government and the selection of the Cabinet. Depending on how well prepared the transition team is for this next step, there should be very little conversation about choosing the Cabinet members, since this will have been sorted out well in advance of the election.

The agenda of the first transition team meeting that took place the day after the 1993 election in the boardroom of the leader of the official opposition can be found in Appendix 4.

TRANSITION TEAM MEETS THE CLERK OF THE PRIVY COUNCIL

This set of meetings is among the most difficult to describe in a general way, since the meetings represent the most idiosyncratic behaviour between two teams of players. As figure 5.1 illustrates, the meeting of these two groups represents the melding of their respective agendas – the political one, which has been validated by the election results, and that of the public service, which is the custodian of the long-term non-partisan administration of the country. As we already know, meetings between the head of the transition team and the clerk may have been going on for weeks before the election (depending on the disposition of the sitting prime minister) or may take place only after the election results are known.

In any case, at some point only a few days after the election the clerk and the head of the transition team will sit down for their first formal meeting. Paul Wells has documented the first telephone contact between the Harper team and Alex Himelfarb, then clerk of the PCO.[18] In a rather jocular manner, Brodie was able to set the wheels in motion for the first meeting:

> But while the strategists worked on strategy, a new government had to govern. Ian Brodie had waited until six days before the election before telephoning Alex Himelfarb, the Clerk of the Privy Council, to start talking about the transition to a Conservative government. The Harper campaign, determined to avoid leaks (except the intentional kind), had been reluctant to reach out to the bureaucracy too soon because they didn't want to read stories about Harper turning arrogant and presumptuous.
>
> Harper's chief of staff had never met the country's ranking civil servant. "I'm Ian Brodie and I'm the chief of staff and I'm on the transition team," he said gamely into the telephone, "and there's a possibility that we could win this thing."
>
> Himelfarb laughed. "There's a *possibility* you could win this thing?"
>
> "Yeah, it looks like there's a possibility we're going to win this thing," Brodie said.

Himelfarb said, "Yeah, I think you've got a pretty good possibility of winning this thing. How are you feeling?"

"Nervous," Brodie said. "If we make it to Thursday without fucking up, I'll believe we might win this." Himelfarb laughed again, and then Brodie gave him the name of the contact person for the Harper transition team, should one be necessary: Derek Burney.[19]

In earlier chapters, considerable space was devoted to the psychological dynamics surrounding these meetings. There is high risk in these first encounters. The clerk is under intense scrutiny from the transition team to demonstrate a willingness to work with the newly elected government and to show loyalty to the new prime minister. The team will also be watching the see if the clerk shows leadership that will result in quick responses to the new government's high-priority agenda items. All actions are magnified in these circumstances, so the clerk will have scripted the encounter in advance, if at all possible, to avoid any missteps.

PRIME MINISTER–DESIGNATE MEETS THE CLERK OF THE PRIVY COUNCIL

The next key meeting will be between the prime minister–elect and the clerk. In many instances, neither will know each other personally, although both will have been extensively briefed by their staff or knowledgeable contacts on the other's personality and key attributes. As already noted, the clerk is the prime minister's principal advisor and agent and will be crucial to determining the prime minister's long-term effectiveness. As with the meeting with the transition team, the clerk will want to show a keen willingness to work for the new government and assure the prime minister of the neutrality of the public service. Moreover, as Glen Shortliffe pointed out to me in a 1993 memo, "once the prime minister takes office, the pressure of events and the demands of the position will make it all the more difficult to focus on the key transition issues."[20]

Once again, the clerk will know that he or she is being heavily scrutinized for signs of partisanship and ideological leanings. The clerk also knows that the prime minister, if coming from the opposition, will already have views that are probably based on flimsy evidence, general impressions, and gossip gathered by staff while in opposition. It is at this moment that all those after-hours get-togethers with political staffers at the Ottawa Sheraton bar, the Brasserie Metropolitain, Hy's Martini Bar,

---

Behind the Scenes: The First Encounter between the Head of the Transition Team and the Clerk of the Privy Council

I had been after Harper about whether I should contact Alex Himelfarb. Finally, on the Thursday before Election Day – the 19th of January – he said, "OK, go ahead and phone Alex, but don't tell him anything! Just tell him who you are, that he should expect to get a call from Derek, and that we have been working on a transition. But don't tell him anything else." So I phoned Himelfarb, though I had never met or talked with him before. In fact, I don't think there was anybody in the PCO, at that point, who I had ever met.

Alex seemed surprised to hear from me. Most of our discussion consisted of me telling him that we were going to conclude the election campaign in Calgary and, in the event that we won, we would come back on the Tuesday morning on the campaign plane. By travelling west to east, we wouldn't get to Ottawa until relatively later in the day.

The rest of our conversation revolved around resolving how the new prime minister would get back to Ottawa. Alex preferred, in the event that we won, that Mr Harper come back on a military plane or on a Challenger. I, however, was quite insistent that he would come back on the campaign plane. There was a long discussion about this, which was ultimately pointless. I knew that we were going to do whatever Harper wanted.

Ian Brodie, interview, 6 April 2011

---

and Darcy McGee's merge into a collective assessment of the degree to which the new government can work with the incumbent clerk. Given the context of the meeting, D'Ombrain observes that the "clerk must be seen as apolitical, and the future of the relationship with the PM depends on the outcome of that assessment."[21]

The clerk must know all the policy and logistical details of the transition and typically does the briefings without help from other PCO staff. The clerk must offer honest advice, and there cannot be any link in his mind between the substance of his advice and his job security. This is the moment when the notions of fearless advice and the independence of the public service are most severely tested. It is truly a high-wire event for the clerk, and for those clerks who like the thrill of risk-taking, the first meetings with the transition team and the prime minister–elect is exhilarating. For those who don't relish being scrutinized, it is a most stressful time. Given the circumstances that surround these first meet-ing, D'Ombrain advises that clerks should be pensionable (or at least know that there is a landing spot if it doesn't work out with the prime minister) and ready to move to another job in order to guarantee that their future does not depend on the PM liking them. In other words, clerks needs to have their resignation letter in the top desk drawer, in order for them to do their job well.[22]

In order to mitigate the potential negative impact of the rumour mill on Harper's view of the public service, Derek Burney sought to bring some objectivity and evidence to the first meeting between the prime minister–elect and the clerk. Accordingly, he asked Arthur Kroeger to meet with Harper to provide an overview of the senior ranks of the public service. Knowing that Kroeger had previously interviewed the deputy minister community for some consulting work, Burney was sure that Kroeger would be able to respond to the full range of Harper's questions.

Ideally, the prime minister will recognize that in this initial meeting the briefing comes from someone who knows the players better than any other single person and who understands the interrelationships and the not-so-obvious complexities of the issues. However, this will all be coloured by the prime minister's inclination to accept (or not accept) the long-standing Canadian tradition that the clerk is a non-political player who has loyally served the previous government and will now transfer this loyalty to the new government.

Bill Neville laid out a precise agenda for Brian Mulroney's use dur-ing his first meeting with the clerk in 1984. In it he suggested that Mulroney give Gordon Osbaldeston (the clerk) "an initial shopping list of the changes you want to accomplish within the agreed timeframe. I would ask him to come back to you with a game plan on how and with whom he would propose to accomplish your wishes. I would ask him to move quickly (this is a bit more delicate, since your prerogatives here are practical and persuasive, rather than legal), to make a couple of changes in the senior personnel of the PCO."[23]

At the end of this first meeting, the two (who may be accompanied by the prime minister's chief of staff and the head of the transition team) begin to get to know each other and to acquire a personal feel for their working relationship. It is also important that the clerk feels assured of the prime minister's confidence and has begun to understand what and how the prime minister likes things done. As a specific outcome of this first meeting, the prime minister should be ready to indicate or reaffirm who the principal contact should be on transition matters and what other staff/advisors (not many) should have access to the briefing books and other materials.

When there has been little or no contact between the transition team and the public service before the election, the incoming transition team is often surprised by the degree to which the public service has anticipated the new government's agenda.

In the United Kingdom, Jonathan Powell recalls the humorous interaction between the prime minister–elect and the Cabinet secretary on the occasion of their first meeting after the Blair victory in 1997. He remembers Robin Butler, the secretary to the Cabinet, producing a number of briefing notes containing a detailed analysis of the Labour Party's election platform. He recalls that the "the civil servants had parsed every aspect of the manifesto and prepared plans to implement even the craziest ideas floated in the heat of the campaign. Far from aiming to frustrate the new government's plans, they had to be restrained from taking each component too literally."[24]

Behind the Scenes: First Meeting between the Prime Minister–Designate and the Clerk of the Privy Council

Maybe this was the way it was always done, but Alex really seemed to realize the importance of relationships. And while we had to seem to be able to produce good quality work, the most important thing was to set the tone. For the first little, while it was only Alex seeing Ian Brodie. After a few days, though, it became less centralized and we all had to start. We used to go up to the fourth floor where they were and hand over some of our stuff. We didn't really get into a lot of discussions, though.

They thought a lot about the machinery issues as well as the Cabinet. In my experience, though, you will get more from the clerks and chief of staff. There is so much work that goes into this, and at a certain point you start to wonder about the value of it, particularly when the new government comes in and they've already thought about it.

Kathy O'Hara, assistant secretary to the Cabinet for Machinery of Government, Privy Council Office, interview, 20 March 2011

Behind the Scenes: Working Together

Everyone in the PCO worked really hard; they were highly motivated. The relations between the second floor – the PMO – and the third floor were excellent in every respect. We all felt that we were in the same business, which was the governance of Canada. The officials knew that they were there to help the government fulfil its objective, and the political staff was respectful to the officials, their duties, and their loyalties. In other words, they understood that the officials were professionally loyal but not partisan, and the officials knew the partisans were professionally competent. To my memory, that was an excellent time in the history of the relationship between the government and the public service.

Jim Mitchell, assistant secretary to the Cabinet,
Privy Council Office, 1991–4

PRIME MINISTER–DESIGNATE MEETS THE GOVERNOR GENERAL

This next meeting has sometimes turned out to be rather drama-filled, although the purpose is straightforward. The formal purpose of this meeting is for the governor general to officially invite the leader of the party with the most seats in the House of Commons to form a government. According to Glen Shortliffe, "The transition formalities highlight the prime minister's relationship with the Governor General which is one of constitutional interdependence."[25] The prime minister is the chief advisor to the governor general, who by convention accepts this advice on almost all matters. Thus, "it is the duty of the Prime Minister to inform the Governor General of all important decisions and to keep him or her informed of issues confronting the Government."[26]

According to convention, the way in which the announcement and timing are made is the governor general's call. Over the years, however, this practice has become the responsibility of the transition team in close cooperation with the clerk. More specifically, the real purpose of this meeting is to finalize the arrangements for the swearing-in – the date, who will attend (in terms of a general policy), where it will be held (if there is a wish to change established practice), and how it will be televised. "And again, while the legal niceties suggest this is her show, it is, in fact, yours beyond any question and you have a right, should it be required, to press very hard for your wishes to be respected."[27]

A few days before the actual swearing-in, it is customary for the prime minister–designate to pay a further call on the governor general to report on the outcome of the Cabinet-making process and to give advance notice of the names of the people that the governor general will be swearing in.

PRIME MINISTER–DESIGNATE MEETS THE OUTGOING PRIME MINISTER

Although there are no formal records of meetings between incoming and outgoing prime ministers, this tradition is not thought to be very long-standing in Canada. In the United States, President Truman was the first president to publicly invite his successor to meet with him to consider transition issues and then call on government departments and agencies to provide information on the status of various programs.[28]

For the two principals, this is a meeting that both would prefer to miss, but good manners and practicality requires both of them to be present for what is usually a short meeting. In some cases, the meeting is perfunctory, with little to be accomplished other than settling on a swearing-in date for the new government and arranging an appropriate time for the moving trucks to arrive at 24 Sussex. At other times, there is last-minute work or some urgent matters to be discussed and transferred from one government to another.

One small example illustrates the pivotal use of this meeting. When Stephen Harper met with Paul Martin to confirm the swearing-in date and to settle on other timing details, Martin took the opportunity to ask Harper to honour Martin's earlier promise to Alex Himelfarb that he would be appointed Canada's ambassador to Italy.

Martin had convinced Himelfarb to stay on as his clerk of the Privy Council during his tenure as prime minister and felt an obligation to carry through with this commitment, but he was aware that making the appointment himself during the dying days of his government would be unseemly and reflect badly on him. As we know, Himelfarb was subsequently appointed ambassador to Italy after serving Harper for six months, during which time he enjoyed an excellent working relationship both with the prime minister and with Ian Brodie, his chief of staff.

Once again, Bill Neville anticipated all of the issues in a briefing note to Mulroney:

At some point on election night, once the results are confirmed, Mr Turner undoubtedly will call you. (Just to be safe, by the way, you should have with you on September 4 phone numbers where both Mr Turner and Mr Broadbent can be reached that evening.) In your conversation that evening, you should agree to meet at the earliest convenience with the outgoing Prime Minister. I would suggest it is both proper protocol and proper generosity for you to go to him, as it were, for this meeting in the Prime Minister's Office.

The key subject on the agenda is the timing of transition. You should tell Mr Turner that you want to take office on Monday, September 17, and ask his cooperation to that end. He will be hard-pressed to refuse it. You then can fill out the rest of the ritual timetable, starting with when he will be calling on the Governor General to submit his resignation.

The second major subject of conversation will be the arrangements for personal transition, i.e., his departure from and your occupancy of 24 Sussex, Harrington Lake, and the Prime Minister's Office on the Hill (although on the latter, you are free, if you so wish, to stay in your present Hill office and simply transform it into the PMO as Clark did). I am sure you need no lecturing on the gains to be had in being seen to be reasonable and even generous to the loser in these arrangements. Since I understand the Turners never really occupied 24 Sussex, the problems should be minimal in any event. You could offer him, if he needs a temporary personal base, the use of either Harrington (as Clark did with Trudeau) or even the Speaker's compound at Kingsmere for a reasonable period.[29]

The consensus about the meetings between incoming and outgoing prime ministers is that they are not particularly friendly, high-minded, or useful. Most in recent years have been tense affairs, with little real conversation between the principal players. Perhaps it is personal animosity that the two leaders have towards one another as a result of years of squaring off during question period that sets the stage for these perfunctory meetings. Or the election loss for the outgoing prime minister still rankles.

As a result, the crucial decisions on the timing of the handover and the transfer of staff in the case of interparty or intraparty transitions is usually left to the incoming and outgoing chiefs of staff to sort out between themselves. In my case, I had an excellent working relationship with Jodi White, Campbell's chief of staff, and our meetings were extremely productive in terms of deciding on a date for the swearing-in ceremony, the move to 24 Sussex, and some personnel issues for staff who had taken a leave from the public service and now wanted to return. Since Campbell had not been prime minister for very long, there were very few things that had to be untangled before her departure.

In the United States, there is much more formal and informal contact between the transition team and the outgoing administration. According to John Burke, "Not only are transitions the occasion for the President-elect to meet with the incumbent president for the traditional policy briefing and tour of the White House, but they are also times when members of the transitions that must work constructively with their counterparts in the outgoing administration. Both levels are critical."[30]

Martha Joynt Kumar goes further than Burke in emphasizing the importance of cooperation between the two parties for the incoming government when she argues, "It's very important to the success of the transition that the president-elect develop a constructive, cooperative relationship with the outgoing president and that an atmosphere of cooperation and mutual respect be communicated to the outgoing transition team and the incoming transition team. If that's not gone well, then you have the potential for really big problems that can screw up the first hundred days of the new administration."[31]

As a final statement on the value of these meetings in the U.S. context, Landon Butler, who was deputy to the chief of staff in the Carter administration from 1977 to 1981, commented about his experience meeting the outgoing government during the 1976, "I think, by and large, we learned far more from our predecessors than we did from any written material. They generally want us to be successful. I think the most important thing would be to try to make sure they talk to their predecessors and to set a tone as I was writing: don't make this a bitter transition, don't walk out the door."[32]

Swearing-In

The swearing-in ceremony is the most visible manifestation of the change in government and as a result the incoming government has increasingly more say in the way in which it unfolds. While it is technically the governor general's event, all details of the swearing-in are negotiated among the PCO, the transition team, and the Governor General's Office. Traditionally a small ceremony is held at Rideau Hall, although there have been many suggestions in recent years to hold the event at other venues where the public could attend.

Attendance at the swearing-in ceremony is limited because of space, and on some occasions even spouses have not been invited to witness it. Since John Turner, the swearing-in has been televised and in some cases has been turned into a major television event.

Behind the Scenes: Lining Up for the Swearing-In Ceremony

It was an incredible day. It was that very morning that I met a lot of my Cabinet colleagues for the first time. One of them arrived in interesting circumstances. We were lining up as directed by the staff at Rideau Hall to go in for the swearing-in. And I was told to keep a spot right in front of me because someone might be coming. And I said, "Well that's odd. I wonder who's going to be here." Five minutes before the doors opened and we walked in for the swearing-in, Anne McLellan was ushered in and stood in front of me. She had just arrived from Edmonton, having been up 'til 2:00 in the morning waiting to see whether she had won, which she did by four votes, subject to a recount. Anyways, she was sworn in as minister of natural resources that day. It was quite a day!

Allan Rock, minister of justice, minister of health, and minister of industry, 1993–2003

In general, the swearing-in unfolds in the following manner:

- The outgoing prime minister makes his final call on the governor general at Rideau Hall (Government House) and formally resigns;
- Very shortly thereafter (usually within minutes) the prime minister-elect arrives at Government House for a brief private meeting with the governor general. At this point, the prime minister-designate may take this opportunity to be sworn in privately, or may wait to be sworn in with his or her colleagues;
- The ministers arrive at Rideau Hall and are collected together for the formal ceremony in one of the ceremonial rooms;
- The Cabinet take the oaths and are formally sworn in as members of the ministry;
- There is a session of formal picture-taking of the governor general with the new government;

- There is a brief, not overly elaborate, reception for ministers and their families;
- The prime minister and many of the better-known ministers run their first initial media gantlet as they leave. However, as Bill Neville shrewdly comments, "Ministers who at this point say anything substantive about the policy aspects of their new portfolios should have their tongues cut out."[33]

Immediately following the swearing-in, a message is sent from the prime minister via the Department of Foreign Affairs, Trade and Development, through Canada House in London, to the Queen's private secretary. On this occasion three key points are typically made. An assurance of continued loyalty to Her Majesty is provided, as well as a promise of respectful duty to Her Majesty, and the prime minister also offers good wishes for the Queen's continued good health and well-being.

Pressing Issues

While it is very difficult to anticipate what issues will emerge during the short time between the election and the swearing-in of the new government, one can be certain that some will arise, needing immediate action from the government. However, it seems inappropriate to ask the outgoing government to make the decision on its own at this juncture. An outgoing government will not be accountable for its actions, and, more important, does not have the legitimacy to make any decision that has long-term implications or ties the hands of a new government. But the newly elected government does not have the legal right to make formal decisions, since it does not yet have direct control of the levers of power.

In some cases, there is a need for some directional guidance from the incoming prime minister, but nothing as formal as a Cabinet decision. A good example of such a situation was during the negotiations around NAFTA. In his book *The Way It Works: Inside Ottawa*, Eddie Goldenberg describes only days after the election of being immersed in Canada–United States relations and the need to pick up the thread of negotiations that had been started by the Mulroney government with the U.S. government.[34]

In all cases, emerging policy issues will need to be handled with the utmost delicacy, making good use of the secretary to the Cabinet's finest skills in order to diplomatically transfer the issues from the office of the outgoing prime minister to the incoming PMO without stressing the system unduly.

Outgoing Governments

The final task immediately after the election is dealing with the outgoing government. While not the direct responsibility of the new prime minister, many loose ends need to be tied up regarding the outgoing group. As has already been mentioned, in some cases the outgoing prime minister may have a request to make of the new prime minister. In other instances, there may be things a generous prime minister could do to ease the transition of the outgoing government, such as the offer of an ambassadorship that Chrétien made to Kim Campbell after she lost both the election and her seat in 1993.

Public Service in Transition

The public service has been focusing its time and efforts during the election period on developing briefing books and departmental or portfolio books for each individual minister. But as Phase Three begins, the

---

Behind the Scenes: Life before and after Politics

You have a life before and you also have to have a life after. And it can't define you. How many former politicians, former political aides, do we know, who after that whole episode in their lives, they find it hard to re-enter normal, everyday life? And in transitions you see kings being made but then eventually the reign ends. I think political parties in this country are very good at transitioning to power. They're not so great at transitioning out of power, because even though no one wants to transition out of power, unlike in business, there isn't a proper succession-planning process. And so you're kind of left hanging. And that's why I think in Canada you find that it takes sometimes a whole generation to rejuvenate a political party. The cycle seems to be like that.

Simone Philogène, interview, 29 April 2011

public service is able to fine-tune its efforts to welcome and support the incoming government.

First and foremost, the transition team is provided with as much logistical support as is necessary. Elizabeth Roscoe, who served on Harper's transition team, remembers the days immediately following the election:

> The heavy lifting didn't start until January 24, the day after the election, whereby we were all asked to meet on the fourth floor of the Langevin Block. We started about 9:30 on the morning of the 24th and proceeded immediately to be facilitated by very competent PCO staff, led by Roberta Santi of the Machinery of Government Secretariat in the PCO. They were waiting for us with long checklists of things to be done, phone support systems, and the offer to help with all our questions. For the next two weeks we had daily meetings among ourselves and although PCO's presence wasn't constant it was very responsive when we asked for help or advice. It was clear what we needed to get done, and the PCO was there to support our efforts.[35]

In these days, the public service has an opportunity to shine. And it starts with anticipating every detail in advance, such as transition space for the team, phone and computer support. Tony Dean, who was the secretary to Cabinet for the Ontario Public Service from 2002 to 2008, calls this the "business service ethic," and it goes a long way when developing trust and good first impressions. He describes the system and the environment that he endeavoured to create during the transition exercise in 2003:

> The pencils have to be sharpened and people have to be available twenty-four hours a day to deal with everything from answering questions about how much money was spent on X and Y to "I'm going to need a briefing or a meeting room available at 5:00 a.m. tomorrow morning and I understand that it's now 11:00 p.m. the evening before but, you know, this would be helpful."
>
> We gave them high-powered, service-oriented, action-oriented, results-oriented concierge service. We provided a senior concierge who was the go-to person for anybody on that incoming transition team who needed anything. And behind that person was every phone number and support function that they could possibly need.[36]

While the PCO is operating at full speed to support the transition exercise at the centre, the deputy minister community is coming together to prepare to greet a "new" government. This is particularly critical when the election has brought a new party into power. A good example of this occurred when the Liberals won a majority in 1993. Glen Shortliffe, then clerk of the Privy Council, brought all deputy ministers together over the lunch hour to set the stage for the new administration. His goal was to review the actions that Chrétien was taking to place his personal stamp on the new administration and to give the deputies a taste of the way in which the new government would work.

Shortliffe described to the assembled deputies Chrétien's decision to have a small twenty-three-member Cabinet supported by a small number of secretary of state positions. The emphasis was on an efficient Cabinet structure, with maximum scope for ministers to be innovative but with strict enforcement of rules for Cabinet solidarity and close control of key files. Smaller ministerial offices were to be the norm, along with a renewal of the classical minister–deputy-minister relationships. Shortliffe also reinforced Chrétien's commitment to integrity, beginning with a detailed vetting of potential ministers and continuing with conflict-of-interest provisions, merit in GIC appointments, and sensitivity to stories about lobbyists selling access to ministers and officials. At the end of the meeting, Shortliffe challenged the deputy minister community to rise to the occasion and to provide wise, thoughtful, and decisive support to the new administration. He assured them that their advice would be welcome.[37]

Conclusion

At this point in our narrative the election is over, the winning party declared the victor, and, barring any serious constitutional crises, the elected or party-chosen prime minister is poised to take over the government. At this juncture the transition team needs to do one more survey of the environment and to then initiate the formal transition process which includes organizing and attending a number of first meetings with the clerk of the Privy Council, the governor general, and the deputy minister community.

In addition, the transition team needs to finalize the plans for the swearing-in ceremony, deal with pressing policy issues that may await the prime minister, sensitively administer to the outgoing government with as much care and understanding as possible, and give some thought to whether there are human capital issues to consider within the public service.

We now move to the core series of activities that are the most visible part of the transition exercise and most crucial to a successful launch. Most important, they represent the merging of the political and public service agendas to facilitate the transition.

7 Post-Election Phase: Getting the Fundamentals Right

To judge a president by a transition is like judging dinner by the noise out in the kitchen; the clatter is fascinating, but it doesn't guarantee what's about to appear on the table.

– Newsweek[1]

Thinking well is wise; planning well, wiser; but doing well is the wisest and best of all.

– Persian proverb

Introduction

This chapter discusses the three most critical activities to take place during the third phase of the transition exercise. These are the Cabinet selection, the staffing of the Prime Minister's Office and ministers' offices, and the appointment of key positions in the government that are made by the governor general on the recommendation of the prime minister. There should be no doubt that the prime minister makes the key decisions; however, each important decision is supported by the transition team, and by the clerk of the Privy Council who, in turn, is advised by the secretariats in the Privy Council Office, notably the Machinery of Government Secretariat.

This period, which is usually less than two weeks, is the crucial test of the transition team, since it is the time when it has its greatest impact on the careers of many individuals who have aspirations to be Cabinet ministers and influence on the machinery of government. In the end, the decisions taken at the transition meetings have consequences for all 260,000 full-time federal public servants.

Cabinet Selection

By now the prime minister–designate should be in the proper frame of mind to tackle these important decisions, especially choosing from among his party colleagues for the key positions in the government. As David Docherty pointed out in a 1997 article, "The attractiveness of a cabinet career is almost self-evident ... A seat at the federal cabinet table, therefore, represents the only chair that allows an individual to satisfy both political and policy ambition."[2] As a result, most of those appointed to Cabinet are thrilled with the opportunity to serve, but many others will be angry and disappointed at being left out. The prime minister soon realizes after the swearing-in ceremony that some of this disappointment could later become the source of some difficult interpersonal conflict if it is not attended to early in the mandate.

Eddie Goldenberg served as a senior policy advisor and chief of staff to Jean Chrétien over a ten-year period and had the privilege of a front-row seat during the formation and selection of all of Chrétien's Cabinets. Goldenberg writes that he was struck by the humorous reference of Canada's first prime minister, Sir John A. Macdonald, to his occupation as that of "cabinet-maker." Goldenberg concurs with Macdonald: "Cabinet making is one of the most difficult and loneliest parts of the prime minister's job, with the government success or failure hanging on the success of the selection. A prime minister's cabinet making produces instant and very public winners and, in some instances a number of public losers. Ambitions are satisfied in some cases, but are disappointed in many more, because there is hardly a single backbencher, no matter how limited his or her talents may be, who does not believe that he or she deserves to be in the cabinet."[3]

Needless to say, for those who hope or expect to be called to join the Cabinet, these days are agonizing. While some MPs assume that they will be called, because of their proven loyalty to the prime minister or because of the need for gender or geographical balance, others will nervously sit by the phone, waiting for it to ring. This situation was captured beautifully in an early episode of *Yes Minister*:

I've been sitting by the telephone ever since breakfast. No potential cabinet minister ever moves more than 20 feet from the telephone in the 24 hours following the appointment of a new prime minister. If you haven't heard within 24 hours, you're not going to be in the cabinet.

Annie kept me supplied with constant cups of coffee all morning, and when I returned to the armchair next to the phone after lunch she asked me to help do the Brussels sprouts for dinner if I didn't have anything else to do. I explained to her that I couldn't because I was waiting for the call.[4]

Behind the Scenes: Interview Time

I was sitting in the outer office when Paul Martin appeared in front of me, looking for the meeting with Mr Chrétien. My first reaction was that he did not appear as sure of himself as I'd expected him to look. I mean, you know, Paul Martin was already heavily rumoured to be the finance minister, so I expected that someone with his credentials would not be worried about a meeting where the outcome was known. But again, this is a job interview, and it is someone else making the choice about your political future.

In fact, all of the ministers that I saw that morning had the same look. Sheila, John, Paul – they all had that look: "What's about to happen to me?" So in the end, no matter how well known they are and how successful they've been, they are still human beings whose future is in the hands of another person.

And that's one of the ironies about the Canadian political system. In theory, our prime ministers have a very limited role. But in practice, they have extremely powerful jobs, including the ability to appoint the entire Cabinet without any constraints.

Simone Philogène, interview, 29 April 2011

It goes without saying that this phase of the transition is a very delicate one and requires complete confidentiality on the part of the transition team and the PCO. As well, all potential candidates for the cabinet have to agree that the entire procedure be done "under a cone of silence." Derek Burney described how he was able to impose confidentiality during the Harper transition: "Cabinet-making is an exceedingly delicate process and, above all, we were determined to prevent leaks. Those interviewed were told bluntly that if any word of their meeting became public, whatever offer had been discussed would be withdrawn – that helped! I had also recruited a media spokesperson for the transition team and directed her explicitly to say nothing, politely, for two weeks. She did, and I am happy to say that we succeeded in launching the new Cabinet without any leaks."[5]

As noted earlier, the first step in the process is to determine the Cabinet's size and structure. The size is one of the most controversial issues that the transition team will have to deal with. The pressures for a large Cabinet are obvious. More seats at the table allow for a greater number of appointments. Moreover, the larger the size of the caucus the greater the pressure mounts on the prime minister to appoint a large Cabinet.

However, large Cabinets have their own drawbacks. First, every additional seat that is created means that someone competent must be found to fill it. The harsh reality is that only a few MPs are qualified for the job, in the sense that they have the requisite skills to lead a large department and to adequately defend the actions of the portfolio in the House of Commons. As a consequence, most experts argue that a smaller Cabinet produces a more efficient and effective government.

However, the large increase in the size of the Harper Cabinet in June 2011 illustrates that it is difficult to hold the line on Cabinet size, even when there is a strong disposition for smaller government. The tables in Appendix 2 illustrate how much the size of Cabinet has varied over the years.

It is also important during this phase of Cabinet-making that the prime minister approves the decision-making mechanisms for the Cabinet. This means articulating the role and size of Cabinet committees, naming a deputy prime minister, and setting parameters around who will attend what meetings. All this work should have been done in Phase One and Phase Two of the transition process. Having failed to do so at that time will complicate Phase Three of the transition and will greatly distract the prime minister–designate and the transition team from their primary activities.

Months before the 1993 election, Jean Chrétien made a number of important transition decisions. He wanted a smaller Cabinet because he felt that the large Trudeau Cabinets did not produce improved decision-making and simply took too much time from busy ministers. At the same time, he thought that Cabinet was a valuable way to discuss broad policy issues, keep ministers informed, and provide a political context for ministerial work. As a consequence, he settled on a Cabinet of twenty-three, but created a number of non-Cabinet "secretary of state" positions. While the size of his Cabinet grew over the next two mandates, its relatively small initial size gave him a highly responsive and effective Cabinet and started his government off on the right foot.

Several criteria are typically applied to Cabinet appointments in Canada. First, prime ministers are mindful of their need to keep the party onside. In practical terms, this means including key figures in the prime minister's party, even political rivals (such as former candidates for party leadership). The risk of excluding rivals is too high, but to balance the potential impact of including them, efforts are also made to include people who can be counted on to throw their support behind the prime minister. While expertise and experience are important criteria for the job of minister, some consideration must also be given to the ethnic, gender, and regional balance of the Cabinet. If there is room for an additional member or two, then the prime minister, looking to the future, may also give some fresh faces the opportunity to demonstrate their potential in the Cabinet.

David Collenette sees Cabinet-making from the perspective of someone who was a central Cabinet minister over a ten-year period in the Chrétien government. In our interview he reflected on the importance of a good working relationship with the prime minister.[6] Although it is difficult to generalize the complex and personal nature of the individual relationships established between prime ministers and their Cabinet colleagues, Collenette believes that successful ministers are those who quickly learn to appreciate the dynamics of the power relationships around the Cabinet table and can exploit it to their advantage. Characterizing an influential minister as being particularly "political" (not necessarily partisan) is simply shorthand for describing someone who fully understands how to exercise power in our Westminster system.

Collenette uses a unique typology for describing how prime ministers have organized their Cabinets. While the traditional model analyses the Cabinet from a regional, language, or gender perspective, Collenette argues that, in his experience, prime ministers use a four-tiered system in selecting their Cabinet. The first tier and the foundation for the other layers is populated with the prime minister's loyalists who have distinguished themselves during a leadership campaign or other venue by providing unwavering support for the prime minister's ambition to lead the party.

The second-tier of the Cabinet is occupied by people who the prime minister feels must be appointed because they represent certain constituencies in the party or have a power/regional base of their own within the party,[7] and excluding them might cause an irreparable split within the party. The third tier, which is a relatively small group, is chosen from among MPs who are respected for their particular expertise in a policy area that will be crucial to the government's success. The fourth tier comprises the most diverse of the groupings because it represents individuals whom the prime minister sees as having high potential and deserve to be given a chance to demonstrate their abilities. This tier also contains people who represent key subgroups of voters such as ethnic groups whose support the government would like to acknowledge.

As a general rule, the first tier or "A team" has a huge advantage over the other three groups because their established loyalty and guaranteed support give them special access to the prime minister and more than likely allow them to be less circumspect or restrained.

Collenette is quick to point out that Cabinet ministers are competing not only with each other for the prime minister's attention, but also with multiple sources of influence that in some cases are more important to the prime minister than those that emanate from Cabinet. The successful Cabinet minister soon learns to cultivate and seek alliances with these influential individuals – some of whom will work in the prime minister's office and others who have their own direct line of communication to the prime minister from outside the government.

Cabinet-making is also made more difficult if the incoming prime minister shares Tony Blair's view that the skills and characteristics that helped some members of Parliament distinguish themselves as particularly effective members of the opposition can become strong ministers and collegial members of the Cabinet. Based on his experiences, Blair warns future prime ministers, "The skills that bring you to the top of the greasy pole in Parliament are not necessarily those that equip you to run a department with a workforce number in thousands, in the budget numbered in billions."[8] In recent years as prime minister, Stephen Harper has come to a similar conclusion. Derek Burney tells us, "Harper has learned that this is not an ideological game. It's a management game. Government is about management."[9]

With all of this preparatory work done, the transition team prepares a draft plan of the Cabinet, the decision-making process, and the Cabinet committee system. This phase may take days if only limited work has been done before the election. Well-prepared teams will have sketched out potential Cabinets and Cabinet committees well in advance of the election, if only to familiarize themselves with the profile of potential Cabinet members and to test the decision-making processes with the clerk of the Privy Council. These draft plans can go back and forth between the prime minister–designate and the transition team many times before the prime minister is satisfied with the overall structure.

Candidate Interviews and the Vetting Process

The interview process can be organized in three coordinated stages. The first consists of general discussions between the prime minister and the candidates. The second phase, known as the vetting process, may involve candidates being interviewed by a committee appointed by the leader that will ask about the candidates' personal, educational, and professional background and will probe for potential problems. The committee reports its findings back to the prime minister, who assembles them with the other information provided by the security branch of the RCMP, who will have completed their own security checks. In the final stage of this important process, the prime minister advises the potential ministers of the decision shortly before the swearing-in ceremony.[10]

To begin this part of the process, only a few days after the election, telephone calls are made by a member of the transition team or another trusted aide to each of the potential Cabinet ministers, asking each to come to Stornoway, to a parliamentary office, or other location on Parliament Hill at an agreed time. As a general rule, the prime minister meets each potential minister personally to discuss the appointment, unless that person is physically absolutely unavailable.[11]

The meetings themselves should, of course, be one-on-one between the prime minister–designate and the prospective minister, with a transition member nearby who can record and convey the results of the discussion to the waiting transition team. In preparing Mulroney for his meetings with potential Cabinet ministers in 1984, Bill Neville provided the following advice:

1. While you have the results of the pre-clearance process (and you can so inform the prospective ministers that there is nothing there to disqualify them), the prime minister must go beyond the limited security / national revenue check and ask each prospective minister whether there is anything in his or her background, past or

present, which could prove embarrassing to you or the government or which possibly could disqualify him or her from membership in the cabinet.

Before speaking to any prospective ministers you should have come to a decision on the guidelines you intend to impose respecting conflict of interest. You should ensure that ministers receive a copy of the guidelines and tell them that you want to hear from them within 48 hours if they foresee any significant problem with compliance.

2. My advice would be not to invite any initiative from the prospective minister on what portfolio he or she might like. Rather, you inform them that you would like them to be a member of your government and minister of X – period. You are exercising your most central prerogative here and, in that sense, bestowing your favour on the minister. These are not bargaining sessions.

3. You are under no obligation to tell any minister whom you are proposing to appoint to any other portfolio and I see no reason for you to do so. It just begs comparisons and bargaining – and invites leaks. The sole exception may be a situation where you are offering a ministry of state position which will operate in a subordinate role to a departmental minister. But even there, you very well could restrict yourself to simply describing the relationship you envisage – minus the names.

4. You do not want at this stage of the process to get into a lengthy discussion about specific plans or policies for the ministry in question. You might simply invite the prospective minister to give some quiet – and private – consideration to the job against the early need and opportunity within the cabinet structure for him to submit his initial analysis and priorities.

5. Ministers should be told that they are not to discuss their appointments with anyone except members of their immediate family and that any breach of that code will be grounds for reconsidering the appointment.

You should emphasize that ministers are *not* to approach potential personal staff and that you have established a process through which ministers must clear their choice of their chief of staff before any approaches are made. This means that ministers will have to endure a short, but essential, delay in approaching potential personal staff.

6. If you are offering the individual a position that does not carry full ministerial salary (you personally can determine the salary of ministers of state), you had better note that fact in passing. It could be grounds for future misunderstanding (this happened to Clark).

7. While this is not absolutely necessary, I would strongly recommend that you end the conversation with all but the core ministers with a statement that you will confirm this conversation by brief telephone call on the weekend (i.e., the Saturday/Sunday before swearing-in). It is just possible that one or more of these appointments could come unstuck for some unforeseen reason and this way leaves you at least an opening to make portfolio adjustments if necessary without being open to the charge of "breaking your word."[12]

It is up to the prime minister to decide whom to interview first. However, it is recommended to begin with the most crucial Cabinet positions such as finance, industry, and foreign affairs, and move out from there. Obviously any problem in confirming the nominee for a critical ministry may well affect the other choices, requiring one or even more changes in that list. That problem clearly lessens as the importance of the portfolio in question moves down.[13]

Once the requirements of the job have been covered in the interview and the prime minister has a good sense if the proposed position is going to fit with the overall Cabinet plan, areas may be summarized in the interview if time allows. In particular, the prime minister might want to review administrative rules and conventions that might affect their behaviour as a minister, should they be invited to join the Cabinet. For example, there are three major areas that fall in this area of conversation.

MINISTERIAL BEHAVIOUR

What ministers can and cannot do in the discharge of their duties has become a moving target over the years but the trend has been to ensure ministers act in ethical and principled ways. Fortunately, for the past decade the Privy council office has produced a very readable document entitled *Accountable Government: Guide for Ministers and Secretaries of State* that anticipates the kinds of issues that might challenge a new minister. For example, it covers topic such as responsibilities, duties, and functions of ministers, with particular emphasis on the ongoing principles, practices, and expectations concerning their individual and collective responsibilities. Along with the *Conflict of Interest and Post-Employment Code for Public Office Holders*, these documents provide ministers with the basic rules to govern their official and personal conduct.

Ministers should be made aware that they must comply with Treasury Board policies on the operation of their offices, particularly on contracting, travel, and staffing. A separate document titled *Guidelines for Ministers' Offices* details the requirements and should be provided to ministers.

The prime minister may also want to emphasize the requirement that ministers consult the caucus and other stakeholders on policy proposals, and the need for ministers to have an active and effective partnership with their junior ministers (if applicable) and parliamentary secretary, who can provide valuable support.

Finally, the prime minister may emphasize that all appointment recommendations are subject to the prime minister's concurrence, and that they cannot be announced until the governor general has approved them.

Further guidance and support will be provided to new ministers and staff through an orientation session held shortly after the swearing-in ceremony.

CONFLICT OF INTEREST

Ministers should be reminded that they are subject to the *Conflict of Interest and Post-Employment Code for Public Office Holders*. The prime minister–elect can indicate that they will receive a copy of the code, and that the expectation is that they will read it carefully. Ministers may also receive expert advice and guidance on the arrangement of their personal affairs from the ethics counsellor, who will also brief them personally.

All prospective ministers will be asked whether there is any conflict of interest, or appearance of a conflict of interest, that would prevent them from taking up their proposed portfolio responsibilities. At this point, the prime minister may engage in a more detailed conversation with a particular minister in this regard.

MINISTERIAL STAFF

The prime minister may remind colleagues that nowhere will their individual responsibility be more open to public scrutiny than in the selection and management of their political staff. Because of this possible political vulnerability, the selection of their chief of staff will be carried out jointly with the PMO. As staffing initiatives continue, the PMO should be advised as appointments of other staff members are made to their offices.

Ministers are accountable to the prime minister for ensuring smooth relations between political staff and departmental officials. The prime minister may counsel them to choose their political staff wisely. The capacities and conduct of a minister's staff are not only vital to his or her effectiveness, but, as a reflection of the minister's personal capacities and conduct, are also likely to be publicly scrutinized.

Ministers should understand that the government must not be diverted from its agenda by difficult relationships with the public service, which is ready to serve each minister loyally by providing both policy advice and administrative follow-through. The prime minister may emphasize that deputy ministers are as much policy advisors and firefighters as they are administrators. A good deputy minister is one of the minister's best means of staying out of trouble.

In 1993, Jean Chrétien introduced a new element in the Cabinet selection process. He was very aware that Brian Mulroney had lost more than half a dozen ministers over the course of his two mandates as a result of ethical lapses. Chrétien was determined that he would ensure, to the extent it was possible, that his ministers act in the best interests of Canada and avoid the ethical potholes that had plagued the Mulroney government.

Since all Mulroney appointees had been subjected to a security check by the RCMP, it was apparent that a new system had to be developed that would bring to the light potential problems before they were exposed by the media. After some discussions with Chrétien and Herb Gray, whom Chrétien valued as a wise advisor, I was asked to develop an additional screening process, to identify whether any of Chrétien's proposed Cabinet ministers would be problematic once they were appointed to Cabinet. Effectively this meant that each potential cabinet minister would have to agree to be subjected to vigorous questioning from a neutral source about their past behaviour.

Chrétien asked his mentor and close friend, Mitchell Sharp, and then lawyer Allan Lutfy[14] to take on this important task. Being a very well-organized professional, Lutfy kept notes from his early meetings with Chrétien and Sharp, which now provide us with insights into the reasoning behind the decision to subject potential Cabinet ministers to a very rigorous selection process. On 22 October 1993 in a note to file

Lutfy provided five reasons for interviewing each potential Cabinet minister before being appointed:

- The process provides a small, first step towards enhancing integrity in government;
- It communicates a clear message to ministers about the importance of integrity in government;
- It may disclose relevant information not otherwise available through the PCO verification process;
- It will assist the government if any personal problems of ministers are disclosed publicly during the mandate;
- There is a likelihood that many candidates will be first-time parliamentarians and would are relatively unknown to the Leader.[15]

He also described in some detail the process that would be used during the vetting of potential Cabinet ministers:

> After receiving instructions from the Prime Minister designate, the Chief of Staff will invite candidates to meet with the interviewers. (For Privy Council members or senior parliamentarians, the Prime Minister designate may wish to initiate or, in some instances, carry out the interview process himself.) The candidates will have the burden of disclosing any relevant information in response to certain questions. After receiving oral reports from the interviewers (and PCO reports from Revenue Canada, RCMP and CSIS verification of convictions or investigations), the Chief of Staff will communicate the results to the Prime Minister designate who will then proceed with formal invitations to the cabinet. The Prime Minister designate will want to reiterate the importance of integrity and ask the future minister one general question to obtain a personal commitment that there is no embarrassing information to disclose.[16]

Ever mindful of the potential impact that public disclosure of this vetting process might have on the reputation of the incoming government, Lutfy also had some communications advice for the prime minister–delegate. Recognizing that there was growing cynicism about the integrity of politicians in the 1990s, Lutfy wrote to Jean Pelletier on the advantage of informing the public about the rigorous nature of the vetting process. He concluded that, "while the process should stand the test of scrutiny, there is no apparent advantage to its immediate disclosure. Critical or other comments concerning the process in the short term can only distract from more important announcements in the early days of the government. There is likely to be an occasion during the mandate of the government where disclosure of the process may be helpful in resisting criticism that may result from a personal problem of a minister."[17]

For those readers with an interest in the details of the questions that were asked to each potential candidate for Cabinet in 1993, the questionnaire used by Sharp and Lutfy has been reproduced below.[18]

Disclosure of Personal Financial Information (Conflict of Interests)

1. Are you prepared to conform fully with the *Conflict of Interest and Post-employment Code for Public Office Holders* (1985)?
2. Would you be prepared to disclose publicly your assets, liabilities, and income and its sources, without quantification, should Parliament adopt legislation to this effect? Including those of your spouse and minor children?
3. Have you ever filed for personal bankruptcy? Has a company controlled by yourself or your family members declared bankruptcy? If so, in what circumstances?
4. Are you currently involved in litigation? Have you ever been involved in litigation that, if brought to public attention, would cause you embarrassment?
5. Are you currently acting in a fiduciary capacity for any other person?
6. Are you the beneficiary of trust funds raised on your behalf during your political career?
7. Are you currently or have you been previously engaged in any activity that would place you or have the appearance of putting you in a conflict of interest with a particular government institution?

Security Clearance

8. Have you ever been refused a security clearance?
9. Are you a citizen or the equivalent of a permanent resident of any country other than Canada?
10. Are you or have you been a member of an association that to your knowledge may have been a target of the Canadian Security Intelligence Service?

Personal Health

11. Have you been treated for drug or alcohol abuse within the last ten years? Or has any such treatment been recommended but refused by you?
12. Have you been treated by any mental health caregiver within the last ten years?

General information

13. Are you aware of any information that, if disclosed publicly, would embarrass you, your family, or the government?

In the end of the process, five individuals revealed details of their personal circumstances that were considered material enough to be raised with the prime minister–designate. Three of the five were financial, having to do with tax disputes, trust funds, and the nature of a candidate's share holdings. One case involved a severance package from a previous employer, and the last one concerned a membership at a private club.

Ian Brodie provides interesting insight into the process used by Harper in 2006, and the limitations of having the prime minister–designate in the room:

> With the PM in attendance, Derek [Burney] asked all the questions to the potential Cabinet member. The PM wanted to be around for all of those discussions and, at the time, I didn't appreciate the change in dynamics between the candidates and Harper.
>
> Nobody wants to say, "Yeah, Prime Minister, I've got a quarter of a million dollars of unpaid taxes." Derek was asking the questions and was on a different end of the table than the prime minister, so that people had to turn away from the prime minister and talk to Derek. He set this up carefully.
>
> Nevertheless, knowing that the future prime minister is with you at a table, people responded to him when Derek brought up a background check. "Have you got anything that would prevent you from serving in my Cabinet?" "No, Prime Minister." Except for one candidate, everyone said, "No, Prime Minister."
>
> It could turn out that you have five outstanding legal liens against your property, but you didn't want to bring that up with the PM in the room.

I see now the wisdom in separating the candidate from the PM and, if I went back and did it again, we would insist on separating them. It is unfeasible to hash out any problems with the PM in the room.[19]

As a final thought on the topic about what one should expect from the vetting process, Tony Blair offers a straightforward assessment. About the lives of politicians, he says, "Here's the shocking or not so shocking thing: politicians really are like everyone else. Some are in marriages of love, some are in marriages of convenience, some are having affairs, some are straight, and some are gay."[20]

Informing Individuals Who Are Not Selected for Cabinet

Once these meetings are completed and the appointments are made, the prime minister faces one optional but very important additional task. It is good manners and probably good politics for the prime minister to take the time to make at least brief telephone calls to those who were not interviewed but were known to be expecting a Cabinet post, or who were but did not survive the process, to break the bad news and briefly tell them why they were not chosen, without disclosing the names of those who were. This may be an occasion to suggest that the appointments process is not yet complete, and that there are many other positions yet to fill (parliamentary secretaries, deputy speaker, committee chairs, and so on). This is not a pleasant task, but I think it pays dividends. And as Bill Neville says in his briefing materials to Mulroney, "Besides, who said being prime minister was all pleasantries?"[21]

Staffing

Prime Minister's Office

The fundamental challenge faced by a prime minister beginning to staff the PMO is that the people who helped to get you elected are not necessarily best suited to help you govern.

At this juncture, it is not likely that the prime minister will be looking for a chief of staff to fill the crucial role in the PMO. In almost all cases, chiefs of staff simply pack their books and files from their fourth-floor offices in the Centre Block (if the party is the official opposition) and move down one floor to a third floor office in the PM's suite of government offices. In these circumstances, the only time that the chief of staff appointment might offer some challenging moments for the prime minister–elect is in the case of intraparty transitions if incoming prime ministers do not have a suitable candidate from within their own offices – presuming that they are already a Cabinet minister.

Behind the Scenes: Relationship between the Clerk of the Privy Council and the Chief of Staff

It is important to get clarity on who has what function and also to realize that, as chief of staff, you are going to have a say on a lot of different things. When I looked at my situation as a new chief of staff, it was clear that the previous prime minister had appointed all of the deputy ministers. As well, the role of the clerk of the Privy Council had expanded over the previous two years. For me, one of the issues in the transition was figuring out the relationship with the clerk who had worked for the prior prime minister and was now working for us, and he was used to working with the previous chief of staff in a particular way. Part of our challenge was working out our relationship over the first few months. We had some bumps along the way, but eventually we had some very honest discussions and it ended up being a great working relationship.

It did take awhile to figure out what each of us did. Part of that was because he had worked with the prior prime minister in a certain style, and I was coming in and taking back some power that he had by virtue of his strong personality and skills. Within the dynamics of the PMO and PCO there is a triangular relationship with the prime minister where a change in one of the players will change the dynamics of the entire relationship. As a result, it is not surprising that there is uncertainty and apprehension. The difference we had was that Alex, as a clerk, was not a new clerk. He had come in with a certain set of assumptions based on who he worked with before and he, like all of us, had to learn the new trend.

Tim Murphy, chief of staff to Prime Minister Martin, 2003–6

Brian Mulroney learned the hard way that a chief of staff, no matter how well meaning, must have very particular attributes. Early in his first mandate he was forced to bring in a new chief of staff to run his office. While no one predicted it would be Derek Burney, everyone who is in the business of watching (and critiquing) government knows that

Mulroney rarely makes the same mistake twice. He hit a solid home run in his choice of Burney to fix the problems at the PMO. While Mulroney recognized that while he was more than capable of taking the lead on strategy, he recognized that he needed help in organizing the office and leaving him to focus on major issues – tax reform and free trade, not tainted tuna.[22] Burney brought both a familiarity with the bureaucracy and an understanding of the major policy issues to the table.

Derek Burney reports that his experience as chief of staff was his "'most foreign assignment': the most demanding, the most exhausting, and the most exhilarating of all."[23] Mulroney gave him free rein to do whatever he needed to do to get the office organized. Burney brought much-needed discipline and control over the prime minister's precious time. He describes the job of chief of staff in a nutshell:

> Most of all, I endeavoured to become the single funnel of views and deci-
> sions to and from the Prime Minister and the regular controller and coor-
> dinator of his ever-changing agenda, conscious at all times of a principal
> rule of politics: the need to concentrate his time and his message on key
> items and not be diverted, as he had put it, by "tainted tuna." Some have
> suggested that I was a control freak and overdid the concentration of
> power in the PMO. There is some validity to both charges, but the latter
> goes with the territory. As to the control aspect, it was presumably the
> objective of my appointment. In any event, as Mr Mulroney was a "phone-
> aholic" with a network all his own, my control of his agenda and face-to-
> face meetings was never total.[24]

How the prime minister chooses to staff the PMO has wide-ranging implications for government. The chief of staff is the most visible position, and the incumbent is the most senior official in the office, with the rank of deputy minister. All senior advisors and directors report directly to the chief of staff, who attends all Cabinet meetings and receives copies of all PCO and PMO briefing notes to the prime minister. Everything that moves forward to the prime minister must go through the chief of staff.

As mentioned elsewhere, there will be great pressure on the incoming government to hire people who had worked tirelessly during the election to help the party win. Many of them will lobby hard for jobs in the PMO, ministers' offices, or an appointment to the many positions that are available just after the election or soon after. Unfortunately, most of them are not qualified for a government job because they will have little

Behind the Scenes: Staffing the PMO

There were people that worked for her [Prime Minister Kim Campbell] that I knew quite well. Miles Kervin had been in her office, and so I reached out to him and brought him in to run policy. She was extremely pleased about that. I wasn't going to bring in somebody who was going to be problematic for her. Plus, I really liked Miles and I had known him for a long time, which made her feel more comfortable. Michael Farrabie was more junior but had also been very close to her, so I brought him in. It would have been natural to bring in some Charest people, but none were brought in. It's a big job to suddenly try to put it all together. And there wasn't an obvious press secretary, so I reached out to Paul Fraser, who had been the ambassador in the Czech Republic, and I brought him home.

Janice Charette, who was in the PCO, then came on board as my executive assistant. Suzanne Hurtubise said to her, "Not over my dead body. Your career will be over if you do this." Janice told me this and I said that it didn't make any sense. I phoned Glen [Shortliffe, secretary to Cabinet], who I knew from Foreign Affairs, and said, "So Glen, I've got a win-win offer for you." And he said, "Oh, what's that?" I said, "You let me have Janice Charette as my EA. It means you've got a spy in my office and it also means that I've got somebody in my office who understands the system, so that I follow all the rules and don't do stupid things around you." Glen replied, "Of course! You can have her tomorrow."

To me, getting those relationships right is the richness of the job. I can't remember if Glen and I had disagreements that summer, but you're working with a real professional. I believed in building up relationships and, over time, we did better when we were listening to the public servants.

Jodi White, chief of staff to Prime Minister Campbell, interview,
10 February 2011

appreciation of the difference between elections and governing. This issue is a universal problem with all newly elected governments, and the degree to which they can differentiate between the two skill sets the more likely the transition will succeed. As Wellford has written, "Both the Carter and Clinton White House staffs were initially stacked with campaign veterans who had little Washington experience, and their on-the-job training was sometimes painful to watch."[25]

Ministers' Offices

In the same way that the PMO is closely tied to the prime minister, a minister's staff must bring the necessary skills and experience to the office to support the minister. A minister's office is not nearly as large as that of the prime minister, but it plays a similar function in helping its minister with effective, ongoing management of the political agenda.

This all sounds logical and straightforward. However, put yourself in the shoes of a newly appointed minister for a moment and try to think through the process of staffing your office. You've finished a gruelling election campaign and have just found out you made it into Cabinet. You are heading up a department (and a portfolio of related agencies) that makes billions in budget expenditures and may employ 20,000 staff. You may be given a portfolio within a policy area you are familiar with – or you may be facing a variety of subject areas that are completely new to you. The natural tendency will be to staff your office with people you know and trust. You'll tell yourself you're doing this just to get things up and running in the busy and confusing first days as a minister, but the challenge is to push back on that tendency and reach out to find people who can truly make you a better leader and help your office function as effectively as possible. In the same way, a prime minister must realize that the people who helped win an election are not necessarily the right ones to help govern. A minister must also be disciplined enough to look for individuals who have the right mix of skills, experience, and working style to make the task of governing as successful as possible.

Behind the Scenes: The Advantage of Leading with a Majority

I think we even have a chance of attracting better political staff to the city. Why? Because they can now look at a two-, three-, four-year lease on life. Whereas previously in a minority government situation, would you give up your job in Toronto and come here for three months? I don't think so. You've got a young family, you're going to say, "No way." But I think instead of a bunch of kids working in ministers' offices, you're going to get some of the more seasoned talent. Guys in their fifties are going to spend four years here, doing something good for the country.

Derek Burney, transition team leader for the Conservative Party

The ability to hire qualified staff is greatly affected by the size of the electoral victory of the winning party. Derek Burney has commented that the minority government status of the first Harper victory greatly hampered ministers' abilities to hire experienced and knowledge-able staff, which, in turn, led to the greater centralization of power in the prime minister's office that would have been the case if the Conservatives had won a majority.

Robert Reich, who served as secretary of labour through Bill Clinton's first term as president of the United States, captured this dilemma in his book *Locked in the Cabinet*. He describes the process of staffing his office:

Part of my problem is I don't know exactly what I'm looking for and I certainly don't know how to tell whether I've found it. Some obvious criteria:

1. *They should share the President-elect's values.* But how will I know they do? I can't very well ask, "Do you share the President's values?" and expect an honest answer. Even if they contributed money to the campaign, there's no telling. I've heard of several middle-aged Washington lawyers so desperate to escape the tedium of law practice by becoming an assistant secretary for Anything That Gets Me Out of Here that they've made whopping contributions to both campaigns.

2. *They should be competent and knowledgeable about the policies they'll administer.* Sounds logical, but here again, how can I tell? I don't know enough to know whether someone *else* knows enough. "What do you think about the Employee Retirement Income Security Act?" I might ask, and an ambitious huckster could snow me. "I've concluded that Section 508(m) should be changed because most retirees have 307 accounts which are treated by the IRS as Subchapter 12 entities." Uttered with enough conviction, bullshit like this could sweep me off my feet.

3. *They should be good managers.* But how to find out? Yesterday I phoned someone about a particular job candidate's management skills, at her suggestion. He told me she worked for him and was a terrific manager. "Terrific?" I repeated. "Wonderful. The best," he said. "You'd recommend her?" I asked. "Absolutely. Can't go wrong," he assured me. I thanked him, hung up the phone, and was enthusiastic for about five minutes, until I realized how little I had learned. How do I know *he* recognizes a good manager? Maybe he's a lousy manager himself and has a bunch of bozos working for him. Why should I trust that he's more interested in my having her on *my* team than in getting her off his?

I'm flying blind.[26]

Key Appointments

During the weeks following the swearing-in, the government will have to make a number of appointments that may have become vacant as the result of resignations and term completions. At any given moment, there are always many high-profile full- and part-time governor-in-council positions that need to be filled immediately or even urgently (such as the commissioner of the RCMP in the summer of 2011).

To help the transition team advise the prime minister, the high-profile appointments are usually grouped into three categories:

- Current vacancies that need to be filled *urgently*, where appointments have expired and it will require considerable time and effort to find a suitable candidate;
- Current vacancies that will need to be filled *soon* (within three months), including appointments about to expire that will also require some time and effort to find a suitable candidate to fill the position; and
- Positions that will need to be filled in the medium term (within six months), and will require some time to find a suitable candidate.[27]

Conclusion

This chapter concludes the post-election phase of the transition process and signals that most of the events on the critical path have been implemented. This is a most exciting and stressful time for the transition team, since there is so much to conclude in the relatively short time between election day and the swearing-in of the government. While voters across the country have returned to their day-to-day activities and the media have turned their attention to projects that languished while they were on the election trail, the transition team has been working closely with the prime minister–elect to put the finishing touches on the elements that will collectively define the government. This period also sharpens and brings into focus the need for a smooth merging of agendas between the political players and the public service. This phase also reveals whether the relationships among the key players, the prime minister, the chief of staff and the clerk of the Privy Council Office, are going to be effective, trusting, and respectful. If not, this will also be the time that serious considerations are given to making a personnel change or two.

At this point in the transition, a new government has also completed the complex and crucial selection process for the Cabinet by vetting all potential members using any number of different processes. As well, the key positions for the Prime Minister's Office will have been staffed, making sure that the office has the right balance of skills and other important attributes to properly serve the prime minister.

Finally, the PMO should also be aware of pending appointments and have begun, in collaboration with the PCO, to develop a process for each of the key positions. The next chapter captures the last phase of the transition that consolidates the transition and ensures that all the work and planning is fully implemented and "holds" when the pressures to government will distract the government away from the principles and practices that formed the basis of the transition.

8 Consolidation Phase: Making the Transition a Reality

But Mouse, you are not alone,
In proving foresight may be vain:
The best laid schemes of mice and men
Go often askew,
And leave us nothing but grief and pain,
For promised joy!

– Robert Burns, "To a Mouse"

Introduction

This chapter describes the last of four phases in the transition process: the consolidation of the work of the transition team so that all decisions taken in the previous three phases are firmly in place and the work of the new ministry is on the right trajectory. In the end, a successful transition will be judged by the degree to which the prime minister was able to assume the reins of power as seamlessly as possible and if, even if there was an initial period of trial and error, the decision-making system operated to the satisfaction of the prime minister. All other activities associated with the transition, such as staffing of the offices and selecting the Cabinet, support this objective.

A number of crucial milestones fall into Phase Four. These include the early Cabinet meetings (which set the tone for future meetings), the first days for a minister as the head of a department, the prime minister's early meetings with the deputy minister community, the distribution of the mandate letters to ministers, dealing with the caucus and defeated candidates, organizing orientation sessions for the Cabinet and their staff, and building trust between the public service and the ministers and their staff. In the case of returning governments it also provides the PMO with an opportunity to evaluate the effectiveness of the office and to determine what changes are needed to successfully implement the government's new agenda. Over time, the consolidation phase fades into a distant memory and the day-to-day challenge of responding to emerging issues and the political pressures of the day will take the work of prime ministers and their staff beyond the reach of the transition team and the advice contained in the briefing materials.

Mandate Letters

Mandate letters are another tool for prime ministers to implement the government's policy and political agenda. In essence, the mandate letters set out the prime minister's expectations for the government and for the individual ministers. Over the past thirty years mandate letters have become more elaborate as successive versions have built on the style and content of previous administrations. Since the PCO has typically managed the production and distribution of the mandate letters, the format has remained fairly constant over the years, despite the changes in prime ministers.

In general, mandate letters follow a certain structure, although each is unique in the sense it is personalized for individual ministers.

- Welcome to the ministry and to Cabinet;
- Reminder of the government's priorities that touch on the portfolio of the minister;
- Description of departmental specific goals and priorities;
- Description of the role the secretary of state or minister of state, if it applies;
- Description of the political duties assigned to the minister, if appropriate;
- House of Commons responsibilities for the minister, if appropriate;
- PM's policy or other priorities for the next two or three years;
- Reminder to ministers that the PM is responsible for all machinery issues;
- Description of the importance of working closely with the deputy minister;

- Notice of upcoming governor-in-council appointments and a description of the process to be followed if the appointment is not considered routine;
- A reminder that ministers' deputy ministers will receive a copy of the mandate letter.

While the format of the mandate letter is generic, the content and tone can be very different. For example, the mandate letters sent out to Stephen Harper's team after they won the 2006 election started out with a call to arms – we won, here are our priorities, and we don't want to deviate from them. Then they described what Harper expected from them and reminded them of the need to adhere to the code of conduct and the confidentiality agreement that came with membership in the Cabinet. According to Derek Burney, the mandate letters also reminded ministers not to open their mouths without checking first with the PCO or the PMO. Contrary to popular belief, this approach appears to have been developed by the transition team and didn't stem personally from Harper.[1]

In 1997, ministers in the second Chrétien government would have received a mandate letter from Prime Minister Chrétien that contained the following:

Introductory Remarks: A warm welcome into the Cabinet as minister of X and a reinforcement of the need to deliver on the commitments that were made in the election policy platform. This meant working together on the Liberals' single most important commitment during that era: Canadian unity. Ministers were reminded that all of their work – collectively as a government, individually as ministers, and in caucus – must be deliberately and carefully designed to support and contribute to the government's unity strategy. Other key priorities were also highlighted, including economic growth, job creation, knowledge and innovation, sound fiscal management, health care, and the well-being of children.

Key Points for the Minister's Portfolio: This section was tailored to each individual minister and emphasized that a minister's responsibilities are critical to the success of the government as a whole. It is within this section that the prime minister outlined the minister's top priority as well as specific issues that needed to be addressed within the portfolio.

Closing Paragraphs: All mandate letters underlined the importance of ensuring that the full range of organizations within a minister's portfolio work together to support both the minister and the government through policy, legislation, and program coordination. Each minister was asked by the prime minister to submit a proposal for how he or she planned to manage the portfolio. Cabinet committee responsibilities were outlined, and changes to the Cabinet committee system were described with a rationale for the need to make adjustments based on feedback from ministers who served from 1993 to 1996.

Where appropriate, the letters also provided clarification on the relationship between a minister and a secretary of state and the expectations that the prime minister held on this approach to governing. Ministers were asked to write formally to their secretaries of state as soon as possible and to provide a copy of this letter to the prime minister. The importance of integrity continued to be emphasized through the mandate letters, and ministers were reminded of their accountability to Canadians. The mandate letters concluded with the prime minister's expectation that ministers work closely with their deputy ministers, who have the capacity to contribute greatly to success within the portfolio.

The draft mandate letters that were prepared for the prime minister in 1997 contained the following sentiments:

- I believe in letting ministers manage their portfolios without interference from me or my officials;[2]
- I expect ministers to bring issues to Cabinet whenever this is necessary and to take decisions themselves whenever appropriate. But I also attach great importance to teamwork and consultation within the ministry and within the community of deputy ministers;
- I want to restore confidence and integrity in government;
- Enhance the role of Cabinet in decision-making by making good use of our Cabinet committees;
- I attach great importance to collegiality, teamwork, and consultation among ministers;
- Deputy ministers will provide you with professional support across the full range of the portfolio;
- A good working relationship with your deputy will contribute greatly to your success in the portfolio.

In recent years, mandate letters have become more important than ever in defining the role of individual ministers. As a consequence, deputy ministers look for ways during the election to influence the content of the draft mandate letters being prepared by the Privy Council

Office for incoming ministers. It is far easier for deputies to influence the behaviour and priorities of ministers if the mandate letters from the prime minister contain directives that are consistent with the needs of the department. As a consequence, deputies do what they can to influence those who draft the mandate letters for the prime minister by being as proactive as possible in providing insights and suggestions that could frame the mandate letters. If they are given an opportunity to provide input, enterprising deputy ministers also look for occasions to influence the configuration of the minister's overall portfolio, which might include looking at the mandates of the agencies, boards, and commissions that fall under the responsibility of the minister.

Not everyone agrees on the usefulness of the mandate letters that the prime minister sends to each minister, and to secretaries of state, if any are appointed. However, over the years, in my estimation they have evolved into a powerful accountability tool a prime minister can use in dealings with ministers. The vast majority of ministers consider them important documents and actively work towards the objectives contained in the letters, which are the only tangible evidence of the prime minister's personal expectations for an individual minister. The fact that the prime minister often reminds ministers that they will be held accountable for their performance against the objectives in the mandate letters often emphasizes the letter's importance in the minister's office.

Cabinet Meetings

The early days for a newly elected prime minister are indeed extremely exciting and at times daunting. Even Tony Blair, an experienced parliamentarian, was struck by the historic importance of his first Cabinet meeting. On entering the Cabinet room for the first time, "I stopped for a moment and looked around, suddenly struck by the sanctity of it, a thousand images fluttering through my mind, like one of those moving picture card displays, of Gladstone, Disraeli, Asquith, Lloyd George, Churchill, Attlee, of historic occasions of war and peace, of representatives of numerous colonies coming through its doors and negotiating independence. This room has seen one of the greatest empires of all time developed, sustained and let go."[3]

The Cabinet room is the best location for the prime minister to consolidate the transition. It allows for a direct interchange within the ministry and also places the prime minister firmly in charge of the proceedings. If there was any question about who is in charge of the

Canadian Westminster system, attendance at a Cabinet meeting will dispel any notions that it is a joint decision-making body.

This is the place for the prime minister to communicate firmly all expectations to Cabinet members and, more important, to inform them of the rules of procedure that will define the way things will be done under the PM's leadership. While each first Cabinet meeting is unique, they all have covered several general topics since 1984:[4]

- An outline of the prime minister's vision for the country and broad direction or themes of the government;
- An overview of the prime minister's expectations on integrity in government, with special reference to guides produced by the PCO for the Cabinet on ethical and other associated issues concerning the behavioural expectations for ministers;
- A description of the role of the PMO and its working relationship with ministers' offices;
- An overview of the prime minister's view of the structure, compensation limits, and size of ministers' offices;
- A strong emphasis on the importance of following the government's administrative codes and, above all, complying with Treasury Board's policy on the operations of ministers' offices to avoid embarrassing the government and especially the prime minister;
- An attempt to regularize the relationship with the senior public service, with emphasis on the need to work closely with deputy ministers, who, if they are allowed to do their work, will provide policy and management advice and support on a wide range of issues across the portfolio;
- An outline of the new Cabinet committee structure and how the decision-making system will operate, to signal the roles individual ministers will play in Cabinet;
- A description of any machinery changes in government structure and the rationale for the changes;[5]
- If appropriate, an explanation of how ministers should work with junior ministers, ministers of state, or parliamentary secretaries, and the purpose of a two-tiered Cabinet system;
- A reminder to all Cabinet ministers of the need to work closely with caucus members and with parliamentary committees on policy issues;
- A discussion of the election results and their impact on the government's policy and political agenda, sometimes followed by a review

of upcoming key events and an overview of the government's
short-term timetable, particularly its legislative agenda;
- The approval of the necessary governor-in-council appointments;
- The need to seek the approval of Cabinet to advance the prime minister's high-priority agenda items.

I sent a draft scenario note for the first Cabinet meeting on 20 October
1993 (five days before the election or twelve days before the actual
Cabinet meeting) to Jean Pelletier, which we subsequently discussed
after the election. The note discussed the tone we wanted to set for this
historic event. The themes that underlie the first Cabinet meeting were
to set a professional tone for all subsequent Cabinet meetings, to make
the ministers aware of the PM's expectations about ethics and behaviour in Cabinet and in the carrying out of their duties, to send clear
messages about working with the public service, to demonstrate that
the prime minister was "in the saddle" and anxious to begin to work
on priorities as set out in the Red Book, to emphasize to ministers (especially new ones) the importance of being well prepared for Cabinet and
to take the time to learn their portfolio, and to follow the ministerial
staffing procedures that would be discussed at a later date.

My draft of the briefing notes was:

Agenda of the Meeting

- Welcome from the prime minister
  - Importance of integrity in government
    - It is fundamental to the credibility of the government
  - Commitment to honest, frugal government
  - Review the value of the vetting process in selecting ministers for
    Cabinet
  - Read the Guidance to Ministers booklet
  - Importance of Security
    - If there are problems, call Jean Pelletier or Glen Shortliffe
  - Pace yourself; you are on a steep learning curve
    - Do your homework and master the issues
  - Be selective, set priorities, and focus on key issues
  - Consult with your caucus members; many of them have great
    talents
- Discuss how Cabinet will operate
  - Explained in mandate letters

- o Matching election commitments to actual performance
  - o Importance of Cabinet solidarity – the importance of speaking with one voice; resignations will be accepted if a minister cannot support the government's decision
  - o Use of both official languages is encouraged
  - o No Priorities and Planning Committee – key decisions to be taken by all ministers
- Basic guidance for running ministerial offices
  - o Set an example of restraint
  - o The office is for political advice and support
  - o It should have regional and linguistic balance
  - o Look to the deputy minister for policy advice and operational support
  - o Ensure that ministerial staff have security clearance before offers of employment are made·
  - o No instances of "paying for access" to a minister in this government
  - o Use public servants in the short term as ministerial staff if necessary
- Use of secretaries of state and parliamentary secretaries
  - o The use of two-tier ministries in Britain, France, and Australia
  - o Secretaries of state and members of the ministry, but not member of Cabinet
  - o They should be active members of the team, can attend Cabinet committees and Cabinet when appropriate, but they are not a replacement for ministers
  - o Make parliamentary secretaries a member of ministers' teams
- Changes to government structures
  - o Discuss the machinery changes
  - o Most important to rebuild trust with the public service
- Discuss key policy files
- Invite secretaries of state to join the meeting to inform everyone of what is expected of them as ministers and of their of staff

In summary, the prime minister will want to accomplish several things at the early Cabinet meetings. First will be setting the tone for Cabinet and ensuring that ministers are aware of expectations. The prime minister will also want to send the appropriate message to the public service about the role the government will want them to play. Finally, the prime minister will want to be in a position to communicate to the public that he or she has taken charge of the government, set a tone for the administration, and made a start on dealing with the major economic issues facing the country.

Behind the Scenes: The First Cabinet Meeting from the Perspective of a New Cabinet Minister

We had to be back on the Hill for 3:00 or 3:30 because the prime minister had called our first Cabinet meeting. So we all dutifully turned up and sat around the Cabinet table for the first time and I saw all of my new colleagues – most of whom I'd met that morning. It was a remarkable experience. I don't remember much about the meeting. It was introductory; there wasn't much business done. But Mr Chrétien set out the tone and told us generally what his expectations were. This is was going to be a clean government, a government of integrity, and he did not work this hard to be prime minister only to preside over a group that was not going to be 100 per cent clean. As a result, there would be zero tolerance for malfeasance. And then he invited people like Herb Gray to make comments, since he had been at the Cabinet table before and had some experience with the system. And I well recall Chrétien saying, "Well, fasten your seatbelts. It's going to be a hell of a ride."

Allan Rock, minister of justice, minister of health, and minister of industry, 1993–2003, interview, 11 June 2011

Each prime minister brings to the job a unique style of presiding over Cabinet. And as discussed in earlier chapters, each time a new prime minister is elected, the entire Cabinet system shifts to reflect the new leadership style. Brian Mulroney came into the role with no prior experience at the Cabinet table. Nevertheless, his career in the boardrooms of corporate Canada prepared him to assume control of the Cabinet process without major missteps. In fact, he did so very quickly by assigning key roles to many of his ministers in the early days.

In Derek Burney's words,

At Priorities and Planning, he moved ministers efficiently through the agenda and usually without extensive debate. Items were rarely brought forward without some degree of advance consensus. In instances where consensus was less apparent, the Prime Minister's position inevitably

carried the day. He also used these meetings with his key cabinet colleagues to deliver a pre-caucus pep talk of sorts, one that he would repeat
with even more flair the next day at caucus. My initial impression of cabinet was that the members were, for the most part, competent but domi-
nated by the Prime Minister – not surprising, given the massive election
victory of 1984. In an age of leadership politics, they (and caucus more
generally) not only knew their place but also recognized clearly that their
future clung to the fortunes, deserved or accidental, of their leader.[6]

The prime minister is not simply the chairman of the most important committee in the land, but is its spiritual and moral leader who
must continually follow the game plan that has been carefully crafted
in advance. This role will be most tested in the Cabinet room, where
the prime minister will be expected to lead. Often, the first meeting
will be the most important, so it is especially crucial to be well prepared and in charge of the agenda. If a prime minister abdicates this
role, the control of the agenda will move to others in the Cabinet room
who have the right skill set. To be successful, a prime minister can and
should count on the support of the chief of staff and the clerk of the
Privy Council. Their advice is crucial and will help to steer a new leader
around unexpected stumbling blocks and bumps in the road. If leadership in the Cabinet room is treated by the prime minister as merely
another job among many, the government will soon lose its focus and
quickly appear rudderless and ineffective.

Early Days as a Minister

Learning on the Job

The new prime minister is not the only individual who faces a daunting task during the consolidation phase – so do those who have been
appointed ministers in the government. Almost overnight, each
becomes the equivalent of a chief executive officer of a large, sprawling
portfolio of companies. The first months of their performance can make
or break them over the longer term. In politics there is only ever the
smallest margin of error allowed for ministers, who are constantly in
the public eye. Michael Watkins, author of *The First 90 Days*, succinctly
captures the importance of this period: "The actions you take during
your first three months in a new job will largely determine whether you
succeed or fail. Transitions are a period of opportunity, a chance to start

afresh and to make needed changes in an organization. But they are also periods of acute vulnerability because you lack established working relationships and a detailed understanding of your new role. If you fail to build momentum during your transition, you will face an uphill battle from that point."[7]

John Manley remembers his first few months as a newly minted minister in the first Jean Chrétien government in 1993. He vividly recalls his first meeting with his deputy minister, Harry Swain, who was an experienced and confident senior executive. Swain was obviously well prepared when they first met only minutes after Manley was sworn in as the minister of industry.

Swain presented the minister with a large number of fat binders filled with briefing materials. With a sweep of his arm he expansively described the size of the department and its portfolio. He impressed the new minister with the range of his ministerial responsibilities and the onerous duty he had to perform on behalf of the department and the thousands of public servants who worked there for him.

At one point, Manley remembers Swain describing the complexity of working through the decision-making process in Ottawa. Swain also offered some observations to his neophyte minister by claiming that the way to succeed in Ottawa was to see the machinations of government as "one big game, where strong ministers win and weak ministers lose. You have to be a player in order to get things done."

Swain also offered some early advice to Manley. Knowing that the new minister's only previous experience as a politician was limited to that of an opposition member of Parliament, Swain provided him with two important observations. He told the minister that although he could suggest many good political science textbooks that would help Manley learn more about the job of being a minister, he suggested that he also purchase a copy of *Yes, Minister*. The popular BBC comedy television series about the U.K. public service was a better reflection of reality than any textbook, said Swain, and beautifully captured the relationship between the minister and the deputy minister.

Swain's second piece of advice was to warn Manley that it was more than likely he would be receiving calls and letters of congratulations from individuals and business groups. While most would be genuine expressions of good luck and offers of help, some would be problematic and should be treated with caution. While it is sometimes difficult to differentiate between people expressing simple good will and those pursuing their own self-interest, Swain was clear that there was at least one well-wisher whom the minister should avoid. Swain told Manley that he would undoubtedly receive a call and most likely a gift from a man called Karlheinz Schreiber. In the event, Swain was adamant that Manley must return the gift and refuse to take the call. Manley took his deputy minister's advice, and the rest is history.

Gerald Kaufman, author of *How to Be a Minister*, gives advice on the early days of being a minister, drawing on his personal experiences during the 1970s Labour governments in the United Kingdom. "You have

---

Behind the Scenes: The First Day on the Job

We got into a bus that took all the new ministers behind the West Block on Parliament Hill. There, thirty chauffeurs were waiting in their limousines to take us from there to our departments. For myself, it was a short drive to the Ministry of Justice, where I was met by John Tait inside the front doors. Tait took me upstairs and brought me to my office. He told me that he was arranging some briefing sessions for me and that he would be in touch soon about where and when they were going to be.

Tait then left me alone with three women who had been the assistant, the office manager, and the director of communications for my Conservative Party predecessor, Pierre Blais. It quickly became apparent that they were quite anxious about their future job prospects, since they assumed that a change in government meant that there would be a "house cleaning" of the ministerial staff. I decided to meet with them, and after a brief conversation I assured them that they were going to keep their jobs because of their reputation as excellent ministerial staff. What I didn't know at the time was the three of them thought that the meeting was intended to inform them of their imminent departure.

They then left me alone in my office and I found myself in front of an empty desk and a silent telephone in a cavernous space that had been occupied by Lionel Chévrier, Pierre Trudeau, Jean Chrétien, Davey Fulton, and a variety of other distinguished Canadians. I said to myself, "So this is where the minister of justice sits. I wonder when he or she is going to arrive!"

Allan Rock, minister of justice, minister of health, and minister of industry, 1993–2003, interview, 11 June 2011

been appointed. For the first time you walk into the government department to which you have been assigned. You are, understandably, highly pleased with yourself. And at that very moment, with your defences down, there on the threshold will await you the bacilli of two potentially debilitating diseases. If you do not very rapidly develop immunities to cocoon yourself in a protective skin, you have been defeated before you have even begun. The diseases to which you are in imminent danger of falling prey are 'ministerialitis' and 'departmentitis.'"[8]

Kaufman goes on to describe the symptoms of ministerialitis as a perceptible swelling of the head and a preoccupation and satisfaction with holding ministerial office to the exclusion of almost all other considerations. It is true that all politicians appointed to ministerial offices aspire to perform well in their new positions. This is expected and certainly warranted. The "disease" starts to creep in when a minister forgets that the world does not revolve around his or her department. Rather, it includes Parliament, the party, and the constituency. As is beautifully articulated by Kaufman, "A whole country is going about its daily business and rarely sweating a thought unless you do something that particularly annoys it."[9]

Departmentalitis is considered a different but equally debilitating ministerial disease. Symptoms include a preoccupation with the department to which the minister is assigned, to the exclusion of all other considerations, including the fortunes of the government as a whole. Ministers with departmentalitis tend to forget that the fortunes of the government are more important than the fortunes of their own departments and that the good of the country may be better served if the interests of one department are subservient to those of another.

The disturbing consequence of a minister falling prey to one or both of these afflictions is that his or her skills and talents will be employed for negative ends. Ministers must always remember that the role is to increase the chance of success for the government as a whole and the citizens in whose interests he or she has been elected.

Orientation: Training and Mentors

One approach that a transition team can implement to get ministers started off on the right foot (and to keep them focused on the priorities of the government) is to provide orientation sessions. Despite the fact that new ministers will have a seemingly endless list of tasks to be addressed early in their mandate, it is critical that there be time allocated to training. The life of a politician is immediately changed by the appointment as a minister, and an orientation session can help to make this transition smooth. In 1993, Chrétien put his entire Cabinet through a mandatory orientation session, and in 1996 it was mandatory for new ministers and secretaries of state to attend a five-hour orientation program. In 1993, the election was held on 25 October and the government was sworn in ten days later. About one week after that, all ministers and secretaries of state found themselves in this all-day orientation session. Chrétien was very aware that, although he had appointed a talented group of ministers, most of them had limited government experience, and given his preference for delegation, he knew they would be vulnerable to rookie mistakes.

Speaking to an audience of ministers and senior public servants in Regina in 2008, I offered my best recollection of the first orientation session for all ministers after the 1993 election:

The session dealt with a wide range of issues, from the Red Book to the Cabinet Committee structure, to ethics, to setting up the minister's office, and how to interact with the public service.

As we went through the training session, I was struck by how uninformed the new ministers were about how the public service was structured, how government worked or about the nature of the relation between politicians and the public service.

New ministers want to make their mark. They want to get to work. But almost instinctively, most of them bring a preconceived management model to their department in which they want to choose their own management team around the ministerial table.

As a result many of them asked, Why I can't I hire my campaign manager to run my office and to instruct the public service what to do? Or why can't I choose my deputy minister since I am ultimately responsible for the performance of the organization?

These questions raised many important issues about the nature of the Westminster system that is the basis for the Canadian form of government.

I shouldn't have been so naïve about the knowledge base of Members of Parliament since I have since learned that very few of them would have had any formal training in government or public administration. I had to keep reminding myself that becoming a Member of Parliament requires a different set of skills than those that are needed to govern. And in 1993, more than 200 of the 295 Members of Parliament were newly elected, parliamentary novices.

The public service lives in the world of public administration. The ministers live in a pressure cooker environment, running from church dinners to caucus meetings to question period. They focus on the drama of high politics. The gritty issues of managing the public service don't usually get on their agenda until the day they become a minister. So, it is not surprising that the topics require a lot of discussion.[10]

For a prime minister to leverage the collective strengths of the appointed team, everything possible must be done to provide them with the tools and information they need to succeed. Minister's school is one tangible and practical way to get them all moving in the same direction.

To give the reader a flavour for the type of issues are covered in an orientation session, the outlines for three orientation sessions and the names of presenters are presented below:

**Orientation Session for New Ministers
and Secretaries of State (1993)**

Agenda

- Introduction (prime minister)
- System of governance in Canada (Mario Dion, Nicole Jauvin)
- Standards of conduct (John Tait, Howard Wilson)
- Cabinet and Cabinet changes (Wayne Wouters, Maurice Rosenberg, and Cabinet committee chairs)
- Policy priorities (Chaviva Hosek)
- Roles of a minister (Mitchell Sharp, André Ouellet)
- Role of the deputy minister (Gordon Smith, Arthur Kroeger)
- Roles of executive assistants (Fred Drummie)
- Wrap up (prime minister)

**Orientation Session for New Ministers
and Secretaries of State (1997)**

Agenda

- Introduction (prime minister)
- Ethics in government (Mitchell Sharp, Howard Wilson)
- Public sector values (John Tait)

- Relations with deputy ministers (Gordon Smith, Roger Tassé, Ercel Baker)
- A day in the life of a minister (Ed Lumley, Marc Lalonde, Serge Joyal, Ron Irwin)
- Managing a minister's office (Doug Kirkpatrick, Terri O'Leary)
- Roles and responsibilities of a minister (Jocelyne Bourgon, Nicole Jauvin)
- The Prime Minister's Office (Jean Pelletier)
- The government's agenda and policy priorities (Chaviva Hosek)
- Government appointments (Penny Collenette)
- Staffing ministers' offices (Penny Collenette)
- New Public Management (Peter Aucoin)
- Wrap up (prime minister)[11]

Assistants to Ministers and Secretaries of State

Agenda (1996)

- Introduction
- Government's agenda
- Role of ministers' and secretaries of state's staff
- Role of the Prime Minister's Office and the Privy Council Office
- Role of the ministers' and secretaries of state's office
- Relations with the deputy minister and the department
- Discussion

I provided the introduction to the session for assistants to ministers and secretaries of state, where I conveyed the following messages:

- You have an important job in the success of the government, so take your job seriously.
- You really do matter to the success of the government.
- Mistakes hurt your credibility and that of your minister and the government, so every task should be done as well as possible.
- Ministerial staff should work together.
- We need a team approach, even though the pressures all work in the opposite direction.
- You are always representing the government and your minister, so you must operate with integrity at all times.

- Work with the deputy minister and get to know the department and its officials.
- Your task is to bring the best from the public service to the attention of the minister.

This sentiment is echoed in observations from the United Kingdom. In 1997 as the election drew close, Tony Blair and his closest advisors became acutely aware that their front bench was very inexperienced in governing. As a consequence, seminars were organized for the shadow ministerial team. The first seminar series was at Templeton College, Oxford, on the theme of "How to Be a Minister." Attendance at this event was disappointing, and notably absent were the "Big Four": Blair, Brown, Cook, and Prescott. Nonetheless, there was a commitment by the transition experts to move ahead with additional training opportunities. The second series involved former civil servants, political advisors, and Labour's front bench and was anchored on two themes: "Hardware and Software of the State" and "How to Get the Best out of the Civil Service."[12]

While the training sessions cover critically important territory, orientation sessions can accomplish only so much. Many former ministers will tell you that the orientation session was helpful, but it is always difficult for them to process the massive amounts of information thrown their way in the days after the swearing-in ceremony. As a result, many transition teams have arranged mentoring to support the ongoing development of new ministers. These mentors and advisors are pulled from the ranks of former ministers, who really are the only people who can possibly understand the day-to-day pressures and challenges that are faced in these positions.

Many successful Cabinet ministers credit former politicians as being a critical factor in their smooth transition from neophyte to well-functioning minister. For example, John Manley recalls his early days in the Department of Industry as a blur of activity and incomprehension. It wasn't until he received a visit from Ed Lumley that things started to fall into place. Lumley had served in the same portfolio some years earlier in the Trudeau administration and was a colleague of Jean Chrétien. The meeting was Lumley's idea, and Manley admits to initially being somewhat sceptical, since he hardly knew Lumley and wondered what his motives would be in wanting to meet.

His suspicions were further aroused when Lumley ordered the minister's executive assistant out of the room, explaining that the meeting was for privy councillors only. As Manley describes it, the value of the meeting was magical for him. In the most colourful language, Lumley outlined what being a minister was all about in the Canadian version of the Westminster system of government. He described the role of Cabinet, how to work with Cabinet colleagues, how to get things done, and how to interact with the prime minister when you wanted a favour.

In addition, Lumley added further insights about the degree to which being a Cabinet minister would change a minister's relationships with his constituents, friends, and most of all, his family. In Manley's estimation, this briefing and subsequent meetings with Lumley were critical in putting his finite time in government in the proper context. They helped him to anticipate the rough patches that would inevitably appear in the course of his work, and prepared him for the stresses that his Cabinet position would place on so many relationships that had previously been easy-going and casual. Lumley also encouraged Manley to establish a good working relationship with his deputy minister and with the public service. Despite pressure from many sources, Manley says that the good relationship he developed with his deputy ministers was instrumental to his being a successful minister.[13]

Prime Minister Meets the Deputy Ministers

In the early days immediately after being sworn in, the prime minister should make an effort to meet with the deputy minister community. This is the prime minister's opportunity to speak frankly about government plans, and expectations, to share the government's short-term game plan and to discuss the long-range view of the challenges the prime minister will be expecting the deputy ministers to manage.

For the deputy ministers, this meeting establishes the importance that the prime minister attaches to the role played by the deputy minister community and the public service, in general. By sharing the government's overall plan, the deputies will be able to organize their departments to reflect the government's needs and better align their activities with government priorities.

As part of our transition planning, we spent a lot of time crafting an approach to the public service, and the deputy minister community in particular, to ensure that the transition from ten years of Conservative government to a new Liberal government would be seamless and perceived as looking for opportunities for the public service and the government to work together on the new agenda.

The public service is the tool the political leadership has to deliver what it wants to do. The prime minister's first address to this community can go a long way towards setting the stage for a smooth and successful transition. As the prime minister prepares for this meeting and in the first weeks and months of governing, there will undoubtedly be a great deal of unsolicited advice on the attributes of the deputy ministers and senior staff from sources outside the government. The prime minister should avoid jumping to conclusions. Little of the advice, good or bad, will come from other than vested interests and may or may not be in the government's interest. A prime minister should proceed on such advice with caution and try not to let it hamper efforts to develop a sound and productive working relationship with the public service.[14]

In order for the government to function effectively in its first months, there needs to be a sense of trust underlying the relationship between the political leaders and the public service. Unfortunately, the natural state of affairs at the beginning of a new mandate is often mutual wariness between these two groups. In Canada this has been particularly troublesome at the provincial level. At the extreme, in the United States the governing party makes wholesale changes to the senior ranks of the bureaucracy, in parallel with how the democratic system works in that country.

In Canada, there has been a wide variation in the degree to which the public service is accepted as neutral advisors by a newly elected incoming government. In Chrétien's case, he had always had a good working relationship with the senior ranks of the public service. Lavoie captured it this way,

> Moi je savais qu'en général les fonctionnaires ne sont pas politisés du tout à Ottawa. Quand je devenais ministre, je disais au sous-ministre: 'Si je réussis, vous aller réussir, et si vous réussissez, je vais réussir. Chrétien avait également dit aux sous-ministres: vous autres, vous êtes responsables de donner les avis administratifs et législatifs aux ministres. Les avis politiques, ce n'est pas de votre affaire. C'est le bureau d'un ministre qui doit donner les avis politiques. Et les avis administratifs et législatifs, ce n'est pas l'affaire des employés politiques du ministre. Si chacun reste sur son territoire tout en ayant une collaboration quotidienne intelligente et productive ... If you remain both on your respective turfs, things will go well, your minister will look good, and if your minister looks good, you will look good.[15]

As a consequence, Chrétien decided to meet with his deputy ministers on the second day of his mandate. Here are the draft notes that were prepared for his meeting:

- Public service of Canada
  - I have had a long-standing and positive relationship with the public service that will continue during my term as prime minister;
  - The Clerk of the Privy Council is the head of the public service and all information to me should go through the Clerk;
  - Stop all across the board restraint programs since they are not effective;
  - I am committed to rebuilding the morale in the public service;
  - I also want to strengthen the policy capacity.
- Role of Deputy Ministers
  - As Deputy Ministers, you are responsible to the Prime Minister for your effective performance in addressing government-wide issues;
  - At the same time, you are responsible to your minister for the effective management of the department and to meet the policy and administrative needs of the government and minister in a timely manner;
  - I will make changes from time to time in the deputy minister personnel but as a general rule it is desirable to leave competent deputies in place as it provides for better departmental management;
  - I have confidence in the vast majority of deputies and your role will be considerably enhanced in terms of system management – you will be called on to creatively manage the budgetary and debt-induced downsizing and rationalization that is required;
  - I expect close communication between the minister and the deputy minister, and the onus is on the both of you to ensure the Prime Minister is well advised on all necessary matters.
- Government priorities
  - Job creation is my first priority;
  - Cut back on professional services;
  - Deal with lobbyists in a professional way.[16]

More often, the election of a new government can result in the perception, and sometimes the reality, of a fundamental clash of world views. The transition experience in Ontario after the NDP Party won a majority in 1990 demonstrates how a government can be debilitated by a difficult relationship between the two pillars of our Westminster system.

Many in the NDP had long seen the senior bureaucracy as a key obstacle to significant social change – as much a part of the conservative establishment as Bay Street financiers. For its part, the bureaucracy often appeared to lack an appreciation of the very real differences between the old-line parties and the NDP ideology, in its social basis of support and its basic approach to governance. Combined with the NDP's ambitious, if not always clearly defined, reform agenda and the almost complete lack of governmental experience on the part of the NDP ministers and their political staff, the mutual suspicion, if not outright antipathy, between important elements in the NDP government and the senior bureaucracy made for a very difficult transition.[17]

In my experience, most federal ministers don't worry about partisanship. They recognize that public servants, like everyone else, have biases, they vote, and they believe. It would be grossly unrealistic to think that people came to the public service with no view of the country and of government. What counts is that they have made a commitment to serve the government of the day, whoever that government is.

The commitment to be a professional, non-partisan public servant is a crucial part of the job and helps to make government work. According to Alex Himelfarb, "It doesn't mean that you're an empty vessel. There's nobody I worked with who didn't know where my biases were. And no one I worked with shared my bias entirely. I would give the best advice I had based on what I learned from the public service, what I learned from research, and from my own experiences, which included my biases. It was all there, laid out honestly. That's the advice portion. And then the democracy portion is when you implement the business of government. You build trust by demonstrating what the public service is all about."[18]

At the same time, ministers know that the public service has learned its way of doing business from the previous administration and that loyalties may well be with the people one has worked with for an extended period of time. But in the long run, government cannot operate effectively if it does not keep the public service challenged and involved in meeting the government's objectives. Building teamwork between ministers and the senior public service is not an easy task. It requires time and the development of trust and confidence between very busy and preoccupied people.

Deputy ministers hold the key to effective and constructive management of the public service. No minister carrying out his of her full responsibilities can become involved in the nuts-and-bolts day-to-day management of the department. It is the deputy who must be responsible for good morale, effective management, creative policy work in response to the requirements of the minister, and the public service's commitment to the priorities established by the government. Ministers also need to remember that deputy ministers report to the prime minister through the secretary to the Cabinet. In effect, they manage their departments and play a corporate role as well. Sometimes this means that deputies are placed in the unenviable position of having to remind their ministers of overall government priorities, but this is not disloyalty to their minister. Tensions caused by this role do occur, although not often, and ministers should be aware that this is simply a legitimate role undertaken by their deputy ministers.

It is critical that ministers establish a one-to-one relationship with their deputy ministers. At times, ministers use their personal staff to

---

Behind the Scenes: Welcoming a New Minister, from a Deputy Minister's Perspective

When the new ministers walk in, their name is on the door to the office. That was magical, because this was the first tangible evidence that they were actually government ministers. Here it was in black and white, on a door, and at the front entrance of a lobby. Those are really tiny things, but they really add up. My mother would always say, "You never get a second chance to make a first impression." This is true in everything, so if you are able to make that first impression, it helps with the first day, the first week, the first month.

Welcoming new ministers made me realize that there was fragility in those first few days. Especially when it's a new government coming in, there are already preconceived notions about everything. You have to ensure in a polite but firm way that they're getting the facts placed in front of them with as much evidence and history as possible, despite their preconceived notions. The ministers have to know when they come in that they may be touching a file that goes back twenty years. Be it the Official Languages Act or any other act, it doesn't work like *Bewitched* where it magically changes. It has taken twists and turns along history, and you have to live with that.

Judith LaRocque, deputy minister of heritage and
chief of staff to the governor general, interview,
8 November 2011

communicate their decisions to the deputy minister and to their department. However, there is no better way of ensuring that the intended message is received than by directly communicating with the deputy minister. Moreover, over time, direct communication enhances trust and avoids the dangers of misinterpretation and reinterpretation. Most ministers choose to meet with their deputies at least once and often twice weekly to review government, ministerial, and departmental needs and to assess emerging problems and opportunities.

While there are many academic descriptions of the relative functions of the two protagonists, very few of them portrayed the drama unfolding between ministers and their deputies in the early days of a new administration. One observer, the former secretary to the Cabinet Gordon Osbaldeston, has exquisitely captured the dynamics in a 1988 essay, "Dear Minister: An Open Letter to an Old Friend Who Has Just Been Appointed to the Cabinet."[19]

In this remarkably insightful memorandum that still resonates with practitioners today, Osbaldeston provides some of the most practical advice about the role of the minister, the prime minister, and the chief of staff. In providing this advice he defines the roles to be played by each and the lines that divide them with the precision of a surgeon.

In so doing, first, he advises newly appointed ministers to rely extensively on their deputy minister and chief of staff. Second, to determine in their mandate how they are going to relate to Cabinet, Parliament, stakeholders, and the department. And third, to decide how much time the minister is planning to devote to each. Osbaldeston underscores the time-management elements in the job by adding, "A good deputy minister will constantly chastise the minister who is overtaxing his physical resources. An exhausted minister is a dangerous minister – to himself and to the government."[20]

With regard to the initial meeting between the minister and their deputies, he has strong views on how the relationship should be anchored. As a starting point, he suggests that ministers come to the meeting "with an open mind – starting with the premise that he or she is there to help you, and wants to serve and support you."[21] Given the neutrality of the public service, Osbaldeston argues the deputy ministers can be counted on to provide professional and evidence-based policy advice to their new ministers. To underscore this point, he also suggests that deputy ministers should not provide a minister with advice on political issues, although it is a requirement of the job that they have well-developed political antennae to fully appreciate the political ramifications of policy options.

Since there remains some sensitivity within the deputy minister community about whether the deputies should excuse themselves when political issues are discussed in their presence, Osbaldeston reminds his readers that in 1988 he would regularly excuse himself from meetings when partisan issues emerged. He went on to add that in order to reinforce the professionalism of the public service, "deputy ministers protect their neutrality and maintain clear ministerial accountability for policy by avoiding promotion of any issue under partisan political debate."[22]

Most observers of the workings of ministers and their offices would argue that a minister should establish an agenda of between three and five items to be accomplished during his or her tenure. Osbaldeston has argued that these items must emerge early in the minister's mandate. He warns that failure to create a personal agenda early on means that someone else will do it instead.

Osbaldeston also points out that when problems arise between ministers and deputy ministers, it is mostly because the minister does not have an agenda, knows little about the department, is suspicious of the public service, and gets involved in day-to-day operations of the organization.

In addition to having a limited agenda, establishing a good working relationship with the deputy minister and the chief of staff, and not trying to manage the department, Osbaldeston suggests that the minister get to know the department well, especially its regional staff, and to establish a clear set of expectations that will guide the relationship between deputy and minister.

On consolidating the minister's relationship with the department and its senior officials, it is best to leave the last word to Jean Chrétien, who was a minister in eight portfolios before becoming prime minister in 1993. On the basis of his experience he felt that ministers had wide discretion on how to do their work and to set their own agenda within the framework set out by the prime minister. His advice was to the point: "To stay strong a minister must show compromise and agility. He may have great authority within his department, but within the cabinet is part of a collectivity, just another advisor to the Prime Minister. He can be told what to do, and on important matters his only choice is to do it or resign. So, survival and success become a matter of judgment."[23]

Here is the checklist distributed to the deputy ministers for discussion at their first meeting with their ministers in 1993.

- The Conflict of Interest rules
- Any security issues

- The role of secretaries of state
- The role of parliamentary secretaries
- The role, size, and hiring in minister's office
- An overview of the department policy priorities
- Pending appointments in the department or portfolio agencies
- The structure and operations of Cabinet and Cabinet committees
- The role of parliamentary committees
- Arranging for an initial meeting with the executive assistant to the minister

Caucus Management

Dealing with Failed Cabinet Candidates

One of the least appealing elements of the transition process is dealing with people who have either failed to be elected in the general election or had expectations of being appointed but were not selected for Cabinet. This is a difficult task, and no newly elected prime minister, in the wake of the celebrations and the congratulatory notes, is ever keen to sit down and recognize those who have failed to meet their political objectives. However, closing the election cycle and Cabinet-selection process is a vital part of Phase Four, so it is a task that has to be done.

Since a prime minister can offer little encouragement to those who lost during a winning election, telephoning failed candidates is difficult to do. In practical terms, a prime minister may have to make more than a hundred calls to individuals he may not know very well, although he may have campaigned with them or sought their counsel in the course of the election. It is hard to explain to a losing candidate why the party prevailed but he or she could not attract enough votes to win. The prime minister may, given the qualifications of the failed candidate, occasionally be in a position to offer a governor-in-council appointment, such as an ambassadorship or a position on the board of a Crown corporation, but this happens increasingly rarely, given the enhanced level of public scrutiny directed to government appointments.

As discussed earlier, the more difficult task than calling failed candidates for the prime minister is speaking directly to those who have been elected but have not been selected for the Cabinet. For one thing, these individuals, as elected members of Parliament, will be present at all caucus activities for the life of the Parliament. In addition, there is little that a prime minister can do to control the behaviour of individual members of Parliament who see themselves as victims and unfairly treated by their leadership. As a result, these one-to-one conversations are crucial to mitigate the negative impact that the hurt feelings and anger of a spurned non-Cabinet member can have.

Aside from the insightful work of Steve Paikin, there is very little consideration given to the negative impact that political events have on politicians. One of the most devastating experiences for an ambitious politician is being excluded from Cabinet, especially for those with high expectations. Many senior Liberals are still critical of Paul Martin for not personally contacting the Chrétien Cabinet ministers he had decided to exclude from his large 2003 Cabinet after winning the leadership. No one suggests that these calls will be pleasant, but one measure of a leader is being prepared to accept full responsibility for his or her actions. Delegating to others the task of informing those not being appointed is a signal that the prime minister does not understand that he alone is accountable to his colleagues for Cabinet selections. The general view in these circumstances is that asking others to do the "heavy lifting" for difficult decisions diminishes the prime minister's authority and power.

It is the responsibility of the prime minister's chief of staff to compile the list of people the prime minister should contact during the consolidation phase of the transition. In addition to those left out of Cabinet, there are several categories of people who should receive some form of communication from the prime minister in the early days following the swearing-in.

If there is enough energy left, the prime minister may also make telephone calls or send messages to several others during the transition period:

- Candidates who defeated major opponents;
- Provincial campaign chairs and other campaign team members;
- Members of the national election-campaign team;
- Members of the provincial election-campaign teams;
- Key local campaign managers.

Evaluating Past Performance

Most returning governments develop a method to evaluate the effectiveness of its administrative and decision-making processes in order to improve on the existing model. The process that is used can be very informal or the result of a formal organization study contracted out to an arm's-length organization in order to avoid possible bias in the data collection and other methodological issues.

In my interviews, it appears that formal internal evaluations are relatively rare in Canada, although prime ministers are constantly informally evaluating the overall performance of their governments, particularly the performance of their ministers, based on their own observations and media reports. One notable exception to the anecdotal approach for performance evaluation is Jean Chrétien, who felt that a systematic approach would improve the performance of his government.

Chrétien asked his staff to prepare a formal evaluation of the government's performance following the 1993 and 1997 election. In the first instance, he asked Chaviva Hosek and Eddie Goldenberg to prepare a document for a Cabinet retreat in 1995. In order to deliver their report for the retreat, they met with "all Ministers, Secretaries of State and the Chair of the National Caucus for an hour each, between May and early June of 1995."[24] At each of the meetings, all ministers were asked the same five questions:

- How they felt things were going for the government as a whole.
- What they wanted the government's record to be, two years hence.
- What issues they perceived were looming on the horizon as potential problems.
- What they felt about the effectiveness of the government's fiscal plan.
- How they felt the Cabinet and Cabinet system was working.

A second example of Chrétien's interest in performance measurement was the exercise that he asked Jean Pelletier to lead immediately after the 1997 general election that secured a second but diminished majority government. Two days after the re-election of the Chrétien government, Pelletier convened a PMO senior staff meeting to review past accomplishments and to plan for the next mandate. I prepared six questions for him to use at the review meeting:

- What has worked well at the PMO during the past three years?
- What areas need improvement?
- Are there any new personnel needs that have emerged as a result of the election?
- Are there ways to improve the relationship between PMO and PCO so that the PM can be served better?

- What are the views of PMO staff on the readiness and ability of the public service to provide policy advice for the next mandate?
- What can the Prime Minister do to make your jobs easier?[25]

These questions led to a series of internal meetings at all levels of the PMO, which in turn led to some restructuring in the office and human resource changes to make the government more responsive to caucus needs and to regional input.

Conclusion

The consolidation phase of the transition is the last in this exciting process that in the extreme may have taken more than twelve months to navigate. At this point, prime ministers should have established a modus vivendi for the Cabinet meetings, made whatever machinery-of-government changes are needed to make the system work for them, and met with the deputy minister community to communicate their expectations and the role of the chief of staff and the clerk of the Privy Council.

Ministers will have carefully read their mandate letter and shared it with key advisors, including the deputy minister, hired their key staff members, established a working relationship with their deputy minister, become familiar with the department and the broader portfolio, and attended an orientation session organized by the prime minister.

To complete this phase, prime ministers should have also communicated directly with potentially disaffected colleagues and supporters, and, in the case of a re-elected government, asked the chief of staff to evaluate the workings of the PMO and ministers' offices and tested the effectiveness of their relationships with key stakeholders in and outside of government.

By now the majority of the transition team members will have returned to their full-time employment outside of government, although they will continue to maintain a watching brief on the functioning of the government, since they are among a small number of people who actually know what the government had intended to accomplish.

The final chapter moves away from detailing the attributes and behaviours of the key players in each of the four phases. Instead, its focus is on highlighting the key elements of transition planning and providing some observations about ways that we can strengthen and institutionalize the system in order to preserve the best of our smart practices.

9 Conclusion

Even the longest journey begins with a single step.

– Chinese proverb

Introduction

The central theme of the book is that government transitions represent the most fundamental element of activity in a democracy: the transfer of power from one political party to another, or in other cases the transfer of power from one leader to another in the same political party. Given the centrality of this event, it is imperative for the key players on both the political and public service sides of the exercise to organize themselves in ways that produce thoughtful plans that allow the agendas of the government and the public service to merge at the appropriate time.

In 1984, Bill Neville provided the first step in the professionalization of transition planning in Canada by building on the earlier efforts of the Clark and Trudeau administrations. Since then, transition planning has become a more professional exercise, especially for political parties, but also for the public service. While transition planning continues to take place out of sight and largely invisible to election watchers, there is an increasing appreciation of the importance of the pivotal moment when governments transfer power from an outgoing government to an incoming one – even when it is the same party and leader.

On the basis of more than forty interviews with political and public service leaders, we know that the intensity and the preparation have varied considerably around the eleven transitions that have taken place since 1984. As might be expected, the transitions following a change in government produced the most intense and best-prepared transition plans. The re-election of a government with the same prime minister produced the simplest and least adventuresome transition.

Transitions are a time of magical opportunity, when a newly elected government can put a public face on its hope and aspirations and begin to fulfil the promises it has made to the Canadian public. History will judge the effectiveness of a transition, but experience teaches us that well-executed transitions give a newly elected government the right trajectory to launch its new mandate. Poorly done transitions will hamper a new government and slow its ability to move forward.

A transition is exhilarating by definition, since it represents the pivotal event in the political agenda of a political party. It opens up infinite opportunities, within government and afterwards, to those who are selected to serve as Cabinet members, and it coincidently confers great administrative powers on their political staff. At the same time, for many participants in the governing process it signals the end of the line – sometimes for the leaders of opposing parties and sometimes because it dashes the aspirations of members of Parliament from the governing party who have not been chosen to serve in the Cabinet. For these individuals the transition can be a most difficult time, since it publicly differentiates between those with power and those without.

Since 1984, a number of outcomes related to elections and transitions appear to characterize our current governance structure. First, it is now rare for a political party to win more than 40 per cent of the popular vote, so the prospect of minority governments is more likely than ever, depending on the strength of the third and fourth parties. Second, governments take about two weeks to be sworn in after a general election, and this length of time seems unrelated to the size of the mandate or whether it is a newly elected government or one that has been re-elected. Third, one area of some variation is in the size of the average Cabinet. There does not appear to be any trend in Cabinet size, and the typical predictors – size of election win or type of transition – are not good predictors of cabinet size. The one general rule emerging from the data is that newly elected governments have the smallest Cabinets. Finally, the number of Cabinet committees also is particular to the style and preferences of the prime minister and doesn't appear to reflect governance trends in the private sector (such as smaller boards of directors).[1]

Personal Reflections

Looking back on my own three experiences in transition planning, there were only a few times where difficult decisions that kept me awake at night had to be made while carrying out my mandate. I attribute this to extensive preparation and being very comfortable with the person for whom the transition is being prepared.

Derek Burney has commented that one of the most challenging aspects of designing a government for Stephen Harper was estimating how the new prime minister would react to his recommendations. In this regard, I was especially fortunate, because not only did I know the work habits of Jean Chrétien extremely well but I also knew that delegation was a core element in his management style and that he believed strongly in his staff providing him with "fearless advice." Individuals such as Jean Pelletier, Eddie Goldenberg, Chaviva Hosek, Peter Donolo, Bruce Hartley, and Patrick Parisot were long-standing (some might say lifelong) staff members because they had the authority to act on behalf of the prime minister, and they also knew that they were expected to provide honest and unvarnished advice when required.

Given the easy access to Chrétien, the most difficult issues I had to deal with could be characterized as strategic. The first involved ensuring that, post-election, the newly appointed PMO staff found themselves in the right job. Matching people to jobs is one of the greatest challenges in any political organization, since the skills needed in the Office of the Leader of the Opposition are not always necessary or desired in a prime minister's office.

Jim Collins, author of some of the most persuasive management books published over the past decade, including *Good to Great*, has always argued that getting the "right people on the bus" is more important than devising impressive organization charts. The value attached to hiring the right people for the key jobs was also crucial to the PMO, as it is to any other organization. As a result, Jean Pelletier as chief of staff spent a lot of his time in the early weeks of the Chrétien government evaluating the skills of the existing OLO staff in light of the attributes needed in the move from an opposition-styled work environment to a governing one. The organization chart designed in advance of the election was prepared to take advantage of the skills and knowledge of these particular people and to suit the management style of the prime minister, at the outset, but it was recognized that some people could not change their behaviour in light of the changes in duties.

The second complex issue was to develop a "policy" or operating principles for dealing with the many former conservative government political staffers who had moved into the public service during Mulroney and Campbell's ten years as prime ministers. Many Liberals felt that some individuals had been badly treated by the Mulroney government because they were seen as liberals, and they wanted to exact some retribution from those seen to be benefiting from their previously easy access to public service jobs or government appointments.

During the 1993 transition, a number of conversations were organized with those who wanted the former political staffers to be removed from their jobs or have their appointments rescinded. After a flurry of activity and a conversation with the leader of the opposition, it was decided that, given the overall high quality of the appointments of former exempt staffers, there seemed no reason to initiate an exercise that would be perceived as highly partisan, would affect public service morale, and would ultimately be a major distraction from more important issues for the government.

Only years later did I learn that, although the prime minister had directed his staff to ensure that former Conservative staffers were not punished or had their careers affected because of their earlier political activities, a number of ministers directed their deputy ministers to move former staffers to jobs that were "out of sight" of the minister. In some cases, the former ministerial staff were moved to other departments or transferred to the Canada School for the Public Service, which ultimately housed a number of them.[2]

The third contentious issue was the appropriate size of ministers' offices and the appropriate job levels and compensation for the senior staff. During the Mulroney years, the prime minister had increased dramatically the size of ministers' offices and had also increased the title, compensation, and responsibilities of the senior staff in a minister's office. The newly coined chiefs of staff were designated as equivalent to assistant deputy ministers and were expected to have the same status of a deputy minister in policy development and interacting with ministers. In 1993, the question was whether a Chrétien government would keep the large offices and chief of staff positions or move to another model of ministerial support.

In the end, after consultation with a number of conservative ministerial staff, senior public servants, and former liberal political staffers, the decision was taken to revert to the system in place during Trudeau's time, when staff played a facilitative role. The reasons were that, first, the prime minister felt that the public service should be his primary source of policy advice, and he didn't want his staff to serve as a counterweight against the public service. Instead, he wanted his office to provide political advice and to work with the public service and to play the role of facilitator. Second, the prime minister felt that the cost of ministers' office had grown to unacceptable levels, and he wanted their size scaled back. He had anticipated the need to cut the overall size of the public service, and he wanted to send clear signals to the public service and to the public at large that smaller, more efficient government offices were going to be a theme during his term as prime minister.

The final difficult issue to deal with during the 1993 transition was getting the approval of Chrétien to vet new ministers for suitability before they were appointed. Early in our deliberations, the transition team identified the issue of integrity in government and the problems that Mulroney had experienced with many of his ministers who had been forced to resign from Cabinet for unethical and inappropriate behaviour. Determined to avoid the embarrassment of having to accepting the resignation of a Cabinet colleague, we developed the idea of implementing a vetting process that would identify potential problem appointments before candidates were sworn into the ministry. When we presented the concept to Chrétien, he was intrigued with the idea and saw the value of the exercise but found our questioning too intrusive and untrusting.

The transition team could see no way other than more onerous surveillance techniques to identify those who present a serious threat to the integrity of the Cabinet. After many weeks of internal debate, Chrétien provided us with a way to resolve our impasse. He said, "If Herb Gray thinks this is a good idea and would allow himself to be subjected to this process, it is OK with me." Fortunately, Gray thought the idea was an excellent one and he strongly endorsed its use in 1993. As a result, variations of this practice are now used when federal ministers are selected for Cabinet.

Key Elements in Transition Planning

This volume has covered a wide range of topics on the ways political leaders and senior public servants look at three kinds of government transitions. In a nutshell, six elements emerge as cornerstones of a transition exercise:

- Developing a leadership style in a world of inexperienced politicians
- Understanding the emerging importance of political advisors

- Establishing respectful and trusting relations among the key players
- Selecting the right transition team
- Making a virtue of planning
- Consolidating the transition by training and mentoring

Developing a Leadership Style in a World of Inexperienced Politicians

Most newly elected governments are not ready to govern for a number of reasons. First, political parties are organized to be election machines and not management organizations, and as a result, the senior party players often lack the skills that would ease their move into management positions in the PMO or ministers' offices. Second, political party officials are fundamentally preoccupied with winning elections and don't want to invite hubris by appearing to be presumptuous or arrogant if it becomes known that they are preparing a transition. Third, the prime minister or party leader may have insufficient management or governing skills to recognize the need to be fully prepared for the responsibilities of office.

Paul 't Hart's analysis of the leaders of many Westminster countries leads to his insightful generalization about the crucial interplay between planning and leadership: "Over-reliance on either a plan, or solely on a leader, is to be avoided. Transition planning can facilitate the bridge into government, but the nature of leadership is also decisive. A leader whose authority is accepted but exercised with a light rein, drawing on plans that are not too rigidly interpreted, and managing talented collaborators, offers the best prospect for transition success and political longevity."[3]

Those who make the journey from opposition leader to heading a government are, by virtue of winning an election, successful leaders. Yet the early months and years of new governments are often mistake-ridden and directionless. Some new prime ministers, like Harper, Mulroney, Australia's John Howard, and Britain's Tony Blair, had little or no prior experience in executive government, and as a consequence, they relied on their instincts or behaviour learned in opposition. Blair's press secretary, Alastair Campbell, observed that Blair's office had "hung on to some of the techniques and ways of opposition for too long" and as a result "the spin thing" became the way in which he managed the government during his early years as prime minister.[4]

Australian Prime Minister John Howard, though an experienced minister in a previous government, struggled to control the issue agenda during his first term. Based on experiences in the United States, Harrison Wellford concludes that the transition team must find a way to prepare the president to lead by learning to take control of the governing levers. He concludes that the primary work of the transition team is to get him ready to do this, as "this is the transition team's only objective."[5]

Understanding the Emerging Importance of Political Advisors

In earlier eras, the transition was led by the clerk of the Privy Council and the senior public service. Now, at both federal and provincial levels, political parties have taken over prime responsibility for the transition process through their own transition teams. As a result, while the public service still plays an important role, it is now secondary. This current reality, the result of more than thirty years of change, has led to a shifting of power away from the permanent public service and to political advisors located in the prime minister's office and the offices of Cabinet ministers.

On the composition of the Prime Minister's Office, a recent study of six countries (including Australia, Germany, the United Kingdom, New Zealand, and Sweden) found that Canada has the highest number of political appointments. While not all staff in Canada's Prime Minister's Office carry out partisan activities, it is notable for its partisanship in comparison to the five other countries. As well, Canada, like Australia and New Zealand, has no public servants working in the Prime Minister's Office, although the foreign policy advisor who is located in the PCO effectively is a member of the PMO.[6]

Given the significance of this new development, the changing role of advisors is becoming an area of interest to the academic community and political observers. In Canada, there have been only a few sporadic attempts to regularize the role of advisors in government, although governments in the United Kingdom and Australia have recognized the importance of these changes and have developed their own codes to regulate the behaviour of political advisors.

The rise of the political advisor as a permanent actor within the machinery of government has also been well documented across a broad spectrum of OECD countries, in addition to Westminster countries. With the increase in the number of political advisors have come greater concerns about their role, the nature of their accountability, and their impact on the relationship between the public service and political leaders. At the heart of this discourse is the recognition that they can exert significant influence over political leaders. As their numbers grow, political observers and citizens alike need to understand how this paradigm shift affects good governance.[7]

It bears repeating that this development does not necessarily deter good governance, since political advisors have the potential to strengthen the functioning of government. They can ensure that the government's agenda is implemented, bring a new vigour to policy development, and maintain the impartiality of the public service by shielding it from pressures to undertake political activities on behalf of ministers. They can also strengthen a minister's ability to manage complex political issues. All of these benefits contribute to good democratic governance.

The challenge is to embrace the benefits that political advisors provide by being more involved in the sharing of power, while minimizing any possible vulnerability. In reality, there are still concerns that political advisors have contributed to a growing separation between the public service and political leaders and the consequent disenfranchisement of the public service from policy development. This worry has been heightened in recent times where minority governments' suspicion of the public service has heightened. In fact, as we have learned from the accounts of many former prime ministers (Chrétien, Mulroney, Martin, Blair), there is no reason for them to distrust their public services as a general rule. While exceptional cases can be found in most jurisdictions, the Westminster countries can count on the strong support of their public service.

Above all, political advisors need to work within an accountability structure that brings clear lines of responsibility to the functioning of these new players. It should no longer be acceptable for political advisors to live in the grey areas between ministers and public servants with uncertainty around their roles, authorities, and allegiances. Good governance demands transparency and openness across the machinery of government and with citizens. As American Supreme Court Justice Louis Brandeis aptly said, "Sunlight is said to be the best of disinfectants."[8] Democracy requires accountability, which itself requires transparency to ensure that citizens are able hold their governments to account. Political advisors are now acknowledged to be permanent and professional government additions. As such, they need to uphold the standards placed on other actors within the system.

The arrival of political advisors in so many OECD countries, in such large numbers and with such influence and proximity to power, has permanently changed the traditional relationship between public servants and its political leadership. Therefore, there is a legitimate need to systematically and rationally develop a policy to foster more effective public policy and more efficient decision-making.

These rules or policies should be anchored by a working environment that is totally committed to integrity in government – that is, in a series of explicit values that champion the primacy of working in the public interest. Many countries have articulated values that guide the work of their public services, but in some cases these don't include political advisors explicitly. As a result, political advisors are seen to operate beyond the good governance practices that have been adopted for other components of the machinery of government.

Establishing Respectful and Trusting Relations among the Key Players

The core purpose of transition planning from the perspective of both the political and public service players is to establish solid working relationships among the key participants in the governing structure. In the end a transition will be judged by the degree to which the relationships are based on trust, respect, and mutual understanding. In most cases, especially when a new government with a new prime minister assumes power, this goal will take much more time to consolidate than the usual fortnight between election day and the swearing-in of the new government.

In particular, the relationships and ways of interacting between the prime minister, the chief of staff, and the clerk of the Privy Council are all crucial elements in a successful transition.

A good working relationship at the outset between and among key participants is crucial to launching a successful government. If the dynamics are not favourable, prime ministers will ultimately have to replace their chiefs of staff or clerks in order to bring order and harmony to this triangular relationship.

In fact, changes in these key jobs should be anticipated, since most long-serving prime ministers have made changes in both. For example, Mulroney had four chiefs of staff and two clerks of the Privy Council during his nine years as prime minister, Chrétien had three clerks and three chiefs of staff over his ten years in office, although Jean Pelletier served for almost eight of those years.

At the heart of the relationship-building dynamic is allowing the transition team to understand and appreciate the personality and needs of the incoming prime minister at a fundamental level. Failure to master these basics will condemn the transition team to errors of judgment and will, in the long term, produce an inefficient governance system that can undermine the government's success.

One of the greatest challenges for the senior public service is preparing for change of leadership at the top. It is often extremely difficult for it to embrace changes within the ministry, particularly a change of prime minister. As we know, most incoming governments are suspicious of the loyalty of the public service. What is less appreciated is that the senior public service often has problems adjusting to a new prime minister, who will have different points of view and a management style different from his or her predecessor.

All these pressures converge during the first meetings of the incoming prime minister (sometimes accompanied by the chief of staff and the head of the transition team) and the clerk of the Privy Council. These early meetings can be extremely formal, tense, and risky for the clerk. At a minimum, they are crucial in setting a tone for subsequent relations between the government and the public service. As a result, there is great pressure on the clerk to perform well, since the eyes of the senior public service are focused on outcomes of these early meetings. For a clerk who enjoys risk, this is a moment to be savoured and remembered. For those for are risk averse, the meetings are extremely stressful and lonely, since they are almost always conducted without the clerk having the support of other PCO staff.

It is worth remembering that there is a natural tension between any newly incoming government and the permanent public service. A central theme in Max Weber's writings during the early twentieth century was that the bureaucracy will manipulate elected politicians by invoking their greater expertise in policy.[9] This long-standing suspicion must therefore be one of the first issues addressed by clerk with a new prime minister.

While most attention is focused on the interaction between the prime minister and the clerk, similar meetings are playing themselves out in every government department and agency, as the deputy ministers and the ministers (often accompanied by their senior staff) meet to work out their own working relationships. Normally, ministers will have met with the heads and the executive committees of all the Crown corporations, agencies, and commissions that make up their portfolio after two or three months of a newly sworn-in government.

Regardless of the relationship developing between the prime minister and the clerk during their early meetings, public servants are being reminded by each of their deputy ministers of their obligation to serve the government of the day. The ethos of the Canadian public service is tested under these circumstances when public servants are asked to implement the agendas of newly elected governments that can be radically different from the familiar agendas of the outgoing government.

Selecting the Right Transition Team

The most effective transition teams are small and made up of people with diverse skills. The team primarily needs individuals who know the prime minister well enough to anticipate his or her needs and aspirations and who have a good appreciation of party politics. The team make-up should reflect the diversity of views that are necessary to provide frank and honest advice to the leader. As a general operating principle, it is useful to have a number of people on the transition team who intend to join the prime minister in the PMO. In addition, they should be able to operate in a pressure-filled environment, be prepared to disappoint people whom they like and respect, and recognize that the transition is not about them. It is not a place for people with egos or with a desire to take advantage of circumstances for their own personal gain.

However, it is strongly preferable for the leader of the transition team not to have aspirations to a job or an appointment in the public service. Nothing can undermine the credibility of the transition team and its work more than a patronage appointment, since it appears as a reward for loyalty and calls into question the objectivity of the transition work. Having lobbyists on the team presents a particular challenge in transition planning, since so many government experts are engaged in government relations. It is therefore probably prudent to avoid including people on the transition team who are currently involved in trying to influence public policy daily.

Making a Virtue of Planning

Planning is crucial for transitions to succeed. It creates the framework for all that follows and, when done well, gives the transition team time to deal with the unexpected that will inevitably intrude into their well-laid plans. Transition teams, especially those representing an opposition party, now spend more than a year planning a transition. As a result, the political side is better prepared than ever before and is clearly in a position to challenge the work done by the public service. While the public service has improved the quality of its own transition materials and analysis, the major changes in transition planning in Canada have taken place on the political side, because it now recruits expert members to its transition teams and has invested the necessary time to produce quality transition materials.

The public service wants to serve all new governments, regardless how they got there, but it is sometimes very difficult in the early days if the incoming groups are hostile or don't know what they want to accomplish while in office. Nothing is more frustrating to the public service than a combination of these two situations.

Consolidating the Transition by Training and Mentoring

One area of consensus among those interviewed for this study from both the political world and the public service is the need for more formal orientation sessions for incoming governments and more training of members of Parliament about public management and good governance. While there have been important new developments at universities, with the creation of a graduate program at Carleton University on political management and five public policy programs over the past five years across the country, there continues to be a need for high-quality training of elected officials and their staff. The success of training programs in the United Kingdom for MPs demonstrates that it can be done.

As a final point on orientation, the lack of knowledge within the political community about the importance of an independent and professional public service is a serious barrier to growing the institution, not in numbers, but as an important public institution. We trust our public services to act professionally in the public interest. To do so means that we need to hire the "best and the brightest," and they will be attracted to the public service only if the work is meaningful and valued. Finding ways to involve ministers and the Cabinet in discussions about public service issues is therefore important in ensuring the healthy development of the public service.

Outstanding Issues

While transition planning has improved in quality and scale over the past thirty years, in the short term, two outstanding issues need to be addressed for Canada to catch up to the practices in other Westminster countries. First, there must be greater clarity about the behaviour of the public service during election campaigns. The independence of the public service from the governing party is a fundamental feature of the Canadian system. While there is a delicate balance to be struck between serving the government of the day and preparing for a new government by meeting with opposition parties before the results of the election are known, there is no evidence that the balance would be disrupted if there were opportunities for the public service to have some contact with the potential governments in waiting.

During two recent federal elections Prime Ministers Harper and Martin refused to allow their clerks of the Privy Council to meet with the leaders of the opposition parties during the election period. While previous prime ministers have given such permission, to provide for a smooth transition should the incumbent government be defeated, in more recent times partisanship has trumped good governance. This is a most unproductive development that only weakens our governance system and politicizes the role of the public service as a stabilizing factor in the transfer of power to an incoming government from the outgoing one.

Specifically, rules or protocols have to be established that prescribe appropriate behaviour of the public service with regard to the opposition parties' transition planning. The Cabinet manuals used in the United Kingdom and Australia clearly describe when and how the opposition parties can interact with the public service. There is no doubt that "conducting discussions with opposition teams while at the same time serving the requirements of an incumbent government requires sensitive handling."[10] However, the U.K. experiences in recent years have demonstrated that the public service understands the limits of its activity while interacting with the opposition parties and its obligation to support the government of the day. As a starting point, rules about what the public service can do (or is permitted to do) during election campaigns to ensure smooth transitions could, along with other issues, be formalized in a policy manual much like they are in the United Kingdom and Australia.[11]

There has been too little conversation in Canada about the value of a set of operating principles or conventions that would define the appropriate behaviour of governments and opposition parties during election campaigns.

The recently published report by the Public Policy Forum on the value of providing guidelines during elections opens up further discussion among parliamentarians and interested observers about the best way to administrative and political interface during elections.[12]

The second major observation that emerges from this study is the immediate need to increase the knowledge base of incoming members of Cabinet and their staff. While most members of Parliament are already familiar with election rules and regulations, very few of them have any real experience in governing, either in the private or public sector. As a consequence, most members of Parliament know very little about parliamentary procedure and even less about governing in our Westminster system. The recognition of a similar need in the United Kingdom prompted a number of the political parties to take advantage of courses offered by think tanks and similar organizations and to engage the senior public servants to share their institutional knowledge.

Neither the publishing of caretaker conventions during elections nor the introduction of formal training sessions for newly elected members of Parliament represents a radical change from Canadian traditions. However, these two changes, in the short term, would help Canadian jurisdictions improve the quality of transition work and would guarantee Canadians that their governments are doing their best in improving the quality of our governance regimes.

It is always important to remember that transitions give life to the most fundamental of our democratic practices – the peaceful transfer of power from one government to another. For this simple reason, we should pay more attention to its well-being and nurture its development in order to ensure that transition planning continues to play a vital role in our pursuit of good government.

Appendices

Appendix 1
Previous Research on Government Transitions

Given the importance of a smooth transition for a newly elected government or one that returns after a general election, it is surprising that there is so little academic and media interest in the details of transition planning. For example, none of the most popular Canadian introductory political science texts contains more than a passing reference to transitions.

Despite it being a relatively unexamined field, there have been a few important contributions in Canada to the transition literature in the past twenty years. The first is a comprehensive IPAC publication, first published in 1993, that focuses on the growing professionalism in government transition planning in the federal government and in the provinces. Donald Savoie's *Taking Power: Managing Government Transitions* provides an excellent overview of the principles of transition planning, followed by specific chapters about transitions in the federal government and four provinces.

The second is the well-crafted analysis of the transition of the Harris government after the defeat of the Rae government in 1995. Thanks to the generosity of a number of the key political players, well-known political scientists David Cameron and Graham White were given unprecedented access to the outgoing and incoming governments. The result was *Cycling into Saigon: The Conservative Transition in Ontario* that gives the reader a level of granularity that is especially insightful, since it taps into the complexity of transition planning that has rarely been captured before in the published literature. In particular, the authors provide a detailed description of the roles played by the political advisors to the incoming premier, with special attention paid to how relations between Harris's advisors and the public service were established.

Their insights into the complex ritual dance between the senior public service and the incoming political advisors as they establish a functional working relationship is one of the highlights of this helpful book.

In 2001, Peter Larson edited the third major contribution to the Canadian transition literature while he served as vice-president of the Public Policy Forum.[1] This publication, *Changing of the Guard: Effective Management of Transitions in Government*, was written for practitioners and especially for those that were directly involved in transition planning. The publication is anchored on three themes: preparing for transitions, managing transitions, and what every minister needs to know. It was based on a series of interviews and an all-day roundtable session involving seventeen experienced transition experts who had worked, at one time, either on the political side or in the public service. *Changing of the Guard* has served as a primer for provincial and territorial governments over the past decade as they prepared for their own transitions.

A number of authors have anchored some of their observations about politics in Canada by referring to transition planning or elements of a transition as part of their description of how things unfolded. For example, Jean Chrétien's *Straight from the Heart*, published in 1985, discusses the skills needed to be a good political leader. Eddie Goldenberg's 2006 book, *The Way It Works: Inside Ottawa*, is, as advertised, an "inside the ropes" accounting of the Chrétien government's ten years in office from the vantage point of Chrétien's senior policy advisor and former chief of staff. His book contains a number of references to transition planning, and his chapter on Cabinet-making is particularly valuable, given his vantage point. And *Double Vision: The Inside Story of the Liberals in Power*, by Edward Greenspon and Anthony Wilson-Smith, has a number of observations about the transition planning that went on before the 1993 federal election.

More recently, in an analysis of the Liberal Party of Canada, Brooke Jeffrey has produced a remarkably detailed look at the development of the party from 1984 to 2008. In the book she devotes a chapter to the Chrétien transition and also offers an analysis of the "uneasy" Martin transition from minister to prime minister after the leadership convention in 2003.[2]

Looking at transitions from a more personal rather than an institutional point of view, Steve Paikin has written a very powerful book, entitled *The Life: The Seductive Call of Politics*, in which he captures the ethos of political leadership and the crushing impact on losing power of politicians and the people around them.

Tom Kent's *A Public Purpose* covers government before transition planning became a professional activity in Canada. In the book he describes how Pearson's poorly planned campaign strategy in 1963 led to him to offer voters a last-minute campaign commitment for "sixty days of decision." The sixty-day declaration was a critical part of the Liberals' final campaign phase, which helped them to win a minority government.

Because the sixty-day declaration was made so late in the campaign, it wasn't until after the election and only one week before the government took office that Pearson asked Kent to prepare for the transition, which contained significant changes to the machinery of government. His account of the casual nature of transitions in the 1960s is an important reminder that it took the efforts of many committed political players and senior public servants to professionalize transition planning.[3]

Two other prime ministers have recently written memoirs of their years as party leaders and prime ministers. In Brian Mulroney's autobiography, *Memoirs: 1939–1993*, he devoted only 9, albeit very interesting, pages to his initial transition, despite an overall heft of more than 1100 pages. This brief chapter describes the period following the 1984 election, which highlights Cabinet-making and the immediate challenges facing the government. Despite the elaborate planning that took place before that election, Mulroney spends little time describing the elaborate preparation that was done on his behalf in 1984 and makes no reference to the transition following the 1988 election.[4]

Similarly, Paul Martin devotes little space to his own transition to prime minister in his autobiography, *Hell or High Water: My Life in and out of Politics*.[5] He does describe in some limited detail some of the struggles of his transition team prior to the 2003 election and in staffing the PMO. For example, he recollects the lack of contact with Chrétien, which made the work of his transition team more difficult. Additionally, Martin describes the challenge of staffing the PMO, his first days in office, and his new Cabinet.

More recently, Lawrence Martin's *Harperland: The Politics of Control* has captured the centralizing power of the prime minister in Canada and the degree to which the Prime Minister's Office has become the heart of government. And finally, Tom Flanagan's *Harper's Team: Behind the Scenes in the Conservative Rise to Power* describes some of the transition challenges for Stephen Harper when he first became prime minister in 2006.

Looking at the recently published international literature of relevance to Canada, only a limited number of publications apply to our Westminster system of government. The most recently published book in this area is the 2011 publication *How Power Changes Hands: Transition and Succession in Government*, edited by Paul 't Hart (a transplanted Dutch scholar who now works in Australia) and John Uhr (a Canadian-trained Australian). They have broadened their academic reach by applying a generalized definition of transitions to all aspects of political life.[6] This has resulted in an eclectic book on a wide variety of transitional issues. It includes chapters on the transition from politics to private life, party leader successions, the rules governing caretaker governments, when and how prime ministers fire their ministerial colleagues, leadership styles developed in opposition, and the dynamics of assuming power in government. An important observation noted in Errington's chapter is that answers to questions about transitions "appear to vary considerably from leader to leader and transition to transition," but opposition experiences are important predictors of prime ministers' early modes of operation.[7] Another author makes the claim that "there probably is some correlation between prime ministerial transition styles and the success, if not the longevity of the governments they lead."[8]

In 2010, former prime minister Tony Blair published his much-anticipated account of his political career, with special emphasis on his ten years as leader of the Labour Party and prime minister of Britain. His account of his ongoing battle to stave off Gordon Brown's attempts to unseat him, the role played by his political advisors, and his uneven relationship with the public service – with which he worked very closely but held at a distance – are all very instructive for students of politics and government. Blair was a consummate politician and explains almost all of his actions in a political context. The notion of "the public interest" was always defined by how an action would affect his party's fortunes in an election campaign.

In addition to the Blair book, Jonathan Powell, who served as chief of staff to Prime Minister Blair for more than a decade, has produced a most engaging and insightful account, *The New Machiavelli: How to Wield Power in the Modern World*, about managing at the centre of government.[9] Powell, weaving his story within a framework that explains the writings of Machiavelli, also provides important observations about government transitions, the role of the public service, and the exercise of power. Like Blair's, his insights have relevance in the Canadian context.

While research on transitions in Westminster systems is generally agreed to be underdeveloped, interest has been sparked among academics and practitioners over the past few years about appropriate behaviour during election campaigns. Sometimes characterized as "caretaker conventions," this relatively new area of academic and central government work has been taken up especially in Australia and New Zealand after a string of minority governments and the dilemma this kind of election outcome poses for governing.

The idea of a caretaker period is central to the idea of responsible government, a core Westminster concept. Responsible government means that the executive is composed of members of Parliament and that the executive requires the confidence of Parliament. Consequently, when Parliament has been dissolved for an election, the executive lacks the capacity to make new laws and the legitimacy to make executive decisions. A neutral public service that continues with routine government business during such periods is another hallmark of Westminster. The simplicity of the model, its emphasis on efficient governance, and the lack of detailed prescriptions made it effective as a means of governance for a wide range of countries during Britain's colonial period.[10]

In the United States, much of the academic thought on transitions has been anchored in that of Martha Joynt Kumar, who has devoted her career to documenting the transitions of presidents, going back to Truman. As a result, she has been recognized as the living repository of everything to do with U.S. presidential transitions. In fact, one of her colleagues has noted, "Over the last decade, Martha Joynt Kumar has become the institutional memory of the modern presidency in transition. The information that the outgoing president makes available to the incoming president is entirely discretionary. Kumar fills the gap."[11]

Harrison Wellford explains Kumar's devotion to this area of work: "Kumar believes that transitions matter and that the newly elected can learn from the successes and mistakes of their predecessors. The complexity of the management, policy, personnel and organization issues increases with every transition." As a consequence, Wellford believes that it is important to have a literature and a place to go to learn from the collective wisdom of those who have gone before.[12]

Appendix 2
Transitions in Canada since 1984

As has been previously mentioned, there has been little comparative work done on the process of government transitions in Canada.
However, all transitions go through the four phases and take place
in the political and public service environment. Beyond the general
issues, each transition is individually tailored to match the needs of
the incoming government and the particular style of the leader. In fact,
Alan Nymark, on the basis of his experiences as a federal deputy minister for more than ten years and his involvement in countless transition exercises in departments and in central agencies, argues that most
transition planning is "80 per cent by formula" and the remainder is a
function of political and socioeconomic contexts that have framed the
election or the leadership campaign that elected the prime minister.[1]
As a consequence, it might be useful to establish, to the extent possible,
norms or average behaviours that typically characterize a Canadian
government transition.

In the concluding portion of this appendix, data gathered from the
last eleven federal elections, commencing with the Mulroney victory
in 1984, are presented in a number of different ways, to illustrate the
range of possibilities that are part of the transition-planning process.
Figure 1 looks at the percentage of the popular vote the winning party
was able to garner.

Generally speaking, in Canada, the percentage of the popular vote
received by the governing party in a general election has decreased
over the past thirty years (see figure 2). As a starting point, Mulroney's
Conservatives received 50 per cent of the popular vote in the 1984
federal election. This result is now the high-water mark for elections
in Canada, and the percentage has steadily decreased over time. The

Figure 1. Percentage of the Popular Vote

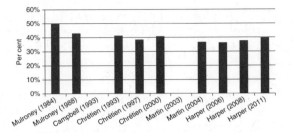

Figure 2. Seats Held by Governing Party (Percentage and Number of Seats)

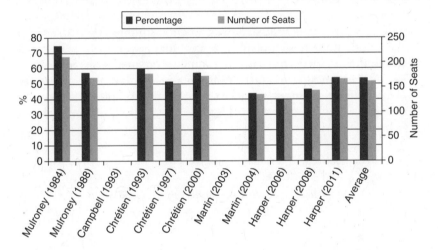

Liberal Party under Chrétien hovered around 40 per cent of the popular vote during its three election wins, and the percentage dropped even further for Martin in 2004 and Harper in 2006.

The 2011 election results, however, yielded a slight increase from the 2008 election, with the popular vote for the Conservative Party now close to 40 per cent. Despite the relatively low level of popular support enjoyed by the winning party, our first-past-the-post system, combined with the increased number of political parties, allows a party to take power and earn a majority government without winning more than 50 per cent of the popular vote.

In addition to lowering the governing party's popular vote over the years, Canada's first-past-the-post system, combined with the plurality of political parties, has also contributed to a trend of fewer seats held by the governing party. In terms of percentage of seats won, Mulroney's 1984 election win was the second largest in Canadian history. Two strong majorities followed – Mulroney in 1988 and Chrétien in 1993 – before the percentage of seats held by the governing party fell even further. Canada underwent three straight minority governments from 2004 to 2008 before the Conservatives obtained more than 50 per cent of the seats in the 2011 election.

It is more difficult today for the governing party to win a large number of seats. Not since 1984 has a party won more than 200 seats, and it does not seem likely that any party will be able to reach this number again anytime soon. The Conservatives' 2011 win was the first time in more than a decade that a party was able to win more than 150 seats. The elections since 1984 appear to suggest that governing parties must live with the reality of minority governments or small majorities.

The next two figures (3 and 4) examine the length of time the newly elected government took to swear in its Cabinet and to reconvene Parliament. The last grouping of figures (5 to 9) looks at how Cabinet

Figure 3. Time between Election and First Sitting

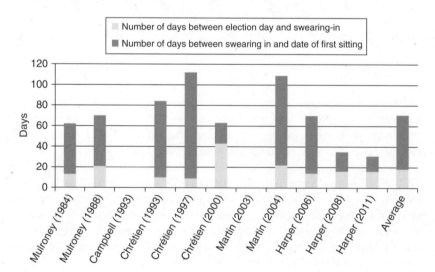

is structured and operationalized. This includes looking at its size, the composition of the ministry, the number and size of Cabinet committees, and the proportion of committees chaired by the prime minister.

The time between election day and the first sitting of Parliament has varied among our prime ministers (see figure 3), with the average being seventy-one days. In the elections since 1984, Chrétien's 1997 win produced the longest period between election day and the first sitting of the new Parliament. While the period of time for the swearing-in was relatively short, more than a hundred days passed from the swearing-in until Parliament actually sat for the first time (see figure 4). After his 2004 minority government victory, Paul Martin almost matched Chrétien's time to recall Parliament when he waited more than ninety days after the swearing-in of his Cabinet to introduce the Speech from the Throne.

While Chrétien took more than a hundred days between the election and the Speech from the Throne, in his other majority government elections, in 1993 and 2000, he took much less time to swear in his Cabinet and to recall Parliament. Interestingly, Chrétien's 2000 election and third majority win produced the longest time period between election day and swearing-in – more than forty days.

Brian Mulroney's 1984 and 1988 elections were more typical of the average seventy-one days for Parliament to first sit following an election. In 2006, Harper's time period was similar to Mulroney's, and it shortened further with the successive Conservative wins in 2008 and 2011. As a result of financial exigencies, Harper recalled Parliament thirty days following the 2 May 2011 federal election.

The first sitting of Parliament tends to take longer for newly elected governments in comparison with re-elected parties, possibly because they need more time to prepare for the swearing-in and for the launching of Parliament. That said, the time gap between the election and first sitting can be attributed partly to the timing of the election. Under most circumstances, Parliament breaks for summer at the end of June, so governments elected in late spring will typically not bother to bring the House back before the summer recess.

A good example was Chrétien's 1997 election win, which produced the longest period between an election and first sitting. The election was held on the second of June and, given the timeframe, there appeared to have been little point in bringing the House back before the late June summer recess. Harper's 2 May 2011 election win would seem to follow a similar pattern, except that the government needed to approve

Figure 4. Time between Election, Swearing-In, and First Sitting by Party

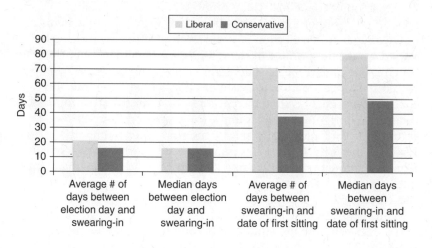

its annual spending estimates, without which it would not be able to expend any money.

Looking at the time between election day and the swearing-in of the government (Cabinet), it is interesting to note that Liberal-led governments have tended to take a longer time than Conservative governments to swear-in the Cabinet and to reconvene Parliament.

There is only a small difference between the parties in the days it takes to swear in Cabinet; in fact, the median number is the same. For the time it takes between swearing-in and the first sitting, however, there is a fairly large discrepancy between the two parties. Liberal governments took an average of seventy-one days to resume Parliament, while it took Conservative governments only thirty-eight days on average. The variance can be attributed partially to the timing of elections. The two longest periods between the election and first sitting – Liberals in 1997 and 2004 – both had June elections. Taking these two out of the equation, there is very little difference between the two parties. The time it takes to reconvene Parliament has more to do with the timing of the federal election than the actions of particular political parties.

With regard to the size of the Cabinet, two indicators are of particular interest in this discussion (see figure 5). First is the number of Cabinet ministers appointed to Cabinet to take on responsibilities for the wide range of federal departments and agencies that make up the

Figure 5. Size and Composition of Ministry

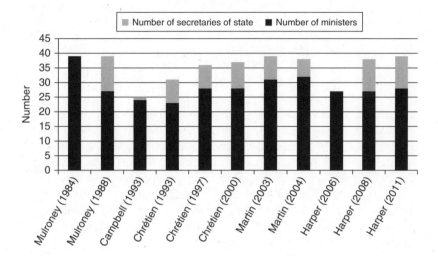

Government of Canada. Interestingly, despite the wide range in interests and priorities of our prime ministers since 1984, the size of Cabinet has stayed approximately the same with little variance among parties.[2]

Between 1984 and 2011, the average size of the federal Cabinet was twenty-nine ministers. In 1984, Brian Mulroney had the envious challenge of dealing with a caucus of 211, the first Conservative majority in twenty-six years, and a political party hungry for power after fifteen years of Liberal administrations, created Canada's largest modern Cabinet. Ironically, Kim Campbell, who succeeded Mulroney without a general election, appointed a considerably smaller Cabinet than her predecessor, perhaps as a way of contrasting her pragmatic and efficient style of managing the country with that of the big-spending Mulroney government.

Finally, when there is a change in the governing party, as there was in 1993 and 2006, the result is a decrease in the size of the Cabinet. As governments win successive elections, it appears that the size of the Cabinet also grows – possibly in response to pressure from the caucus for more chairs in the Cabinet room and the need to reward loyal supporters who have patiently waited for the call to play a role on the "executive team." Of course, it is also possible that a larger Cabinet is also a reflection of an expanded policy agenda that outgrows the government's earlier policy suite.

The second way to look at Cabinet size is to consider the total size of the ministry, including those who are given ministerial responsibilities without full Cabinet duties. Accordingly, when the number of secretaries of state and ministers of state are combined with the number of Cabinet ministers, the variation in the total size of the ministry (Cabinet ministers and secretaries of state) since 1984 is less dramatic than is apparent when looking at the number of ministers alone.

Of note, Mulroney and Harper did not appoint any secretaries of state or ministers of state during their first terms in office, but they added a significant number during their second term. Mulroney added twelve secretaries of state between 1984 and 1988 at the expense of ministers, although he held the total size of his ministry to thirty-nine members. Harper, on the other hand, added eleven ministers of state and secretaries of state to his ministry from 2006 to 2011, bringing the total size of his ministry from an initial twenty-seven ministers to twenty-eight, and eleven ministers of state (for a total ministry of thirty-nine).

As with the size of the Cabinet, the number of Cabinet committees has fluctuated among prime ministers, with no preferences between governing parties (see figure 6). Chrétien had the fewest number of Cabinet committees and made the decision to have his ministers chair

Figure 6. Cabinet Committees

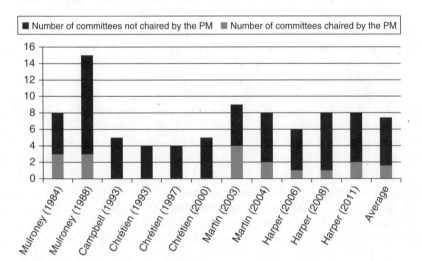

the committees. Kim Campbell also did not chair any Cabinet committees, but the other prime ministers all assumed the role of chair for at least one committee. As an indication of the range in number of Cabinet committees, Mulroney's 1988 government was particularly notable for the fifteen he created to manage the government. Since that time, the number of Cabinet committees has been dramatically reduced, ranging from four under Chrétien to nine for Paul Martin in 2004. Similar to the experience with Cabinet size, the number of members in each of the Cabinet committees tends to increase throughout the duration of a government's tenure, although the variations are insignificant.

The average size of cabinet committees (see figure 7) remained relatively stable between 1984 and 2011, at eleven, but it has ranged from a low of nine to a high of fourteen. There is no real distinction between the Liberals and Conservatives; both parties appear to have settled on about a dozen as the best size for a committee.

Finally, with regard to the role that prime ministers play in the management of their cabinet committees (see figure 8), averages are not particularly useful indicators, since two prime ministers chose not to chair any committees of Cabinet. Of those prime ministers who did so, Mulroney and Martin both chaired more than a third of their Cabinet committees, although they scaled back their level of participation during their second terms.

Figure 7. Average Size of Cabinet Committees

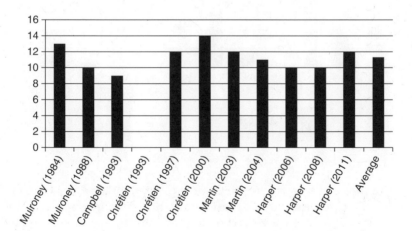

Figure 8. Proportion of Cabinet Committees Chaired by PM

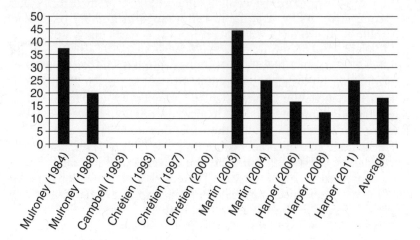

Figure 9. Number of Days between Election and Change in Clerk of Privy Council

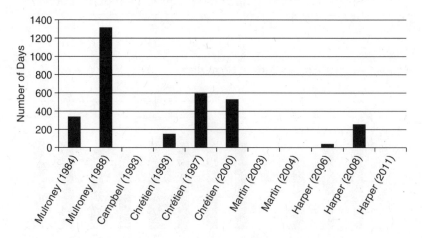

The choice of secretary to the Cabinet (or clerk of the Privy Council) is one of the prime minister's most important appointments. All incoming prime ministers are welcomed to government after an election by the secretary of Cabinet and, depending on circumstances, the two may

never have met before their first transition meeting. Given the pivotal role played by the secretary in the life of a government, the question of who will be tapped to play this key role is always a matter of great speculation among government watchers.

The data are not consistent on the longevity of secretaries to the Cabinet after a government is sworn in (see figure 9). The data suggest great stability in the Canadian context since, on average, in the federal government a secretary to the Cabinet will remain in the job for 462 days before being replaced. However, as the figure demonstrates, there is wide variation in the length of the tenure of modern-day secretaries. These fluctuations suggest that the decision to keep or replace a Cabinet secretary is a function of a wide range of factors that are particular to the tandem relationship between prime minister and Cabinet secretary.

For example, Mulroney waited almost four years to replace his secretary to the Cabinet after his 1988 electoral victory. Campbell and Martin did not replace theirs at all during their relatively short tenures as prime minister. This difference can possibly be attributed to the secretaries having served the same governing party as their predecessors and were therefore known to the incoming prime ministers. As a matter of practice, it appears that the secretary to the Cabinet is replaced more quickly when there is a change in governing party and prime minister.

Appendix 3
Selected Bibliography on Government in Canada

Here is a short list of texts that will satisfy the curiosity of any reader with a passion for a deeper understanding of how government works in Canada:

Aucoin, Peter, Mark Jarvis, and Lori Turnbull. *Democratizing the Constitution: Reforming Responsible Government*. Toronto: Emond Montgomery Publications, 2011.

Barker, Paul. *Public Administration in Canada*. Scarborough, ON: Thomson Nelson, 2008.

Bernier, Luc, Keith Brownsey, and Michael Howlett. *Executive Styles in Canada: Cabinet Structures and Leadership Practices in Canadian Government*. Toronto: University of Toronto Press, 2005.

Bickerton, James, and Alain Gagnon, eds. *Canadian Politics*. 5th ed. Toronto: University of Toronto Press, 2009.

Blakeney, Allan, and Sandford Borins. *Political Management in Canada*. Toronto: McGraw Hill Ryerson, 1992.

Brooks, Stephen. *Canadian Democracy: An Introduction*. 4th ed. Toronto: Oxford University Press, 2004.

Dunn, Christopher. *The Handbook of Canadian Public Administration*. 2nd ed. Toronto: Oxford University Press, 2010.

Dutil, Patrice, ed. *Searching for Leadership: Secretaries to the Cabinet in Canada*. Toronto: University of Toronto Press, 2008.

Dyck, Rand. *Canadian Politics: Critical Approaches*. 6th ed. Toronto: Nelson, 2011.

Inwood, Gregory. *Understanding Canadian Public Administration: An Introduction to Theory and Practice*. 3rd ed. Upper Saddle River, NJ: Pearson Prentice Hall, 2009.

James, Simon. *British Cabinet Government*. 2nd ed. London: Routledge, 1999.

Johnson, David. *Thinking Government: Public Administration and Politics in Canada*. 3rd ed. Toronto: University of Toronto Press, 2011.

Kernaghan, Ken, and David Siegel. *Public Administration in Canada*. Toronto: Nelson, 1995.

Laver, Michael, and Kenneth Shepsle. *Making and Breaking Governments: Cabinets and Legislatures in Parliamentary Democracies*. Cambridge: Cambridge University Press, 1996.

Malcolmson, Patrick, and Richard Myers. *The Canadian Regime: An Introduction to Parliamentary Government in Canada*. 4th ed. Toronto: University of Toronto Press, 2009.

Mallory, J.R. *The Structure of Canadian Government*. Toronto: Macmillan, 1971.

McNaughton, Neil. *The Prime Minister and Cabinet Government*. London: Hodder and Stoughton Educational, 1999.

Osbaldeston, Gordon. "Dear Minister: An Open Letter to an Old Friend Who Has Just Been Appointed to the Federal Cabinet." *Policy Options* (June 1988): 3–11.

– *Keeping Deputy Ministers Accountable*. London, ON: National Centre for Management Research and Development, 1988.

Smith, David E. *The People's House of Commons: Theories of Democracy in Contention*. Toronto: University of Toronto Press, 2007.

White, Graham. *Cabinets and First Ministers: The Canadian Democratic Audit*. Vancouver: UBC Press, 2005.

Whittington, Michael, and Richard Van Loon. *Canadian Government and Politics: Institutions and Processes*. Toronto: McGraw Hill, 1996.

Appendix 4
Transition Book Outlines

Outline of the Chrétien 1993 Transition Book

The transition book prepared for Jean Chrétien in 1993 was 170 pages, with four appendices.

1. Introduction
   a. The failure of the promises of the 1980s
   b. Changes in values
   c. The Conservative government record
   d. The Charter and the rise in importance of interest groups
   e. The status of Canadian society
   f. The business community in Canada
   g. Conclusion
2. Governance in the 1990s
   a. Introduction
   b. The role of government in society
   c. The new economy
   d. Collaboration
   e. The cry for consultation
   f. The demands of the information age
   g. Executive federalism
   h. Five parties in the House of Commons
   i. Governance in the 1990s and the consequences for Jean Chrétien's style of leadership
   j. Conclusion
3. The Role of the Prime Minister
   a. The mechanics of articulating a vision
   b. Setting a tone

   c. Jean Chrétien as prime minister
   d. Conclusion
4. The Cabinet
   a. The role of Cabinet in a Westminster system
   b. The Mulroney Cabinet
   c. Osbaldeston's View: A review of his recent research
   d. The French and British models of governing
   e. Cabinet size
   f. Cabinet structure
   g. Machinery of government: New departments
   h. Deputy prime minister
   i. Cabinet committee system
   j. Ministers' offices
5. The Prime Minister's Office (PMO)
   a. What makes for an effective PMO?
   b. The Mulroney PMO
   c. Chief of staff
   d. Office for Mme Chrétien
   e. Caucus and party liaison
6. The Privy Council Office (PCO)
   a. The role of the PCO
   b. Personnel issues
   c. The clerk of the Privy Council
   d. Organization of the PCO
   e. PCO budget
7. The Public Service
   a. Deputy ministers
   b. Organization of government departments
   c. Special operating agencies
8. Parliament
   a. The House of Commons
   b. The Senate
   c. Reforming Parliament
   d. Your parliamentary personnel
9. The Changeover Process
   a. The transition team
   b. Post-election communications
   c. Appointments
   d. Security

    e. Swearing-in process
    f. First Cabinet meeting
    g. First caucus meeting
    h. Recall of Parliament
    i. Reform of Parliament
    j. Schedule of planned events
    k. Schedule of the first 100 days after the election
    l. Review of current Liberal MPs and those nominated
       for the election
    m. Events during the transition period
    n. Tentative schedule of pre-election events and activities
10. Summary of Recommendations
    a. Principles of governance
    b. Organization of government
    c. Ministers' offices
    d. PMO
    e. PCO
    f. The public service
    g. Parliament
    h. Membership of the transition team

Outline of the Harper 2006 Transition Book

1. Transition Overview
2. Immediate Timetable and Post-Election Activities
    a. Day 1 to day 14
    b. Swearing-in of new Cabinet
    c. Election night analysis
    d. Protocol on who speaks when
    e. Plan for outgoing calls
    f. Calls and messages from world leaders
    g. Complex and uncertain election results:
       i. Results scenarios
       ii. Minority governments, customs, constitutional
         considerations, etc.
3. Ethics and Accountability in Government
4. Upcoming Events and Meetings
    a. Immediate policy issues
    b. Fiscal imbalance

   c. Trade
   d. Productivity
   e. Canada–U.S. Relations, etc.
5. Cabinet
   a. New Cabinet structure
   b. Size
   c. Vetting
   d. Selection
   e. Quebec
6. GIC Appointments and Procedures
   a. Key vacancies to be filled
7. Public Service Overview and Recommendations
8. PMO
   a. Structure
   b. Staffing
   c. Responsibilities
9. Minister's Offices
   a. Structure
   b. Staffing
   c. Orientation and training sessions
10. Caucus
   a. Orientation session, including spouses
11. Name Bank
12. Transition Team coordinates

Derek Burney, Transition Planning,
Harper Government,
28 March 2011

Appendix 5
Agenda for First Meeting of the Chrétien Transition Team

First Meeting of the Chrétien Transition Team

Agenda
26 October 1993
10:00 to 12:00

1. Review of election results
2. Date of the swearing-in
3. Other timing issues
4. Review of Cabinet size and committee system
5. Cabinet selection
6. Vetting process
7. Orientation session: agenda and timing
8. Other business

Appendix 6
Briefing Note 2000 Chrétien
Government Transition

---

22 November 2000
To: Jean Pelletier
From: David Zussman
Topic: Transition 2000

This memorandum sets out the important issues to consider during the critical transition period immediately following the 27 November election. For your convenience, I have prepared a timetable of activities for the Prime Minister from 28 November to 20 December. You will note in the timetable that a number of commitments have been made on behalf of the Prime Minister that cannot be changed.

Given the shortness of time and the delicate issues under consideration, it is very difficult to do a complete analysis of all of the important transition issues. In order to prepare this memorandum, I have consulted a very few individuals who are knowledgeable about the government's agenda and the Prime Minister. I have also drawn on my own observations of the government since its "swearing-in" in 1993.

I have made a number of assumptions about the outcome of the upcoming election. In particular, I have assumed that all Cabinet Ministers will be re-elected but there will be fewer Liberal MPs from Western Canada. I have also assumed that there will be more Liberal MPs from Atlantic Canada and from Quebec. Ontario will be all red.

This memorandum is divided into sections or essential elements in the transition process. In many cases, I have made a recommendation for action when I feel that there is a consensus among informed observers. In those instances where there is no consensus, I have not made any recommendations.

Dealing with the Aftermath of the Election

This election has been characterized by low public interest and intense personal attacks on the integrity of the Prime Minister. As well, there has been considerable speculation within the media concerning the PM's personal plans after his expected majority victory next Monday. As a result, I fear that an undeclared leadership campaign is likely to begin once the new Cabinet is sworn in by the Governor General.

Another likely challenge to the Prime Minister during this upcoming mandate will be finding ways to increase Western participation in the governing of the country. It is possible that there will be only token representation from Western Canada, giving voice to criticisms that the government does not have adequate input from the four western provinces.

Finally, there have been repeated allegations of Prime Ministerial arrogance in dealing with members of his caucus. This is a wedge issue that the media will be very anxious to exploit once the campaign is over. It is also going to be fuelled by some MPs who are not chosen, once again, to hold leadership positions in the government infrastructure and who will immediately begin a campaign to displace the PM.

Prime Minister's Legacy

This is the right time to give some thought to the Prime Minister's legacy, that is, those activities and policies that the Prime Minister would like Canadians to associate with his years as PM. There are a number of areas of possible inclusion but, for argument's sake, let me offer five government initiatives that may serve as the PM's legacy to Canadians:

- Developing a National Learning Strategy for all Canadians that responds to the challenges created by the emergence of the new economy
- Fashioning a first-class health-care system for all Canadians that has the federal government playing as significant a role as in the past
- Increasing the quality of life of Canadians by providing and, in some cases, restoring support for infrastructure programs
- Restoring confidence in our political and public institutions
- Putting youth at the centre of the public agenda

Theme of the Transition

You will recall that in 1993 our transition themes were returning integrity to government, dealing quickly with the immediate problems of the day (Pearson Airport, NAFTA), and a surefooted and an economical government. In 2000, we need a different look. In this instance, I recommend that we design this transition around the following themes:

- Meeting the challenge of the new economy
- Supporting initiatives that preserve our values of compassion and culture
- Bringing honour and civility back to public life for elected officials

Cabinet

The structure and composition of the Cabinet are the most important decisions the PM will make in the weeks following the election. In this section, I have presented a number of Cabinet-related issues for your consideration.

Deputy Prime Minister

The PM has used the position of Deputy PM very effectively since 1993. At this point, there is an opportunity to rethink the position and take advantage of its symbolic title.

Structure and Size of Cabinet

I believe the current number of Cabinet Ministers is appropriate for the PM's style of governing. However, there is some room to add a few more Secretary of State positions to the Cabinet system if there is a need to increase the number of Cabinet-level positions. If you feel an expansion of the number of Cabinet-level positions is warranted, adding a few Secretary of State positions could satisfy the need for greater participation but keep the actual number of Cabinet jobs fixed at the current number. In addition, there are a number of government initiatives and election promises that could benefit from explicit direction from the PM. Therefore, I am suggesting that you consider the appointment of the following new Secretaries of State:

- Public Service Renewal. This is a major challenge for the federal government as so many public servants retire and young Canadians have little appreciation of public service as a career. Without a major initiative, the federal public service will be severely challenged to meet its service obligations.
- Government Online. Based on progress to date, the federal government will not meet its online commitment unless the PM makes a symbolic gesture that government online is one of his priorities.
- International Environmental Affairs. Canada is being constantly criticized for its lack of progress in meeting its international obligations. The appointment of a Secretary of State might signal a change in commitment.

In terms of new areas of responsibility to be assigned to existing Ministers, I suggest the following:

- Official Languages. Both the death of Mr Trudeau and the recent report of the Commissioner of Official Languages demonstrate the support for bilingualism in Canada and the need for the government to act quickly to respond to recent challenges.
- North American Issues. The federal government is not well enough organized to coordinate all of its activities with the United States and those emerging issues with Mexico. A Minister with explicit responsibilities for coordination will help bring the more than fifteen departments and agencies with significant Canada-U.S. activities together to fashion a coherent series of policies.
- Crown Corporations Governance. The election campaign has highlighted a number of governance issues regarding publicly owned organizations. The appointment of a Minister with special responsibilities for governance would send a positive message to Canadians that the government is serious about remedying governance issues.

I have discussed these suggestions with Mel Cappe.

Government Reorganization

There are three important organizational issues that, in the view of many people whom I have consulted, need some "tweaking." HRDC remains a problem for the PM and for the government since it remained an issue during the election campaign. Unfortunately, Canadians still associate the department with shoddy administration and misuse of public funds. In my view, it is unlikely that the department and its Minister, regardless of who it is, will ever be able to operate without the smell of scandal surrounding their work.

Given the centrality of HRDC's mandate to the government's agenda going forward, I suggest that at a minimum, we rename the department – for example, the Department of Social and Labour Market Policy. You may also wish to consider naming an external advisory group to oversee the implementation of the plan outlined by Mrs Stewart some months ago. Finally, the Secretary to the Cabinet may have some views on whether the department is too large to manage as it is presently organized and whether it should be divided in two smaller parts – one for policy, the second for program delivery.

Second, one of the most serious issues facing this government over the next four years is renewing the public service. This could be a legacy program for the PM. Regardless of his commitment to public service renewal, the stark fact is that the federal government must begin hiring immediately in order to keep up with the projected departures over the next few years. Before a major hiring program is initiated there needs to be some change in the mandates of the central agencies (PCO, TBS, PSC, CCMD, Leadership Network) with regards to human resource management in the federal government. You could go so far as to create a new Office of Personnel that reports to the Clerk of the Privy Council Office if you wanted to create a high-profile organization that is seen to be associated with the PM.

The Clerk has already given this matter considerable thought and I would encourage you to work with him to implement a model that eliminates the high degree of overlap and duplication in the public service. I have already shared my views with him so it is sufficient to say that if the government really wants to become the employer of choice and rebuild its reputation for excellence, there is an urgent need for immediate action. This is the opportune time to signal to Canadians that a vigorous and vital public service is crucial to Canada's competitiveness.

Third, the federal government appears to have vacated the important field of consumer protection when it melded the consumer protection branch of Consumer and Corporate Affairs into Industry Canada in 1993. I propose that we consider transferring the Consumer Affairs and Commercial Relations office to the Department of Justice in order to signal the government's interest in protecting consumers who are now made particularly vulnerable by developments in globalization and information technology.

Mandate Letters

Not everyone agrees on the usefulness of the mandate letters that the PM sends to each Minister and Secretary of State. In my opinion, the mandate letters are very powerful accountability tools that the PM could make better use of in his dealings with Cabinet Ministers. Many Ministers consider them very important documents and work towards meeting the objectives stated in the mandate letters that are signed by the PM. Others have paid almost no attention to them.

In my view, the mandate letter gives the PM an opportunity to set the direction and tone of his government by setting down his expectations for his government and for individual Cabinet Ministers. The PCO should be encouraged to develop realistic objectives for each Minister and to develop a system for holding them to account for their performance on a periodic basis. I also suggest, in the interest of addressing the need for greater integrity in government, that the PM give serious consideration to making the mandate letters public along with the Guidance to Ministers manual (which is already in the public domain in an earlier version).

With regards to the mandate letters intended for the Secretaries of State, I suggest that these letters be more explicit than they are at present about the reporting relationship between the Secretaries of State and the Minister in the related portfolio, the level of their mandate to work independently of the Minister, and the degree of delegation.

Decision-Making

The current Cabinet and Cabinet Committee decision-making system needs some changes. Ministers see the process as too transactional and, consequently, they have little opportunity for substantive "political" discussions. There is also considerable resentment building up towards the present resource allocation system that is seen to be entirely negotiated between the Minister of Finance and the PMO at the expense of a wider consultation process. I understand that the Clerk has looked at a number of options to improve the present system of resource allocation. In particular, you may wish to consider moving away from making the budget the only major financial allocation process each year. The current system gives the mistaken impression that the government is not working outside of the budget season since there are almost no major government announcements that are not tied to the Finance Minister's budget.

We have tried other resource allocation systems before. One approach might be to fold the two policy committees (economic and social union) into one policy committee with a once- or twice-a-year allocation to be determined by the members of the policy committee. This approach would give Ministers an opportunity to fund worthwhile projects at other times in the year, other than during the budget.

I recognize the PM prefers an efficient Cabinet system that is not weighed down by lengthy debate. However, there are a number of actions he could take that would preserve his desire for efficient government and, at the same time, encourage greater Ministerial and caucus input. For example, I suggest he look at creating a number of ad hoc Task Forces that would include some backbench Members of Parliament, as is done in a number of provincial jurisdictions. These committees could have a fixed-term mandate, with limited membership (i.e., nine members) and some representation from the caucus.

The following ad hoc Task Forces are proposed for your consideration:

- The future of Agriculture and Rural Life .
- Health Care for Canadians (including public consultations headed by Roy Romanow)
- Aboriginal/First Nations Issues
- North American Economic Integration and its impact on Canada
- Foreign Affairs and Defence

I also suggest that we look into establishing a new Cabinet Committee on Foreign Affairs and Defence. This committee would free up precious full Cabinet time and help to coordinate all of the activities related to our foreign policy. These include:

- Canada's foreign policy, expressed through DFAIT
- Foreign aid (CIDA)
- Peacekeeping activities (Defence)

- Refugee policy (Citizenship and Immigration)
- RCMP (including drug trafficking and organized crime)
- CSIS

Compensation

In 1993, we set in place a structured compensation regime for exempt staff in the PMO and Minister's Offices. Since that time, the public service has endured six years of frozen salaries followed by across-the-board increases and the reintroduction of performance pay. It is now time to review the salary and performance-pay structure for exempt staff in order to bring these salaries more in line with public service compensation. I would extend this review to include Ministers' salaries and all other elected officials.

Training

The training program for the 1993 Cabinet had a very positive impact on the Ministers and gave Canadians a very positive perception of their newly elected government. I suggest that you consider holding a two-day retreat for the newly appointed Cabinet that would help launch the government in its new mandate. Items to be included should be:

- Maintaining integrity in government
- Determining the government's short- and medium-term priorities
- Examining new ways of consulting Canadians
- Managing a Minister's office
- Developing effective ways of consulting with caucus members

Role of the Members of Parliament

The government Members of Parliament, in the next session, will be under constant scrutiny by the media to evaluate the meaningfulness of their contribution to the life of this government. This could be a very severe test for the PM since many caucus members will have their Ministerial ambitions frustrated, once again, by failing to gain membership in the Cabinet and will begin leadership actions. I have already raised the role that the Task Forces could play in getting more caucus members involved in the policy process. In a later part of this memo, I suggest ways in which PMO could be more in tune with caucus.

On the broader issue of the role of MPs there are a few things that could be used to enhance the role of MPs. These could include all-party reviews of new government legislation before it is introduced in the House of Commons and some participation in government appointments by welcoming their observations on significant appointments. You might also provide more funds for staff and MP training, since they often find themselves at a disadvantage when dealing with Ministers and their staff. Since there is no obvious solution, it might be best if the PM were to set up an enquiry, headed by an esteemed parliamentarian, to look into this matter.

Ministers' Offices

It is probably a good time to ask the PCO to undertake a review of Ministers' offices in terms of their size and the adequacy of their budgets.

Prime Minister's Office

As you know, the PMO has been a most stable and effective organization since 1993. There have been very few changes in senior personnel, and when they have occurred, the replacements have moved easily into their new roles without much apparent disruption to the overall effectiveness of the organization.

You are well aware of the pending departures from the PMO, so there is no need for me to suggest replacements. However, two areas within the PMO need strengthening. The first is in Caucus Liaison. In 1993, we created a position of Caucus Liaison modelled after the one used by the Tories in the 1980s. I would suggest that we have not succeeded in establishing a credible link with the caucus. Too many caucus issues are not raised with the Prime Minister, giving the MPs the impression that the PM is arrogant and non-caring about their concerns. We should appoint someone who is trusted by the MPs and who will be able to interpret events taking place in caucus.

The second area in the PMO that needs additional personnel is in communications. I feel that the PM is well served by his current communications staff, but PMO staff is not doing the overall coordination of government communications. Consequently, you depend too much on the PCO to carry out the coordinating function that is difficult for public servants to do. I therefore suggest that you consider designating someone to coordinate explicitly government communications at the political level.

Liberal Party of Canada

The current election campaign revealed some weaknesses within the LPC. In particular, the Party needs to grow in Toronto and in Vancouver. This is a two-year, part-time assignment and I suggest that you ask Gordon Ashworth to do the work on behalf of the Party.

Appointments Process

The PM is going to be under careful scrutiny for all appointments in this next mandate. In my view, there are a number of actions the government could undertake to improve the transparency of the current appointment process without diminishing the PM's prerogative to appoint. In particular, the government should:

- Publish the profiles of vacant positions in all agencies, boards, and commissions
- Offer a governance course to all new appointees
- Create an expert panel to make recommendations regarding compensation and benefits
- Advertise job openings in accessible locations
- Champion best practices in public management and governance

Policy and Legislative Priorities

This will be contained in the PCO documentation.

Swearing-In Ceremony

The swearing-in ceremony offers the government the opportunity to give life to its aspirations. We should consider doing something different this time, such as involving the public in some aspect of the ceremony or making an important policy announcement.

First Thirty Days

I have prepared a timetable for the Prime Minister from 28 November to 20 December. It is located in the attached appendix.

Conclusion

You will recall that in 1997, you and I, along with the Secretary to the Cabinet, met with the Prime Minister in Shawinigan the day before the election. I do not know what you want to do this time, but I am available to travel to Shawinigan if you would like my assistance at the appropriate time.

Appendix 7
First Things First

Memo to: The Party's Nominee
From: Stephen Hess
Subject: Transition Planning
Date: 22 May 1980

In a sense, you are immediately faced with three-dimensional decision-making: there are people decisions, structure decisions, and policy decisions. If you decide first on a person, you may become locked into a structure and/or a policy. Presidents-elect always make people decisions first, then rue many of the consequences ...

Assuming that you will want to get on with appointments, as have your predecessors, are there not ways to group together the consideration of certain jobs so as to keep policy and structure in mind at the same time? For example, by concentrating first on the triangle of State-Defense-NSC [National Security Council]? This mode of arranging your decisions can help you think about what you want of each agency and what qualities you most desire in a secretary of state, a secretary of defense, and a national security assistant. The same principle would apply to thinking about key economic positions.

Other factors enter into the appointing process: Do you want to give your cabinet officers the authority to choose their own deputy/under/assistant secretaries? Are there any jobs that can be best filled by setting up search committees? How much conflict/consensus do you wish to build into your advisory system? What sort of commitments do you want to get from your appointees? When you do not have specific people in mind, what are the most useful questions to ask candidates for each top job? What positions do you wish to abolish? What precedents need to be considered, such as a western governor for secretary of the interior? What part do you want members of Congress and the National Committee to play in people decisions? How do you want to go about screening candidates for conflicts of interest and other disqualifying characteristics? There needs to be a strategy for the announcements of appointments.

Stephen Hess, *What Do We Do Now?*
A Workbook for the President-Elect
(Washington, DC: Brookings Institution Press, 2008)

Appendix 8
Orientation Agenda

Chrétien Cabinet
November 1993

AGENDA

Session.1 (13:00–13:10)   David Zussman
* Welcome and Introduction
* Purpose of the Session

Session 2 (13:10–13:30)   Hon. Mitchell Sharp
* Prime Minister's Philosophy About
  Government
* Integrity in Government
* Personal Behaviour
* Ethics in the Chrétien Government

Session 3 (13:30–14:00)   Hon. Ralph Goodale
* Role of a Minister
* Relations with Caucus and Cabinet
  Colleagues

Session 4 (14:00–14:45)   Chaviva Hosek
* The Government's Policy Agenda   Eddie Goldenberg
* The Red Book   David Zussman
* Key Upcoming Political Events
* Quebec Strategy
* Working with Central Agencies

Session 5 (14:45–15:15)   Peter Donolo
* Communications in Government   Patrick Parisot

Session 6 (15:15–15:45)   Terrie O'Leary
* Management of a Minister's Office   Randy Pettipas

Session 7 (15:45–16:15)   Arthur Kroeger
- Relations Between Ministers and
  Their Deputies

Session 8 (16:15–16:45)   Penny Collenette
- The Appointment Process

Session 9 (16:45–17:15)   George Young
- The Liberal Party of Canada

Appendix 9
Political Advisors and Public Servants
Interviewed for This Book

Political Side

Transition Teams

Gordon Ashworth
Ian Brodie
Peter Burn
Derek Burney
Penny Collenette
Greg Fyffe (also Public Service)
Eddie Goldenberg
Don Guy
David Lindsay
Tim Murphy
Bill Neville
Geoff Norquay
Simone Philogène
Mike Robinson
Elizabeth Roscoe
Jodi White

Former Ministers

David Collenette
John Manley
Allan Rock

Public Service Side

Yaprak Baltacioglu
Margaret Biggs
Richard Dicerni
Michael Horgan
Bill Pentney
Simon Kennedy
Judith Larocque
Jim Mitchell
Alan Nymark
Kathy O'Hara
Richard Van Loon
Michael Wernick
Joe Wild

Clerk of the Privy Council / Secretary to the Cabinet

Alex Himelfarb
Kevin Lynch
Mel Cappe
Tony Dean

Notes

Preface

1 Michael Fenn was the president and CEO of the Canadian Urban Institute at the time.
2 This is my recollection of the meeting I had with Bill Neville in the summer of 1993.
3 Bill Neville, Committee on Government Planning, Office of the Leader of the Opposition, 1984.
4 Bill Neville, interview, 7 January 2011.

1. Introduction

1 See David Cameron and Graham White, *Cycling into Saigon: The Tories Take Power in Ontario* (Vancouver: University of British Columbia Press, 2000), 225, for an excellent overview of the significance of a transition within the context of democratic development.
2 For a fascinating account of how power is exercised in politics, see Steve Paikin, *The Life: The Seductive Call of Politics* (Toronto: Penguin Canada, 2002), 307.
3 I am indebted to Simone Philogène for characterizing transitions in such a theatrical way. For more insight into the value of narratives in learning about public sector leadership and political institutions, see Sandford Borins, *Governing Fables: Learning from Public Sector Narratives* (Charlotte, NC: Information Age Publishing, 2011).
4 Cameron and White, *Cycling into Saigon*.
5 Tony Blair, *A Journey: My Political Life* (Toronto: Alfred A. Knopf, 2010), 107.
6 Ibid., 108.

7 Stephen Hess, *What Do We Do Now? A Workbook for the President-Elect* (Washington, DC: Brookings Institution, 2008), 4.
8 John Burke, "Lessons from Past Presidential Transitions: Organization, Management, and Decision-Making," *Presidential Studies Quarterly* 31, no. 1 (2001): 7.
9 Ibid., 14.
10 Stephanie Smith, *Presidential Transition*, Report no. RS20709 (Washington, DC: Congressional Research Service, 2007), 1.
11 In the late 1980s, Steven Rosell, as the director of the Machinery of Government Unit in the Privy Council Office, had his business cards printed with a black box next to the Canada word-mark as a humorous indication of how mysterious and secret the Machinery of Government's Secretariat's activities were at the time, even to insiders.
12 I have used the terms *secretary to the Cabinet* and *clerk of the Privy Council* interchangeably when describing the role of the most senior public servant in the Government of Canada. For more information about their role, see Patrice Dutil, *Searching for Leadership: Secretaries to Cabinet in Canada* (Toronto: University of Toronto Press, 2008).
13 There is no single or best way to prepare for a government transition since it is so dependent on resources, expertise, personal preferences of key players, and traditions. Instead the intention is to provide examples drawn largely from the federal government that will serve as illustrations of how various transition teams tackled their challenges.
14 By 1984, I am referring to the election of Brian Mulroney on 4 September 1984, and as a result I did not examine the transition of John Turner, who succeeded Pierre Trudeau on 30 June 1984.
15 Anonymous reviewer, May 2012.
16 Public Policy Forum, Roundtable Summary Report on Government Formation, 1 June Roundtable, Ottawa: 2011.
17 There is some debate on whether *caretaker convention* is an appropriate term to describe the rules and policies that dictate government activity during an election period. Peter Russell prefers the term *government formation*, which in his view suggests a more active period than the word *caretaker*, which suggests a period of inactivity.

2. The Context of Transitions: Setting the Stage

1 Also known as exempt staff in Canada.
2 Gordon Ashworth, interview, 8 December 2011.
3 Kevin Lynch, interview, 8 April 2011.

4 Tim Murphy, interview, 15 December 2010.

5 Alan Clark, *Diaries* (London: Phoenix/Orion, 1993), 14.

6 Jodi White, interview, 10 February 2011. In the last years of Mulroney's ten as prime minister, he asked Robert de Cotret, one his most knowledgeable ministers about the workings of government, to review the organization of his government. As a result, he completed an exhaustive examination of the organization of the federal government in close collaboration with the Machinery of Government Secretariat in the Privy Council Office. He produced a twenty-eight section report that served as the blueprint for Kim Campbell's massive restructuring in 1993.

7 Ibid.

8 See Sharon Sutherland, "The Consequences of Electoral Volatility: Inexperienced Ministers 1940–1990," in *Representation, Integration and Political Parties*, ed. Herman Bakvis (Toronto: Dundurn, 1991); and Erik Neilson, *The House Is Not a Home* (Toronto: Macmillan, 1989).

9 Graham White, "Shorter Measures: The Changing Ministerial Career in Canada," *Canadian Public Administration* 41 (1998): 389.

10 Lynch, interview.

11 Ibid. The perceived trend of electing inexperienced members of Parliament was magnified after the 2011 federal election with the arrival in Ottawa of a large number of "new to politics" NDP members. Over the years, Canadians have shown incumbent members of Parliament that there is no guarantee that they will be re-elected. This has led to fragile job security for sitting members of Parliament and, on average, to less-experienced MPs.

12 Alex Himelfarb brought to my attention that John Tait had used this terminology in the 1980s when he prepared his departmental staff for a transition.

13 The notion of transition might imply a defined period of time. In fact, what constitutes the transition period is very fluid and is open to interpretation about when it begins and ends. It could be argued that a transition starts when the leader appoints a transition team, and it ends with the swearing in of the Cabinet. However, I argue in this book that the transition has four phases and, as a result, it starts earlier than the appointment of a transition team, and the transition work continues well past the swearing-in ceremony, perhaps as long as a year, depending on the interest of the prime minister ensuring the lasting impact of the transition.

14 The learning curve is always steep for newly elected government leaders. The slope of the learning curve, however, will depend on external factors that will force the learning to take place during a shorter or longer time

period than anticipated or will be accelerated by crises and emergencies that were created by the external environment. A good example is the case of Barak Obama who in 2008 had to face an international and domestic financial crisis, wars in Iraq and Afghanistan, a huge operating deficit, and inflated expectations from the electorate, especially first-time voters.

15 *Management* and *leadership* are used in this text to reflect an awareness of the distinction made by Burns and others between "transactional" activities characterized by an emphasis on routine procedures applied day-to-day in the workplace and "transformational" behaviour that is characterized by priority-setting and long-term planning. The former is referred to as management skills and the latter as leadership skills. See J.M. Burns, *Leadership* (New York: Harper and Row, 1978).

16 Wayne Errington, "Establishing Prime Ministerial Leadership Style in Opposition," in *How Power Changes Hands: Transition and Succession in Government*, ed. Paul 't Hart and John Uhr (Basingstoke, UK: Palgrave Macmillan, 2011), 71.

17 Mark Bennister, "Blair and Howard: Predominant Prime Ministers Compared," *Parliamentary Affairs* 61, no. 2 (2008): 335.

18 K. Dowding and E. McLeay, "The Firing Line: When and Why do Prime Ministers Fire Ministerial Colleagues?" in 't Hart and Uhr, *How Power Changes Hands*, 254.

19 Jonathan Powell, *The New Machiavelli: How to Wield Power in the Modern World* (London: Bodley Head, 2011), 32.

20 Ibid., 54.

21 Ibid., 56.

22 These included Chaviva Hosek, Peter Donolo, David Miller, and Patrick Parisot.

23 Gilbert Lavoie, *Jean Pelletier: Combattez en Face* (Sillery, QC: Septentrion, 2009), 79.

24 For more information about the search for a chief of staff, see Anthony Wilson-Smith and Edward Greenspon, *Double Vision: The Inside Story of the Liberals in Power* (Toronto: Doubleday Canada, 1996).

25 Lavoie, *Jean Pelletier*.

26 Jean Carle, interview, 16 February 2012.

27 Lawrence Martin, *Harperland: The Politics of Control* (Toronto: Penguin Canada, 2010), 63.

28 Ibid., 54.

29 Ibid., 55. David Emerson was a minister in the Martin government who later crossed the floor after the 2006 general election and served as a minister in the Harper government.

30 Ibid., 62.
31 Derek Burney, interview, 16 June 2011.
32 Richard Neustadt, "Neustadt Advises the Advisers in 2000," in *Preparing to Be President: The Memos of Richard Neustadt*, ed. Charles Jones (Washington, DC: American Enterprise, 2000), 143.
33 Harrison Wellford, "Preparing to Be President on Day One," *Public Administration Review* (July/August 2008): 618.
34 Exempt staff are the political and partisan office staff of federal cabinet ministers. Exempt staff are outside the official public service and are exempt from Public Service Commission staffing guidelines, controls and protection. Cabinet ministers hire their own exempt staff and they are governed by terms and conditions set by the Treasury Board of Canada.
35 While the PSEA no longer allows for exempt staff to join the federal government on a priority basis, there are many examples of former political finding full-time employment in the government and in the government-relations sector, despite the five-year ban on such activities.
36 Blair, *Journey*, 19.
37 Peter Aucoin, "Government and the Evolution of the Westminster System," 11 February 2010, unpublished. The PMO does not publish numbers about its size or the distribution of responsibilities, but most observers estimate the size of the current PMO is more than 150 full-time employees.
38 David Zussman, *Political Advisors*, Expert Group on Conflict of Interest, Public Governance Committee, Public Governance and Territorial Development Directorate (Paris: OECD, May 2009).
39 The most contemporary analysis of the political administrative interface was written by Peter Aucoin and published posthumously early in 2012. See Peter Aucoin, "New Political Governance in Westminster Systems: Impartial Public Administration and Management Performance at Risk," *Governance: An International Journal of Policy, Administrations and Institutions* 25, no. 2 (April 2012): 177–99.
40 Ibid.
41 Blair, *Journey*, 26.
42 Jean Chrétien, *Straight from the Heart* (Toronto: Key Porter Books, 1994), 50.
43 Powell, *New Machiavelli*, 340.
44 Lynch, interview.
45 Jill Rutter, *Are Our Media Threatening the Public Good?* (London: Institute for Government, 2010), 14.
46 Ludger Helms, "Governing in the Media Age: The Impact of Mass Media on Executive Leadership in Contemporary Democracies," *Government and Opposition* 43, no. 1 (2008): 26–54.

47 None of this research, however, explains the remarkable impact that Jack Layton had on the voting public in the May 2011 general election. I will leave it to a more expert observer to explain the "Layton" effect and how the public developed its own narrative about Layton that was not shared by the media until his death. Borins, *Governing Fables*, on the value of narratives in politics, could provide a useful tool in deciphering the NDP surge in 2011.

3. Pre-Election Phase: Kick-Starting the Transition

1 Martha Kumar, "Getting Ready for Day One: Taking Advantage of the Opportunities and Minimizing the Hazards of the Presidential Transition," *Public Administration Review* 67, no. 4 (July/August 2008): 603.
2 Jack Austin was a former chief of staff to Pierre Trudeau and deputy minister, while Arthur Kroeger had been a long-standing federal deputy minister who retired in 1992.
3 Mike Robinson, interview, 21 December 2010.
4 Note from Tom Axworthy to Eddie Goldenberg, 11 November 1992, author's collection.
5 This is true for all recent transition team leaders, save for Derek Burney, who led Harper's transition team in 2006 without knowing him well at all.
6 Carle, interview.
7 Bill Neville, interview, 7 January 2011.
8 Ibid.
9 Burney, interview.
10 Undated notes, 1992, author's collection.
11 See Brooke Jeffrey, *Divided Loyalties: The Liberal Party of Canada, 1984–2008* (Toronto: University of Toronto Press, 2011), 243–5.
12 Ibid.
13 Tim Murphy, chief of staff to Prime Minister Paul Martin, interview, 15 December 2010.
14 Simone Philogène, interview, 29 April 2011.
15 Wellford, "Preparing to Be President," 61–2.
16 Carle, interview.
17 Wellford, "Preparing to Be President," 63.
18 Tony Blair, *Journey*, 109.
19 Jeffrey, *Divided Loyalties*, 207.
20 Geoff Norquay, interview, 24 March 2011.
21 Robinson, interview.
22 Ibid.

23 Burney, interview.

24 Ibid.

25 Since the 1970s, the most powerful way of describing the relationship between the professional public service and ministers was by borrowing Aaron Wildavsky's term of "speaking truth to power." Recently, in Canada, this relationship has been characterized as providing "fearless advice and loyal implementation." I attribute the first-time use of this phrase to the former secretary to the Cabinet Alex Himelfarb, when he was a member of the federal government's Task Force on Values and Ethics (also known as the Tait Task Force) in 1996. It is now enshrined in the mission statement of Correctional Services in Canada and has become an important element in the orientation of recent hires into the federal public service.

26 Nicholas D'Ombrain is one of Canada's leading experts on the Westminster system of government and was deputy secretary to the Cabinet for machinery of government in the Privy Council Office (1990–4) and a key participant in the Campbell and Chrétien transitions.

27 Nicholas D'Ombrain, interview, 6 December 2011.

28 Ibid.

29 Ibid.

30 Judith Larocque, interview, 18 November 2010.

31 Alex Himelfarb, interview, 19 September 2010.

32 Name withheld, interview, December 2010.

33 Ibid.

34 Himelfarb, interview.

35 Sir Robert Armstrong, quoted by Marcel Berlins on BBC Channel Four *Questions*, 1 July 1984.

36 Nicholas D'Ombrain, "Ministerial Responsibility and the Machinery of Government," *Canadian Public Administration* 50, no. 2 (2007): 215.

37 Lynch, interview.

38 During the recent U.K. election, the civil service conducted scenario-planning exercises for a number of possible electoral results, in anticipation of a hung Parliament outcome.

39 Lynch, interview.

40 Ibid.

41 Australia, Department of the Prime Minister and Cabinet, "Guidance on Caretaker Conventions," 2010, 9–10.

42 David Richards, "Sustaining the Westminster Model: A Case Study of the Transition in Power between Political Parties in British Government," *Parliamentary Affairs* 62, no. 1 (January 2009): 108–28.

43　Ibid., 7.
44　Tony Dean, interview, 17 November 2010.
45　Himelfarb, interview.
46　This assertion is based on a number of conversations with members of the Harper transition team.
47　For example, in the first Harper government Bob Nicholson, John Baird, Tony Clement, and Jim Flaherty all had previous Cabinet experience.
48　A good example is Paul Martin, who expanded the number of Cabinet Committees and made himself the chair of many of them. Another is Stephen Harper, who dispensed with the deputy prime minister position and deeply centralized the decision-making system.

4. The Transition Plan

1　Derek H. Burney, "Managing Transition in Government," SCDS-CCISS Strategic Analysis Seminar, Ottawa, 2 February 2011.
2　Bill Neville, Briefing Book, 1984, 3. Personal collection of Jodi White.
3　See chapter 2, note 34.
4　Examples of governor-in-council appointments are the president of the CBC, the president of Export Development Canada, the CEO of Telefilm Canada, and the chair of the CRTC.
5　The rank ordering of these three entities in terms of importance is a significant consideration for prime ministers in signalling their priorities.
6　Powell, *New Machiavelli*, 92.
7　John Manley, interview, 6 July 2011.
8　Neville, Briefing Book, 1984, s. 3, p. 1.
9　Robinson, interview.
10　Ian Clark, "Recent Changes in the Cabinet Decision Making System in Ottawa," *Canadian Public Administration* 28, no. 2 (1985): 185–201.
11　Burney, interview.
12　D'Ombrain, "Ministerial Responsibility," 210.
13　Neville, Briefing Book, chap. 3, pp. 6–7.
14　Ministerial careers have been understudied in Canada. One recent study identified the importance of gender, academic training, age, previous experience, and leadership challenger status in "accelerating" an appointment to Cabinet. See Matthew Kerby, "Worth the Wait: Determinants of Ministerial Appointments in Canada, 1935–2008," *Canadian Journal of Political Science* 42, no. 3 (September 2009): 593–611.
15　Gerald Kaufman, *How to Be a Minister* (London: Faber and Faber, 1997).
16　Powell, *New Machiavelli*, 126.

17 Ibid., 30.
18 Ibid., 68.
19 Blair, *Journey*, 340.
20 Ibid.
21 Former federal deputy minister, interview, January 2011.
22 Interview with two deputy ministers who have worked for the Martin and Harper governments.
23 Ibid.
24 Draft version of *A Guide for Ministers*, PCO, 27 May 1997.
25 Nicholas d'Ombrain, "Cabinet Secrecy," *Canadian Public Administration* 47, no. 3 (2004): 332–59.
26 Chrétien, *Straight from the Heart*, 85.
27 United Kingdom, Cabinet Office, *Machinery of Government Changes: Best Practice Handbook*, 4.
28 Jim Mitchell, interview, 11 January 2011.
29 Ian Brodie, Interview, 6 April 2011.
30 They were the Ministry of State for Social Development (MSSD) and the Ministry of State for Economic and Regional Development (MSERD).
31 Prime Minister's Office, press release, 23 June 1993.
32 Patrick Dunleavy and Anne White, *Making and Breaking Whitehall Departments: A Guide to Machinery of Government Changes* (London: Institute for Government, 2010), 102.
33 Peter Hennessy, *Whitehall* (London: Pimlico, 2001), 23.
34 Paul Barker, *Public Administration in Canada, Brief Edition* (Toronto: Thomson Nelson, 2008), 147.
35 Ibid. As Barker points out, the politics/administration dichotomy has playing out in different ways recently as a result of the growing emphasis on separating policy development from program delivery. One important consequence has been the now popular view of political leaders that public servants "wield too much power and that the participation of the bureaucracy in the formulation of policy should be severely limited" (Barker, *Public Administration*, 152).
36 Neville, Briefing Book, 1984.
37 Burney, interview.

5. Election Phase: Putting the Building Blocks in Place

1 Sir Gus O'Donnell, interview, 3 June 2011.
2 Himelfarb, interview.
3 Senior deputy minister, name withheld.

4 Richard Dicerni, interview, 29 June 2011. He served as deputy minister of the Department of Industry, 2006–12.
5 Michael Wernick, interview, 27 June 2011.
6 Dicerni, interview.
7 Ibid.
8 Deputy minister, name withheld.
9 The second book closely approximates the work that Judith Larocque undertook with her staff in their transition-planning at Canadian Heritage.
10 Glen Shortliffe, Cabinet secretary, 1992–4.
11 Morris Rosenberg, interview, 8 July 2011.

6. Post-Election Phase: Electioneering to Governing

1 This honeymoon is an unspecified period of time after the government is sworn into office, when the public and the media do not apply as much scrutiny and hold the government to the same level of accountability as they will later. The reasoning is that new governments should be given some "slack" or a "breaking in" period to put their transition and policy plan into action.
2 "News in a Time of Terror," *Media Monitor* 15, no. 2 (2001): 4.
3 Neville, Briefing Book, 1984, s. 2.2: "Media/Communications Requirements," 1.
4 Ibid.
5 Carle, interview.
6 Paul Wells, *Right Side Up: The Fall of Paul Martin and the Rise of Stephen Harper's New Conservatism* (Toronto: Doug Gibson/McClelland & Stewart, 2006), 380.
7 Wellford, "Preparing to Be President," 622.
8 Kumar, "Getting Ready for Day One," 609.
9 Ibid., 610.
10 Hess, *What Do We Do Now?*, 5.
11 Martin, *Harperland*, 19.
12 Robert Reich, *Locked in the Cabinet* (New York: Vintage Books, 1998), 84–5.
13 Carle, interview.
14 *Ready to Govern: Improving the Presidential Transition* (Washington, DC: Partnership for Public Service, 2010), 12.
15 Based on interviews with those involved in recent transitions.
16 Philogène, interview.
17 Derek Burney, head of the transition team for Prime Minister Harper and chief of staff to Prime Minister Mulroney, interview, 28 March 2011.

18 Wells, *Right Side Up*.
19 Ibid., 245.
20 Glen Shortliffe, undated memorandum, 1993. Personal papers.
21 D'Ombrain, interview.
22 Ibid.
23 Neville, interview.
24 Powell, *New Machiavelli*, 18.
25 Shortliffe, undated memorandum, 1993.
26 Ibid.
27 Neville, 1984, Briefing Book, 3–4.
28 Stephanie Smith, *Presidential Transitions*, Report RS20709 (Washington, DC: Congressional Research Service, 2007).
29 Neville, Briefing Book, 1984, s. 2, pp. 2–3.
30 Burke, "Lessons from Past Presidential Transitions," 17.
31 Martha Joynt Kumar, White House Interview Program, Washington DC, 30 April 1999. For more information on this fascinating project, see Martha Joynt Kumar and Terry Sullivan, "Source Material: The White House Interview Program: Objectives, Resources and Releases," *Presidential Studies Quarterly* 30, no. 2 (June 2000): 382–7.
32 Ibid.
33 Neville, interview.
34 Eddie Goldenberg, *The Way It Works: Inside Ottawa* (Toronto: Douglas Gibson Books, 2006), 52.
35 Elizabeth Roscoe, interview, 25 January 2011.
36 Dean, interview.
37 Notes for address by Glen Shortliffe, clerk of the Privy Council and secretary to Cabinet, Deputy Ministers' Lunch, 5 November 1993. Personal collection.

7. Post-Election Phase: Getting the Fundamentals Right

1 "Warm-Up Lessons: Clinton's Transition Was a Slow and Messy Process. But a Glimpse inside His Administration-in-Progress Provides Clues to How He May Govern," *Newsweek*, 25 January 1993.
2 David Docherty, *Mr Smith Goes to Ottawa: Life in the House of Commons* (Vancouver: UBC Press, 1997), 95–6.
3 Goldenberg, *The Way It Works*, 57.
4 Jonathan Lynn and Antony Jay, *The Complete Yes Minister: The Diaries of a Cabinet Minister* (London: British Broadcasting Corporation, 1984), 11.
5 Derek Burney, interview, 28 March 2011.

6 David Collenette was a member of Parliament for more than twenty years and served in the Cabinet of three prime ministers, where he held five ministerial positions.

7 These might include Paul Martin, Sheila Copps, David Anderson, and Roy Maclaren.

8 Blair, *Journey*, 20.

9 Burney, interview, 16 June 2011.

10 In some cases, members of Parliament arrive at the swearing-in ceremony not knowing what their Cabinet position will be. Anne McLellan, for example, arrived in Ottawa only hours before the ceremony, after having survived a recount that she won by twelve votes.

11 Bill Graham was in Mexico when Chrétien wanted to appoint him to the Cabinet. The vetting was done over a crackling telephone line from a language school in rural Mexico.

12 Neville, Briefing Book, 1984, s. 3: Populating the Cabinet Positions, 9–11.

13 Ibid., 8.

14 Allan Lutfy retired in 2011 as chief justice of the Federal Court after serving eight distinguished years there.

15 Allan Lutfy, personal notes, 1993. Personal collection.

16 Ibid.

17 Ibid.

18 Personal collection. We consulted with Professor John Langford, an ethics expert at the University of Victoria. In a note to Langford, he was asked to prepare a "questionnaire that would ask all of the tough questions which must be asked of modern day politicians" (23 July 1993).

19 Brodie, interview.

20 Blair, *My Journey*, 130.

21 Neville, Briefing Book, 1984, 11.

22 Derek Burney, "Getting It Done," *Diplomatic and International Canada Magazine*, May–June 2005, 84. The tainted tuna issue revolved around the decision of Minister of Fisheries John Fraser to sell a million cans of tuna that were possibly tainted. In the end, the government recalled the tuna from the store shelves, the minister resigned, and the rules were changed so that ministers could not overrule the decisions of food inspectors.

23 Ibid., 85.

24 Ibid., 88.

25 Wellford, "Preparing to Be President," 621.

26 Reich, *Locked in the Cabinet*, 52–3.

27 Privy Council Office, 2003.

8. Consolidation Phase: Making the Transition a Reality

1 Burney, interview, 28 March 2011.
2 Some generic text has been used from draft mandate letters to give readers a sense of the tone of these letters.
3 Blair, *Journey*, 18.
4 These messages are a broad summary of examples drawn from transitions since 1984 and from notes from conversations that I had with Glen Shortliffe in 1993.
5 Since the U.K. coalition made so many machinery changes, to inform their civil service and the interested public they decided to issue a separate document outlining the features of the changes.
6 Burney, "Getting It Done," *Diplomatic and International Canada Magazine*, May–June 2005, 91.
7 Peter Daly and Michael Watkins, *The First 90 Days in Government: Critical Success Strategies for New Public Managers at All Levels* (Cambridge, MA: Harvard Business Press, 2006).
8 Gerald Kaufman, *How to Be a Minister* (London: Faber and Faber, 1997), 2.
9 Ibid., 10.
10 David Zussman, "The New Governing Balance: Politicians and Public Servants in Canada" (Tansley Lecture, Johnson Shoyama Graduate School of Public Policy, University of Regina, 13 March 2008).
11 David Zussman, personal notes, 21 June 1997.
12 Richards, "Sustaining the Westminster Model," 108–28.
13 Manley, interview.
14 Neville, 1984, Briefing Book, s. 3.5.5: Minister's Relations with Deputy Ministers, 1–3.
15 Lavoie, *Jean Pelletier*, 89.
16 David Zussman, personal notes, 1993.
17 David Cameron and Graham White, "Cycling into Saigon: The Tories Take Power in Ontario, 1995" (paper delivered at the Annual Meeting of the Canadian Political Science Association, Brock University, St Catharines, Ontario, 1996).
18 Himelfarb, interview.
19 Gordon Osbaldeston, "Dear Minister: An Open Letter to an Old Friend Who Has Just Been Appointed to the Cabinet," *Policy Options*, 9, no. 4 (June 1988): 3–11. Osbaldeston is a highly respected former deputy minister in the federal government and was clerk of the Privy Council from 1982 to 1985, where he served three prime ministers during those years: Trudeau, Turner, and Mulroney.

20 Ibid., 4.
21 Ibid., 7.
22 Ibid., 8.
23 Chrétien, *Straight from the Heart*, 85.
24 Zussman, personal notes, 1995.
25 Zussman, personal notes, 1997.

9. Conclusion

1 See Appendix 2 for more detailed information.
2 Greg Fyffe, a former chief of staff, senior public servant, and current colleague at the university, provided me with very important insights into the careers of former political advisors who joined the federal public service after working in ministers' offices.
3 Paul 't Hart and John Uhr, eds., *How Power Changes Hands: Transition and Succession in Government* (Basingstoke, UK: Palgrave Macmillan, 2011), 53.
4 *BBC News*, 9 May 2002.
5 Wellford, "Preparing to be President," 622.
6 Emma Trusswell and David Atkinson, "Supporting Heads of Government: A Comparison across Six Countries" (working paper, Institute for Government, London, 2011).
7 See Zussman, *Political Advisors*.
8 Louis Brandeis, *Other People's Money and How Bankers Use It* (New York: F.A. Stokes, 1914).
9 G. Roth and C. Wittich, eds., *Max Weber: The Theory of Economic and Social Organizations*, 2 vols. (Berkeley: University of California Press, 1968).
10 Richards, "Sustaining the Westminster Model."
11 Peter Riddell and Catherine Haddon, *Transitions: Preparing for Change in Government* (London: Institute for Government, 2009), 65.
12 See Public Policy Forum, *Towards Guidelines on Government Formation: Facilitating Openness and Efficiency in Canada's Governance*, Final Report (Ottawa: Public Policy Forum, April 2012).

Appendix 1. Previous Research on Government Transitions

1 It should be noted that I was the president of the Public Policy Forum at the time and I was one of the three authors of the publication. The other two authors were Nicholas D'Ombrain, former deputy secretary for machinery of government in the Privy Council Office, and Bill Neville,

head of the Mulroney transition and long-time advisor to the Conservative Party of Canada.

2 Jeffrey, *Divided Loyalties*.

3 I am indebted to Duncan Edmonds, a long-standing advisor to Liberal and Conservative governments in Ottawa, for reminding me of Kent's book. For more information about the Pearson government transition, see Tom Kent, *A Public Purpose: An Experience of Liberal Opposition and Canadian Government* (Montreal and Kingston: McGill-Queen's University Press, 1988).

4 Brian Mulroney, *Memoirs: 1939–1993* (Toronto: Douglas Gibson Books, 2007).

5 Paul Martin, *Hell or High Water: My Life in and out of Politics* (Toronto: Douglas Gibson Books, 2008).

6 't Hart and Uhr, *How Power Changes Hands*.

7 Ibid, 57.

8 Ibid. 30.

9 Powell, *New Machiavelli*.

10 't Hart and Uhr, *How Power Changes Hands*, chap. 6.

11 Wellford, "Preparing to Be President," 618.

12 Ibid.

Appendix 2. Transitions in Canada since 1984

1 Alan Nymark, former deputy minister of Environment Canada and commissioner of the Canada Revenue Agency, personal communication, 16 June 2011.

2 For an excellent historical overview of the Cabinet system, see Clark, *Recent Changes in the Cabinet Decision Making System*, 185–201.

Select Bibliography

Canada

Aucoin, Peter. "New Political Governance in Westminster Systems: Impartial Public Administration and Management Performance at Risk." *Governance: An International Journal of Policy, Administrations and Institutions* 25, no. 2 (2012): 177–99.

– "New Public Management and the Quality of Government: Coping with the New Political Governance in Canada." Presented at the Conference on New Public Management and the Quality of Government, University of Gothenburg, Sweden, 13–15 November 2008.

– "Prime Minister and Cabinet: Power at the Apex," in *Canadian Politics*, ed. James Bickerton and Alain Gagnon, 3rd ed., 109–26. Peterborough, ON: Broadview, 1999.

Barker, Paul. *Public Administration in Canada, Brief Edition.* City: Thomson Nelson, 2008.

Bartleman, James. *Rollercoaster: My Hectic Years as Jean Chrétien's Diplomatic Advisor.* Toronto: Doug Gibson Books, 2005.

Benoit, Liane. *Ministerial Staff: The Life and Times of Parliament's Statutory Orphans.* Phase II Report, Commission of Inquiry into the Sponsorship Program and Advertising Activities, 2006.

Bernier, L., K. Brownsey, and M. Howlett, eds. *Executive Styles in Canada: Cabinet Structures and Leadership Practices in Canadian Government.* Toronto: University of Toronto Press, 2005.

Bickerton, J., and A.G. Gagnon. *Canadian Politics.* 5th ed. Toronto: University of Toronto Press, Higher Education Division, 2009.

Blakeney, Allan, and Sandford Borins. *Political Management in Canada.* Toronto: McGraw Hill Ryerson, 1992.

Borins, Sandford. *Governing Fables: Learning from Public Sector Narratives.* Charlotte, NC: Information Age Publishing, 2011.

Bourgault, Jacques. *Taking Power: Managing Government Transitions.* Ottawa: Canada School of the Public Service, 1993.

– "The Role of Deputy Ministers in Canadian Government," in *The Handbook of Canadian Public Administration,* ed. Christopher Dunn, 2nd ed., 504–52. Don Mills, ON: Oxford University Press.

Brooks, Stephen. *Canadian Democracy: An Introduction.* 6th ed. Don Mills, ON: Oxford University Press, 2009.

Burney, Derek. *Getting It Done: A Memoir.* Montreal and Kingston: McGill-Queen's University Press, 2005.

– "Getting It Done." *Diplomatic and International Canada Magazine,* May–June 2005.

– "Managing Transition in Government." SCDS-CCISS Strategic Analysis Seminar, Ottawa, 2 February 2011.

Cameron, David, and Graham White. *Cycling into Saigon: The Conservative Transition in Ontario.* Vancouver: UBC Press, 2000.

Cameron, Stevie. *Ottawa Inside Out: Power, Prestige and Scandal in the Nation's Capital.* Toronto: Key Porter Books, 1989.

Chrétien, Jean. *Straight from the Heart.* Toronto: Key Porter Books, 2002.

Clark, Ian. "Recent Changes in the Cabinet Decision Making System in Ottawa." *Canadian Public Administration* 28, no. 2 (1985): 185–201.

Courtney, David C., and David E. Smith. *The Oxford Handbook of Canadian Politics.* Don Mills, ON: Oxford University Press, 2010.

Craft, Jonathan. "Canadian Partisan Advisers and Policy-Making: Currency in the Policy Process or a New Public Governance Bargain?" Presented to the Canadian Political Science Association Annual Meeting, University of Waterloo, May 2011.

Davey, Keith. *The Rainmaker: A Passion for Politics.* Toronto: Stoddard, 1986.

Docherty, David. *Mr Smith Goes to Ottawa: Life in the House of Commons.* Vancouver: UBC Press, 1997.

D'Ombrain, Nicholas. "Cabinet Secrecy." *Canadian Public Administration* 47, no. 3 (2004): 332–59.

– "Ministerial Responsibility and the Machinery of Government." *Canadian Public Administration* 50, no. 2 (2007): 195–217.

Dunn, Christopher. *The Handbook of Canadian Public Administration.* 2nd ed. Don Mills, ON: Oxford University Press, 2010.

Dutil, Patrice, ed., *Searching for Leadership: Secretaries to the Cabinet in Canada.* Toronto: University of Toronto Press, 2008.

Dyck, R., *Canadian Politics: Critical Approaches.* 6th ed. Scarborough: Nelson College Indigenous, 2010.

Flanagan, Tom. *Harper's Team: Behind the Scenes in the Conservative Rise to Power*. 2nd ed. Montreal and Kingston. McGill-Queen's University Press, 2007.

Fraser, Graham. *René Lévesque and the Parti Québécois in Power*. Toronto: Macmillan of Canada, 1984.

Goldenberg, Eddie. *The Way It Works*. Toronto: McClelland and Stewart, 2006.

Inwood, Gregory. *Understanding Canadian Public Administration: An Introduction to Theory and Practice*. 3rd ed. Toronto: Pearson Prentice Hall, 2009.

Jeffrey, Brooke. *Divided Loyalties: The Liberal Party of Canada, 1984–2008*. Toronto: University of Toronto Press, 2011.

Kent, Tom. *A Public Purpose: An Experience of Liberal Opposition and Canadian Government*. Montreal and Kingston: McGill-Queen's University Press, 1988.

Kerby, Matthew. "Worth the Wait: Determinants of Ministerial Appointments in Canada, 1935–2008." *Canadian Journal of Political Science* 42, no. 3 (September 2009): 593–611.

Kernaghan, Ken. "East Block and Westminster: Conventions, Values and Public Service" in Dunn, *Handbook of Canadian Public Administration*, 289–304.

Lavoie, Gilbert. *Jean Pelletier: Combattez en Face*. Quebec, QC: Septentrion, 2009.

Loat, Alison. *The Outsiders Manifesto: Surviving and Thriving as a Member of Parliament*, Report #4. Toronto: Samara, 2011.

Maister, David, Charles Green, and Robert Galford, *The Trusted Advisor*. New York: Touchstone, 2000.

Malcolmson, Patrick, and Richard Myer. *The Canadian Regime: An Introduction to Parliamentary Government in Canada*. Toronto: University of Toronto Press, 2009.

Malkin, Alissa. "Government Reorganization and the Transfer of Powers: Does Certainty Matter?" *Ottawa Law Review* 39, no. 3 (2008): 537.

Mallory, J.R. *The Structure of Canadian Government*. 2nd ed. Toronto: Gage, 1984.

Martin, Lawrence. *Harperland: The Politics of Control*. Toronto: Penguin Canada, 2010.

Martin, Paul. *Hell or High Water: My Life in and Out of Politics*. Toronto: Douglas Gibson Books, 2008.

Neilson, Erik. 1989. *The House Is Not a Home*. Toronto: Macmillan.

Osbaldeston, Gordon. "Dear Minister, Letter to an Old Friend Who Has Just Been Appointed to the Federal Cabinet." *Policy Options* (June–July 1988): 3–11.

– *Keeping Deputy Ministers Accountable*. London, ON: National Centre for Management Research and Development, University of Western Ontario, 1988.

– *Organizing to Govern*. Toronto: McGraw Hill, 1992.

Paikin, Steve. *The Life: The Seductive Call of Politics*. Toronto: Penguin Canada, 2002.

Popp, Brian. *How We Almost Gave the Tories the Boot: The Inside Story behind the Coalition*. Toronto: James Lorimer, 2010.

Privy Council Office. *Accountable Government: A Guide for Ministers and Ministers of State*. Ottawa: Queen's Printer, 2011.

– *Governing Responsibly: A Guide for Ministers and Ministers of State*. Ottawa: Queen's Printer, 2003.

Public Policy Forum. *Directions for Reform: The Views of Current and Former Deputy Ministers on Reforming the Ontario Public Service*. Ottawa: Public Policy Forum, 1995.

– *Towards Guidelines on Government Formation: Facilitating Openness and Efficiency in Canada's Governance*. Final Report. Ottawa: Public Policy Forum, April 2012.

Rae, Bob. *Exporting Democracy: The Risks and Rewards of Pursuing a Good Idea*. Toronto: McClelland and Steward, 2010.

– *From Protest to Power: Personal Reflections on a Life in Politics*. Toronto: McClelland and Stewart, 2006.

Savoie, Donald. "First Ministers, Cabinet and the Public Service," in *The Oxford Handbook of Canadian Politics*, ed. John C. Courtney and David E. Smith. Don Mills, ON: Oxford University Press, 2010.

–, ed. *Taking Power: Managing Government Transitions*. Toronto: IPAC, 1993.

Sharp, Mitchell. *Which Reminds Me ...* Toronto: University of Toronto Press, 1994.

Sossin, Lorne. "Bureaucratic Independence," in Dunn, *Handbook of Canadian Public Administration*, 364–79.

Sutherland, Sharon. "The Consequences of Electoral Volatility: Inexperienced Ministers 1940–1990," in *Representation, Integration and Political Parties*, ed. Herman Bakvis, 303–54. Toronto: Dundurn, 1991.

Wells, Paul. *Right Side Up: The Fall of Paul Martin and the Rise of Stephen Harper's New Conservatism*. Toronto: Doug Gibson/McClelland & Stewart, 2006.

Whittington, Michael, and Richard Van Loon. *Canadian Government and Politics: Institutions and Processes*. Toronto: McGraw Hill, 1996.

White, Graham. *Cabinets and First Ministers: The Canadian Democratic Audit*. Vancouver: UBC Press, 2005.

- "Shorter Measures: The Changing Ministerial Career in Canada." *Canadian Public Administration* 41 (1998): 369–94.

Wilson-Smith, Anthony, and Edward Greenspon. *Double Vision: The Inside Story of the Liberals in Power.* Toronto: Doubleday Canada, 1996.

Zussman, David. "The New Governing Balance: Politicians and Public Servants in Canada." The First Tansley Lecture, Johnson-Shoyama Graduate School of Public Policy, University of Regina, 13 March 2008.

- *Political Advisors.* Expert Group on Conflict of Interest, Public Governance Committee, Public Governance and Territorial Development Directorate. Paris: OECD, May 2009.

United Kingdom

Barker, Anthony, and Graham Wilson. "Whitehall's Disobedient Servants? Senior Officials' Potential Resistance to Ministers in British Government Departments." *British Journal of Political Science* 27 (1997): 223–46.

Bennister, Mark. "Blair and Howard: Predominant Prime Ministers Compared." *Parliamentary Affairs* 61, no. 2 (2008): 335.

Blair, Tony. *A Journey: My Political Life.* Toronto: Knopf Canada, 2010.

Clark, Alan. *Diaries.* London: Phoenix/Orion, 1993.

Dunleavy, Patrick, and Anne White. *Making and Breaking Whitehall Departments: A Guide to Machinery of Government Changes.* London: Institute for Government, 2010.

Errington, Wayne. "Establishing Prime Ministerial Leadership Style in Opposition," in *How Power Changes Hands: Transition and Succession in Government,* ed. Paul 't Hart and John Uhr. Basingstoke, UK: Palgrave Macmillan, 2011.

Hazell, Robert, and Akash Paun, eds. *Making Minority Government Work: Hung Parliaments and the Challenges for Westminster and Whitehall.* London: Institute for Government, 2009.

Hennessy, Peter. *Cabinet.* London: Basil Blackwell, 1986.

- *Whitehall.* London: Pimlico, 2001.

James, Simon. *British Cabinet Government.* 2nd ed. London: Routledge, 1999.

Kaufman, Gerald. *How to Be a Minister.* London: Faber and Faber, 1997.

Kavanagh, D., and A. Seldon. *The Powers behind the Prime Minister: The Hidden Influence of Number Ten.* London: Harper Collins, 2000.

Laver, M., and K.A. Shepsle, eds. *Making and Breaking Governments: Cabinets and Legislatures in Parliamentary Democracies.* Cambridge: Cambridge University Press, 1996.

Marsh, D., D. Richards, and M.J. Smith. "Unequal Power: Towards an Asymmetric Model of the British Polity." *Government and Opposition* 38 (2003): 306–22.

Mcnaughton, N. *The Prime Minister and Cabinet Government*. London: Hodder Education, 1999.

Parker, Simon, Akash Paun, and Jonathan McClory. *The State of the Service: A Review of Whitehall's Performance and Prospects for Improvement*. London: Institute for Government, 2009.

Powell, Jonathan. *The New Machiavelli: How to Wield Power in the Modern World*. London: Bodley Head, 2010.

Rhodes, Rod A.W. *Everyday Life in British Government*. Oxford: Oxford University Press, 2011.

– *Understanding Governance: Policy Networks, Governance, Reflexivity, and Accountability*. Bristol, PA: Open University Press, 1997.

–, ed. *Public Administration: 25 Years of Analysis and Debate, 1986–2011*. Oxford: Wiley-Blackwell, 2011.

Richards, David. *New Labour and the Civil Service: Reconstituting the Westminster System*. London: Palgrave, 2008.

– "Sustaining the Westminster Model: A Case Study of the Transition in Power between Political Parties in British Government." *Parliamentary Affairs* 62, no. 1 (2009): 108–28.

Riddell, Peter, and Catherine Haddon. *Transitions: Preparing for Changes in Government*. London: Institute for Government, 2009.

Robinson, Geoffrey. *The Unconventional Minister: My Life inside New Labour*. London: Penguin, 2001.

Rutter, Jill. *Are Our Media Threatening the Public Good?* London: Institute for Government, 2010.

Trusswell, Emma, and David Atkinson. "Supporting Heads of Government: A Comparison across Six Countries." Working paper, Institute for Government, London, 2011.

United Kingdom, Cabinet Office. *Machinery of Government Changes: Best Practice Handbook*.

United States

Brandeis, Louis. *Other People's Money and How Bankers Use It*. New York: F.A. Stokes, 1914.

Brauer, Carl. *Presidential Transitions: Eisenhower to Reagan*. Oxford University Press, 1986.

Burke, John. *Becoming President: The Bush Transition, 2000–2003*. Boulder, CO: Lynne Rienner, 2004.

– "Lessons from Past Presidential Transitions: Organization, Management, and Decision-Making." *Presidential Studies Quarterly* 31, no. 1 (2001): 5–24.

– *Presidential Transitions: From Politics to Practice*. Boulder, CO: Lynne Rienner, 2000.

Burns, James McGregor. *Leadership*. New York: Harper and Row, 1978.

Daly, Peter, and Michael Watkins. *The First 90 Days in Government: Critical Success Strategies for New Public Managers at All Levels*. Cambridge, MA: Harvard Business Press, 2006.

Held, David. *Models of Democracy*. 3rd ed. Stanford: Stanford University Press, 2006.

Helms, Ludger. "Governing in the Media Age: The Impact of Mass Media on Executive Leadership in Contemporary Democracies." *Government and Opposition* 43, no. 1 (2008).

Hess, Stephen. *What Do We Do Now? A Workbook for the President-Elect*. Washington, DC: Brookings Institution, 2008.

Johnson, Clay. "Recommendations for an Effective 2008 Transition." *Public Administration Review* 68, no. 4 (2008): 624–6.

Jones, Charles, ed. *Preparing to Be President: The Memos of Richard Neustadt*. Washington: American Enterprise Press, 2000.

Kumar, Martha. "Getting Ready for Day One: Taking Advantage of the Opportunities and Minimizing the Hazards of the Presidential Transition." *Public Administration Review* 68, no. 4 (2008): 603–17.

Kumar, Martha Joynt, and Terry Sullivan, eds. *The White House World: Transitions, Organization, and Office Operations*. College Station: Texas A & M University Press, 2003.

Light, Paul. "Recommendations Forestalled or Forgotten? The National Commission on the Public Service and Presidential Appointments." *Public Administration Review* 67, no. 3 (2007): 408–17.

Ludger, Peter. "Governing in the Media Age: The Impact of Mass Media on Executive Leadership in Contemporary Democracies." *Government and Opposition: An International Journal of Comparative Politics* 43, no. 1 (2008): 26–54.

Morehouse, M. "The Transition: Preparing for the Next President." *Congressional Quarterly Weekly Report* 45 (1987): 2745–6.

Neustadt, Richard. "Neustadt Advises the Advisers in 2000," in *Preparing to Be President: The Memos of Richard E. Neustadt*, ed. Charles Jones, 143–72. Washington, DC: American Enterprise Institute, 2000.

– "Presidential Transitions: Are the Risks Rising?" *Miller Center Journal* (Spring 1994): 4–7.

Newsweek. "Warm-up Lessons: Clinton's Transition Was a Slow and Messy Process. But a Glimpse Inside His Administration-in-Progress Provides Clues to How He May Govern." 25 January 1993, 30.

Pfiffner, James P. *The Strategic Presidency: Hitting the Ground Running.* Studies in Government and Public Policy. Lawrence: University Press of Kansas, 1996.

Reich, Robert. *Locked in the Cabinet.* New York: Vintage Books, 1998.

Roth, Guenter, and Claus Wittich, eds. *Max Weber: The Theory of Economic and Social Organizations.* 2 vols. Berkeley: University of California Press, 1968.

Smith, Stephanie. *Presidential Transitions.* Report no. RS20709. Washington, DC: Congressional Research Service, 2007.

Wellford, Harrison. "Avoiding the Hazards of Transition: Neustadt's Lessons," in *Guardian of the Presidency: The Legacy of Richard E. Neustadt*, ed. Matthews Dickenson and Elizabeth Neustadt, 52–74. Washington, DC: Brookings Institution, 2007.

– "Preparing to Be President on Day One." *Public Administration Review* (July/August 2008).

Woodward, Bob. *Obama's Wars.* New York: Simon and Schuster, 2010.

Australia

Australia. Department of the Prime Minister and Cabinet. *Cabinet Handbook.* 6th ed. Canberra: Department of the Prime Minister and Cabinet Government, 2009.

– "Guidance on Caretaker Conventions, 2010.

Davis, Glyn, and Michael Keating, eds. *The Future of Governance: Policy Choices.* St Leonards, New South Wales: Allen and Unwin, 2000.

Holland, Ian. Government of Australia, Department of Parliamentary Library, *Accountability of Ministerial Staff?* Research Paper, No. 19, 2001–2002.

't Hart, Paul, and John Uhr, eds. *How Power Changes Hands: Transition and Succession in Government.* Basingstoke, UK: Palgrave Macmillan, 2011.

Tiernan, Anne. *Power without Responsibility: Ministerial Staffers in Australian Governments from Whitlam to Howard.* Sydney: University of New South Wales Press, 2007.

– "Problem or Solution? The Role of Ministerial Staff," in *Motivating Ministers to Morality*, ed. J. Fleming and I. Holland, 91–106. London: Ashgate, 2001.

Tiernan, Anne, and Jennifer Menzies. *Caretaker Conventions in Australasia: Minding the Shop for Government.* Canberra: Australian National University Press, 2007.

Tiernan, Anne, and Patrick Weller. *Learning to Be a Minister: Heroic Expectations, Practical Realities.* Melbourne: Melbourne University Press, 2010.

Weller, Patrick. *Australia's Mandarins: The Frank and the Fearless?* Sydney: Allen and Unwin, 2001.

– *Cabinet Government in Australia, 1901–2006.* Sydney: University of New South Wales Press, 2007.

New Zealand

New Zealand. Cabinet Office. *Cabinet Manual.* 2008

Index

Page numbers in boldface refer to figures and tables.

Access to Information Act, 116–17
Accountable Government: Guide for Ministers and Secretaries of State, 162–3
Archdeacon, Maurice, 44
Armstrong, Sir Robert, 62–3
Ashworth, Gordon, 14–15, 46
Aucoin, Peter, 31–2
Austin, Jack, 41
Australia: public service guidelines, 64–5, 216; three-tier Cabinet, 88
Axworthy, Tom, 41–2
Aylmer Conference, 45, 55

Bank of Canada: governor appointment, 85
Bennister, Mark, 24
Bichard, Michael, 65–6
bilingualism policy: deputy ministers, 117
Blair, Tony: Cabinet-making, 91, 93, 159, 168; first meetings, 143, 180; guidelines for meeting the opposition party, 65–6; inexperience of newly elected government, 5–6; leadership style, 24, 209; political advisors, 31, 33; time management style, 53–4; transition team, 7
Blunkett, David, 65–6
Boudria, Don, 28
Brandeis, Louis, 211
briefing materials. *See* transition materials
Brodie, Ian, 44, 96–7, 132–5, 138, 141, 143, 167–8
Bryce, Bob, 33
Burke, John, 6, 147
Burn, Peter, 44
Burney, Derek: advisor on deputy minister appointments, 101; appointment as chief of staff, 169–70; political staff of majority government, 172–3; transition team, Brian Mulroney, 48, 131, 169–70, 184–5; transition team confidentiality, 156–7; transition team, Stephen Harper, 29–30, 43, 75, 87, 138, 142, 167–8, 178, 206
Bush, George H.W.: role of spouse, 57
Bush, George W., 7

Butler, Landon, 147
Butler, Robin, 7, 143

Cabinet: confidentiality, 94–5;
ministerial behaviour code of
conduct guidelines, 162–3, 166;
newly elected ministers' inexperience, 217; performance measurement, 202–3; size, 41, 86–7, 97, 152,
157–8, 205; swearing-in ceremony
procedures, 147–9
Cabinet-making: appointment of
secretary, 99; candidate interviews,
160–2, 164–8; candidate interviews with prime minister-elect,
167–8; criteria for selection, 89–93,
155–68; decision making, 75–6;
influence of spouse, 56; input
from clerk of Privy Council, 67–8;
key Cabinet positions, 92–3, 162;
mandate letters, 93–4; Minister of
Finance, 92; Minister of Foreign
Affairs, Trade and Development,
93; ministers' personal health
disclosure, 167; ministers' security
clearance, 166–7; one-tier ministry,
87; prime minister-elect informing
candidates, 168; shadow Cabinet
ministers, 91; size, 41, 86–7, 97,
152, 157–8, 205; structure, 87–9;
swearing-in ceremony, 144–5;
three-tier ministry, 88–9; tiers of
Cabinet, 158–9; transition team
confidentiality, 156–7; two-tier
ministry, 87–8, 89; vetting process,
160, 165–8, 208
Cabinet secretary, 34, 66, 95, 99
Cameron, David, 5
Campbell, Kim: Cabinet-making,
87; governor-in-council appointment, 108; leadership race, 15, 17;

leadership style, 108; machinery-
of-government restructuring, 18,
97; outgoing government request,
150; outgoing prime minister,
146–7; Prime Minister's Office
(PMO) staff selection, 171; transition planning, 113
Carle, Jean: expectations of transition team, 42–3; head of operations, PMO, 28; post-election
phase, 52, 129, 137; security for
prime minister-elect, 135
Carson, Bruce, 44, 132
Carter, Jimmy, 6, 52
caucus and party liaison: role in
Prime Minister's Office (PMO), 81
caucus management: prime minister,
70, 200–1
Charette, Janice, 171
chief of staff. See under Prime Minister's Office (PMO)
Chrétien, Jean: consolidation phase:
first Cabinet meeting, 182–3, 184;
government priorities, 195; leadership style, 184; newly elected ministers, advice, 199; newly elected
ministers' orientation sessions,
189–92; relationship with public
service, 194–5; role of deputy
ministers, 195; management style
as leader of the opposition, 26–8;
memoir, 8; performance measurement of re-elected government,
202–3; post-election phase:
appointment of Kim Campbell,
108; Cabinet-making screening
process, 164–8; Cabinet-making
size, 28, 152, 157–8; governor-in-
council reform, 84; machinery-of-
government restructuring, 97;
management style, 26–8, 206;

mandate letters, 93–4, 178–9;
media strategy, 101–3; opposition parties, 137; public service
as source of policy advice, 207–8;
security for prime minister-elect,
135; size of ministers' staff, 207–8;
transition team, 46–7; vetting
process for new ministers, 208;
pre-election phase: expectations
of transition team, 42–3; policy
commitments, 52–3; policymaking skills, 54–5; relationship with
caucus, 70–1; relationship with
Jean Pelletier, 26–8; relationship
with public service, 33–4; transition planning: communication
style, 71; Gantt chart, 71; transition
materials, 112; transition team
mandate, 44–5; transition team
media strategy, 36; transition team
meetings, 41–3, 46–7; transition
team priority setting, 51–2
Clark, Ian, 87
Clark, Joe: transition teams and
media coverage, 128
clerk of the Privy Council Office
(PCO). *See under* Privy Council
Office (PCO)
Clinton, Bill, 6, 7, 52, 134
Collenette, David, 70, 158–9
Collenette, Penny, 46, 84
Collins, Jim, 206
communications director: role in
Prime Minister's Office (PMO),
80–1
communications tool, 119–24
*Conflict of Interest and Post-Employment
Code for Public Office Holders,* 163
Conservative Party of Canada, 4, 14,
15, 17, 172, 187, 207. See also *names
of party leaders*

consolidation phase (Phase Four):
activities during, 176–7; caucus
management, 193–200; chief of
staff role, 201; conclusion of transition team, 203; consolidation of
power, 21–2; deputy ministers,
193–200; first Cabinet meetings,
180–5; government priorities, 195;
mandate letters, 177–80; newly
elected ministers' inexperience,
185–8; newly elected ministers'
orientation sessions, 188–93;
newly elected ministers' training and mentoring, 215, 217; one
hundred days, 4–5; public service
partisanship, 196

Dean, Tony, 62, 66, 67, 151
DeCotret report, 17–18
Department of Finance: election
phase transition planning, 113
deputy ministers: appointments,
101; assistant deputy minister,
117–18; bilingualism policy, 117;
first meeting with newly elected
ministers, 199–200; mandate letters, influencing, 179–80; relationship with ministers, 69, 115–24,
186–7, 193–200; role of, 195; support to incoming government, 152;
transition materials for ministers,
59–61, 116–24; transition planning,
114–18
deputy prime minister (DPM), 84,
92, 103, 112
deputy secretary of plans: appointment, 58
Dicerni, Richard, 115
Docherty, David, 155
D'Ombrain, Nicholas, 58–9, 63,
141–2

Donolo, Peter, 46, 206
"Douglas Home rules," 65–6

Ehrenworth, Shelley, 45
election phase (Phase Two): ac-
    tivities during, 4, 18–19, 105–10;
    departmental perspective, 118–24;
    government policy decisions,
    107; governor-in-council appoint-
    ment, 108; level of effort, 105–7,
    111–12; partisanship of public
    service, 105–9, 216–17; political
    perspective, 110–12; public service
    perspective, 113–18; role of public
    service towards opposition party,
    216–17; transition planning and
    opposition party, 106–7, 111–12;
    transition planning and Privy
    Council Office (PCO), 113; transi-
    tion team review of government
    pr' cesses, 110–11
election team: relationship with tran-
    sition team, 52–3
ethical standards, 79, 162, 164, 181,
    208
executive assistant: role in Prime
    Minister's Office (PMO), 80
exempt staff: appointments, 76;
    ministers' offices, 82

failed candidates: communication
    from prime minister, 200–1
Fairburn, Joyce, 46
Farrabie, Michael, 171
Federal Accountability Act (FAA), 31
federal departments: election phase
    transition planning, 114–18
first meetings: Cabinet, 180–5;
    deputy ministers with ministers,
    199–200; prime minister-elect,

135–9, 140–7, 194–5; transition
    team and clerk of the Privy
    Council, 139–40, 141
Fitzpatrick, Ross, 46
Fortier, Michael, 89–90
Fraser, Paul, 171

Gagnier, Dan, 45
Gallant, Edgar, 33
Gantt chart: transition planning
    model, 71
Goldenberg, Eddie: author, *The Way
    It Works*, 8; Cabinet-making, 155;
    performance measurement of
    re-elected government, 202–3;
    policy issues, 149; Prime Minister's
    Office (PMO), 46; staffing Office
    of the Leader of the Opposition
    (OLO), 26; transition planning,
    41–2
governance structure: characteris-
    tics, 205
Governor General: relationship with
    prime minister-elect, 144–5
governor-in-council (GIC): appoint-
    ments, 82–5, 108, 174
Gray, Herb, 70, 85, 208
Guidelines for Ministers' Offices, 163

Harper, Laureen: role of spouse, 56
Harper, Stephen: election phase:
    relationship with public service,
    107; rules of behaviour of public
    service, 216; *Harperland*, 28;
    leadership style, 29; lobbyists, 44,
    47; management style, 26, 29–30,
    159; minority prime minister vs.
    majority prime minister, 29–30;
    National Citizens Coalition, 47;
    post-election phase: first meetings

with clerk of the Privy Council,
139–40, 141; meeting with outgoing prime minister, 145; newly
elected minority government,
131–2; planning strategy, 129;
prime minister-elect first meetings, 142; prime minister-elect
security, 134–5; prime minister-
elect stature, 133; psychological
change, 130–2; role of spouse:
Laureen Harper, 56; transition
planning: Cabinet-making, 87,
89–90, 156–7, 167–8; deputy
minister appointments, 101; lack
of planning, 110; machinery-
of-government restructuring,
96–7; mandate letters, 93–4, 178;
relationship with clerk of Privy
Council, 69; transition materials,
75; transition team: meets prime
minister-elect, 138; public service
support, 151
Harris, Mike, 5
Hartley, Bruce, 206
Hess, Stephen, 130
Himelfarb, Alex: appointment as
ambassador to Italy, 145; consolidation phase: public service partisanship, 196; election phase: level
of effort of deputy ministers, 114;
post-election phase: first meetings with transition team, 139–40,
141, 143; relationship with chief
of staff, 169; pre-election phase:
meeting with opposition, 68; relationship with prime minister, 69;
transition materials, 60, 62
Hnatyshyn, Ray, 118
Hosek, Chaviva, 46, 202–3, 206
Howard, John, 210

"Hundred and Fifty Day Book," 60
Hurtubise, Suzanne, 171

incoming government. See newly
elected government
intra-party leadership change, 4, 15,
16–17, 97

Jeffrey, Brooke, 55
Joynt Kumar, Martha, 129–30, 147
judicial appointments, 85

Kaufman, Gerald, 90, 187–8
Kervin, Miles, 171
Kroeger, Arthur, 41, 46–7, 101, 128, 141

LaRocque, Judith, 59–60, 197
Lavoie, Gilbert, 27–8
Liberal Party of Canada: leadership,
14–16; level of effort during election phase, 106–7; mandate letters,
178–9; as opposition party, 26, 45;
policymaking, 55, 207; transition
planning, 193. See also names of
party leaders
lobbyists: connection to government,
47; connection to transition teams,
36, 44; legislation, 47
Lumley, Ed, 70, 192–3
Lutfy, Allan, 164–7
Lynch, Kevin, 16, 20, 34–5, 63

Macdonald, Sir John A., 155
machinery-of-government: DeCotret
report, 17–18; principles of, 95–6;
restructuring and transition planning, 95–8
Major, John, 7
majority government: staff recruitment, 172–3

mandate letters: prime ministers to ministers, 22; structure of, 177–9; timing of, 93–4

Manley, John, 84–5, 186–7, 192–3

Martin, Lawrence, 28–9, 131–2

Martin, Paul: Cabinet-making, 17, 41, 86–7, 97, 156; intra-party transition, 15, 17; machinery-of-government restructuring, 97; management style, 28–9; media relations, 36, 128; meeting outgoing prime minister, 145; Minister of Finance, 156; ministers not appointed to Cabinet, 201; prime minister-elect stature, 133–4; public service partisanship, 216–17; role of spouse, 56; transition planning, 8, 113; transition team, 41

Martin, Sheila: role of spouse, 56

Maxwell, Judith, 45

McGuinty, Dalton, 66

McLellan, Anne, 148

media: coverage during post-election phase, 127–8; prime minister-elect, 36, 128; role in transitions, 12, 35–7, 101–3; transition planning strategy, 76; U.S. president-elect, 127

Members of Parliament. See ministers

Miliband, David, 7

ministerial staff. See under ministers; ministers' offices

Minister of Finance: appointment, 92–3; candidate interview, 156

Minister of Foreign Affairs, Trade and Development: appointment, 93

Minister of Justice: Rock, Allan, newly elected minister, 187

ministers: ethics, 164; failed candidates, 200–1; mandate letters,

93–4; ministerial staff selection guidelines, 163–4; not appointed to Cabinet, 200–1; performance measurement of re-elected government, 202–3; relationship with deputy minister, 69, 115–24, 186–7, 193–200; relationship with political advisors, 32–3; relationship with public service, 115–18, 164; vetting process, 208. See also newly elected ministers

ministers' offices: departmental assistants, 82; exempt staff, 82; political staff, 81–2; staff selection and experience, 172–3

Ministry of Foreign Affairs, Trade and Development: appointment, 93

minority government: emergence of "permanent election," 37–8; leadership style, 29–30; management style, 131–2; outcome of popular vote, 205

Mitchell, Jim, 96, 122, 131, 144

MP. See ministers

Mulroney, Brian: leadership style, 184–5; lobbyists, 108; management of caucus, 81; management style, 29; ministers' staff, 207; partisanship of PMO, 78; patronage appointments, 84; post-election phase: Cabinet-making, 90, 160–2, 164; chief of staff selection, 131, 169–70; decision-making, 128–9; first meetings with clerk of the Privy Council, 142; meeting outgoing prime minister, 145–6; public service staffing changes, 100–1; role of spouse, 55–7; transition materials, 75; transition planning, 8; transition team, 43, 48

Mulroney, Mila: role of spouse, 55–7
Murphy, Tim, 16, 46, 169
Muttart, Patrick, 129

National Citizens Coalition, 29, 47
Neustadt, Richard, 30
Neville, Bill: Cabinet-making, 86, 91, 160–2, 168; first meeting with clerk of the Privy Council, 142; leader of transition team, 43; prime ministers and decision-making, 128–9; professionalization of transition planning, 204; public service staffing, 100–1; relationship with clerk of the Privy Council Office, 131; transition materials, 145–6
New Democratic Party of Canada: level of effort during election phase, 106
newly elected government: leadership style, 209–10; ministers' offices staff selection and experience, 170–4; newly elected ministers' training, 215, 217; policy issues, 149–50; relationship with public service, 213–14. See also prime minister-elect
newly elected ministers: early days, 185–93; inexperience, 19–20, 21; knowledge base, 217; mentoring, 192–3; orientation sessions, 190–2, 215; reaction to first Cabinet meeting, 184; relationship with deputy minister, 193, 198–200; relationship with public service, 189–90; transition materials and training, 121–3. See also ministers
newly elected prime minister. See prime minister-elect
Nicholson, Peter, 128

Nielsen, Eric, 43
Norquay, Geoff, 55–7

Obama, Barack, 135–6
O'Donnell, Sir Gus, 11, 113
Office of the Leader of the Opposition (OLO): chief of staff, 26–8; management style of leader, 26; post-election phase, 137
Official Languages Act, 117
Official Opposition party: level of transition planning during election, 106–7; pre-election relationship with Privy Council Office (PCO), 64–8. See also Office of the Leader of the Opposition (OLO); opposition parties
O'Hara, Kathy, 143
OLO. See Office of the Leader of the Opposition (OLO)
one hundred days. See transition periods: consolidation phase
Ontario: government transition: relationship with public service, 195–6; government transition planning, 5, 62, 66, 67
Ontario New Democratic Party: transition and relationship with public service, 195–6
opposition parties: psychological change in post-election phase, 132–4; transition planning in election phase, 106–7, 111–12; transition planning rules for public service behaviour, 216–17; transition team, 137. See also Office of the Leader of the Opposition (OLO); Official Opposition party
orientation sessions: newly elected ministers' outlines, 190–2
Osbaldeston, Gordon, 142, 198–9

outgoing governments: policy
issues, 149–50; requests, 150
outgoing prime ministers: meeting
prime minister-elect, 145–7; moving out of official residences, 146;
rituals of transition, 137–8

Paikin, Steve, 201
Panetta, Leon, 6–7
Parisot, Patrick, 206
partisanship: appointments, 83–4;
public service during consolidation
phase, 196; public service during election phase, 105–9, 216–17;
public service during post-election
phase, 140–2; public service during
pre-election phase, 42
patronage appointments, 83–4
PCO. See Privy Council Office (PCO)
Pelletier, Jean: chief of staff, 80,
212; chief of staff, Office of the
Leader of the Opposition (OLO),
26–8; evaluating staff, Office of
the Leader of the Opposition
(OLO), 206; Liberal candidate,
70–1; performance measurement
of re-elected government, 202–3;
relationship with Jean Chrétien,
26–8; transition materials, 122;
transition planning, 41–2; transition team, 46, 137
performance measurement, 202–3
"permanent election" campaign:
minority governments, 37–8
phases of transition. See transition
periods
Philogène, Simone: prime minister-
elect and Cabinet-making, 155;
transition in Office of the Official
Opposition, 137; transition team
member, 22, 45; transition teams,

personal and professional relationships, 47–9; transitioning out
of power, 150
PMO. See Prime Minister's Office
(PMO)
policy advisors: role in Prime Minister's Office (PMO), 80
policy issues: bilingualism, 117;
Liberal Party policymaking, 55,
207; newly elected government,
149–50; policy advisors, 26–7,
30–5, 80; policy decisions, 107,
108, 212; policy development, 49,
77–8, 207, 211; prime minister and
policymaking skills, 54–5; public
service advice, 207–8
political advisors: accountability,
211–12; Federal Accountability Act
(FAA), 31; historical context, 31–2;
importance of role in transition
planning, 210–12; policy advice,
31; recruitment, 31–2; relationship
with ministers, 32–3; relationship
with public service, 32–3; role of,
30–3
political parties. See *individual party
names*
political staff. See *under* ministers;
ministers' offices
post-election phase (Phase Three):
activities during, 20, 126, 154–5; appointments, 174; Cabinet-making,
90, 155–68; length of, 130; media
coverage, 127–8; ministerial behaviour, 162–8; outgoing government
requests, 150; policy issues, 149–50;
prime minister-elect first meetings, 135–47; psychological change,
132–4; public service and partisanship, 140–2; public service support
to transition team, 150–2; staffing

ministers' offices, 172–3; staffing Prime Minister's Office (PMO), 168–71; stature of prime minister-elect, 133–4; swearing-in ceremony procedures, 147–9

Powell, Jonathan, 7, 24–5, 79, 91, 92, 143

power transfer. *See* transition periods

pre-election phase (Phase One): activities during, 18, 39–40; deputy secretary of plans in PCO, 58; partisanship during, 42; preparation for leadership, 53–5; priorities, 51–2; public service guidelines for meeting the opposition party, 65–6; role of clerk of the Privy Council Office (PCO), 57–8; role of public service vs. role of transition team, 63; transition materials, 59–61, 60, 62; transition planning duties, 58–63; transition planning in Privy Council Office (PCO), 58–63; transition team expectations, 42–3; transition team relationship with caucus, 70–1; transition team relationship with election team, 52–3; transition team relationship with opposition, 68; transition team relationship with public service, 39, 75–6; transition team timing, 40–9

Presidential Transitions Act, 7

prime minister-elect: activities during consolidation phase, 176–7; appointment of chief of staff, 168–70; Cabinet: first meetings, 180–5; management, 180–1; Cabinet-making: candidate interviews, 160–2, 165–8; choosing party colleagues, 155–6; informing candidates, 168; key Cabinet positions, 162; selection criteria, 155–68; vetting process, 160, 165–8, 208; first Cabinet meeting, 184–5; first meetings with Privy Council Office (PCO), 140–4; first meetings with the Governor General, 144–5; mandate letters to ministers, 177–80; meeting transition team, 138–9; preparation for leadership, 53–5; psychological change, 132–4; relationship with chief of staff, 136–7; relationship with outgoing prime minister, 145–7; relationship with Privy Council Office (PCO), 136–7, 213–14; relationship with the Governor General, 144–5; rituals of transition with outgoing prime minister, 137–8; security, 134–5, 141; stature, 133–4. *See also* post-election phase

prime ministers: appointments to the Prime Minister's Office (PMO), 78; Cabinet-making planning phase, 75–6, 86–95; caucus management, 200–1; chief of staff selection, 75; communication skills, 25, 71; decision-making, 21–2, 75–6; decision-making, governor-in-council appointments, 85; deputy prime minister (DPM) appointment, 92; failed candidates, meeting with, 200–1; first Cabinet meeting goals, 183–4; interpersonal skills, 25; intra-party transitions, 4, 15, 16–17; leadership style, 23–30, 53–5, 94, 209–10; machinery-of-government restructuring, 95–8; management skills, 24–6, 50, 53–7, 72; mandate letters, 22, 93–4; media relations, 128;

ministers not appointed to
Cabinet, meeting with, 200–1;
personal relationship with clerk of
the Privy Council, 68–70; philosophy of government, 50; policymaking skills, 54–5; re-elected,
15–16; relationship with caucus,
70–1; relationship with clerk of
the Privy Council, 22, 42, 98–101,
212–14; relationship with deputy
minister, 193–5; relationship with
public service, 33–6, 42, 46–7,
50–1, 193–5; relationship with the
media, 36–7; relationship with
transition team, 50; role of spouse,
55–7; time management, 53–4, 80
Prime Minister's Office (PMO):
caucus and party liaison, role of,
81; chief of staff: relationship with
prime minister, 26–8; relationship
with prime minister-elect, 136–7;
relationship with the clerk of the
Privy Council, 169, 212–14; role,
79–80, 201; selection, 75, 168–9;
communications director, role of,
80–1; executive assistant, role of,
80; exempt staff appointments, 76;
first meetings with Privy Council
Office (PCO), 140–4; leadership
roles, 78–82; partisan appointments, 78, 210–12; performance
measurement of re-elected government, 202–3; policy advisors,
80; principal secretary, 41; relationship with Privy Council Office
(PCO), 22, 77–8, 98–101, 131; role,
77–9; senior policy advisor, role of,
80; staff selection, 22, 31–2, 40, 75,
76–7, 168–71, 206
principal secretary. See under Prime
Minister's Office (PMO)

Priorities and Planning Committee,
88, 89, 95
Privy Council Office (PCO): clerk of
the Privy Council Office (PCO):
advisor on deputy minister appointments, 101; first meetings
with prime minister-elect, 140–4;
first meetings with transition
team, 139–43; meeting with opposition, 20; partisanship, 69, 99–100;
relationship with chief of staff,
169, 212–14; relationship with
Official Opposition party, 64–8;
relationship with prime minister,
33–5, 68–70, 98–101; relationship
with transition team, 57–8, 113,
150–2; role, 34–5; role during pre-
election phase, 57–8; timing of
appointment, 99; deputy secretary
of plans, appointment, 58; ideology and incoming government, 61;
transition material preparation,
59–61; transition planning duties,
58–63. See also public service
Public Policy Forum, 11, 216–17
public service: caretaker role during
election phase, 109; code of conduct, 100; departmental assistants
in ministers' offices, 82; hallmark
of, 62; ideology and incoming
government, 61; importance of
orientation for newly elected
ministers, 215; key appointments,
98–101; partisanship during
consolidation phase, 196; partisanship during election phase,
105–9, 216–17; partisanship during
post-election phase, 99–100, 140–2;
policy advice, 207–8; relationship
with newly elected government,
22, 33–6, 193–5, 213–14; relationship

with political advisors, 32–3; relationship with Prime Minister's Office (PMO), 69–70, 212–14; role during election phase, 109; role of, 34–5; rules for behaviour with opposition party, 65–6, 216–17; support to incoming government, 152; support to transition team, 150–2. *See also* Privy Council Office (PCO)

Rae, John, 41–2, 46
Rasminsky, Louis, 33
Reagan, Ronald, 6
Red Book, 182, 189
re-elected governments: ministers' performance measurement, 201–3; type of transition, 4, **15**–16
Reich, Robert, 134, 173
Reisman, Simon, 33
Robinson, Mike, 17, 41, 55–7, 86–7
Rock, Allan, 148, 184, 187
Roscoe, Elizabeth, 44, 46, 48
Rosenberg, Morris, 123
Roy, Bernard, 131
Royal Canadian Mounted Police (RCMP): security for prime minister-elect, 134–5

Santi, Roberta, 151
Savoie, Donald, 45
Schreiber, Karlheinz: gifts to minister, 187
secretaries of state: orientation sessions, 190–2
Segal, Hugh, 48
senior policy advisor: role in Prime Minister's Office (PMO), 80
Sharp, Mitchell, 70, 164–8
Shortliffe, Glen: clerk of the Privy Council Office (PCO), 108, 140, 144–5, 152, 171

Speaker, Ray, 44
Swain, Harry, 186–7
swearing-in ceremony: first meetings with prime minister and Governor General, 144–5; procedures, 147–9

Tait, John, 20, 187
Tellier, Paul, 131
't Hart, Paul, 24, 209
The First 90 Days, 185–6
The Way It Works, 8
Tobin, Brian, 70
transfer of power. *See* transition periods
transition materials: amount of, 122–3; deputy ministers for ministers, 59–61, 182–3; importance of, 118–24; legislation, 116–17; outline, 112; preparation, 60, 62, 75
transition periods: consolidation phase (Phase Four), 4–5, 21–2, 176–203; election phase (Phase Two), 4, 18–19, 105–25; evolution of four phases, **106**; guidelines, 66; key players, 23; length of, 4–5; political advisors, 30–3; post-election phase (Phase Three), 20, 126–75; pre-election phase (Phase One), 18, 22, 39–73; types, 12, **15**. *See also* consolidation phase (Phase Four); election phase (Phase Two); post-election phase (Phase Three); pre-election phase (Phase One)
transition planning: changes in, 214–15; communication, 71; cornerstones of, 208–9; facilitating leadership style, 209–10; federal vs. provincial transitions, 9–10; Gantt chart, 71; historical analyses, 8–9; issues for transition team, 206–8;

objectives of, 9; outstanding issues of transition planning, 215–17; parallel issues with transition teams and public service, 63; perceptions of, 7–9; phases of, 11–12; policy issues for political staffers, 207–8; political advisors, changing role, 210–12; professionalization of, 204; relationship with public service, 39, 75–6; relationship-building with key players, 212–14; reluctance to discuss, 7–9; rules for public service behaviour with opposition parties, 216–17; seminars, 11; staffing issues, 206; success of, 30, 205

transition process: departmental perspective, 118–24; phases of, 4–5, 18, **19**–23; political perspective, 110–12; public service perspective, 113–18; as Shakespearean play, 4; strategy, 5; types of transitions, 4, 14–18, **15**

transition teams: Cabinet-making plans, 90, 159–60; Campbell, Kim, 17; Chrétien, Jean: expectations, 42–3; Gantt chart model, 71; mandate, 44–5; media strategy, 36; meeting agenda, 45; post-election team, 46–7; priority setting, 51–2; reaction to transfer of power, 137; secrecy, 22; transition materials, 112; transition planning, 41–2; working with, 206–8; consolidation phase: conclusion of team, 203; newly elected ministers, mentoring, 192–3; newly elected ministers' orientation sessions, 188–93; criteria for selection of members, 214; election phase: role

during, 109–10; Harper, Stephen: first meetings, 139–40; lack of transition planning, 110; leader of team, 43; management style, 29–30; public service support, 151; relationship with Privy Council Office, 61; working with, 206; issues, 206–8; key players, 23–35; mandate letter preparation, 93–4; mandates, 44–5; Martin, Paul: Cabinet-making, 17; media strategy, 36; members, 46; transition planning, 41; media strategy, 35–7, 101–3, 128; member experience, 47–8; Mulroney, Brian, 43, 48; outstanding issues of transition planning, 215–17; personal and professional relationships, 47–9; post-election phase: first meetings with clerk of the Privy Council, 139–40; meeting prime minister-elect, 138–9; pre-election phase: appointment, 22; meeting with clerk of the Privy Council, 57–8; priority setting, 51–2; recruitment, 43–4; relationship with caucus, 70; relationship with election team, 52–3; relationship with Privy Council Office (PCO), 57–8, 61–3; relationship with public service, 39, 75–6; role of, 49–52; secrecy, 7–8, 22–3, 36–7, 47–8; selection of leader, 49; timing, 40–9

Trudeau, Pierre Elliott, 26–7, 97
Truman, Harry S., 145
Turner, John, 97, 145–6
types of transitions: intra-party leadership change, 4, 15, 16–17; transitions as a result of general

election: change in governing party, 4, 14–**15**; re-elected government, 4, **15**–16

United Kingdom: consolidation phase: newly elected ministers' orientation sessions, 192; newly elected ministers, advice, 186–8; election phase: rules for public service behaviour with opposition, 216; transition planning, 113; post-election phase: Cabinet-making, 92, 93; first meetings with prime minister-elect and Cabinet secretary, 143; three-tier Cabinet, 88; pre-election phase: public service guidelines for meeting the opposition party, 65–6; transition planning, 5–6, 11, 113; transition planning and public service, 62–3

United States: Congress, 91; post-election phase: president-elect first meetings, 135–6; president-elect media coverage, 127; president-elect relationship with outgoing president, 145, 147; president-elect stature, 134; president-elect transition, 129–30; staff selection criteria, 171, 173; transition funding law, 7; transition planning, 6–8, 30, 52

Values and Ethics Code, 100

Watkins, Michael, 185–6
Weber, Max, 213
Wellford, Harrison, 30, 52, 53, 129, 171, 210
Wells, Paul, 129, 139–40
Wernick, Michael, 115, 121–3
White, Graham, 5, 19
White, Jodi, 17, 18, 108, 111, 146–7, 171

Yes, Minister: advice to newly elected ministers, 122, 186; Cabinet-making, 155–6

Zussman, David: Cabinet screening process development, 164; transition materials for first Cabinet meeting, 182–3; transition planning: agenda issues, 41–2; meeting with chief of staff, 146–7; newly elected ministers' orientation sessions, 189–92; outstanding issues, 215–17; performance measurement of re-elected government, 202–3; personal reflections, 206–8; transition team: chair, 46; media strategy, 127–8; priority setting, 51–2; recruiting members, 45

The Institute of Public Administration of Canada Series in Public Management and Governance

Networks of Knowledge: Collaborative Innovation in International Learning, Janice Stein, Richard Stren, Joy Fitzgibbon, and Melissa Maclean

The National Research Council in the Innovative Policy Era: Changing Hierarchies, Networks, and Markets, G. Bruce Doern and Richard Levesque

Beyond Service: State Workers, Public Policy, and the Prospects for Democratic Administration, Greg McElligott

A Law unto Itself: How the Ontario Municipal Board Has Developed and Applied Land Use Planning Policy, John G. Chipman

Health Care, Entitlement, and Citizenship, Candace Redden

Between Colliding Worlds: The Ambiguous Existence of Government Agencies for Aboriginal and Women's Policy, Jonathan Malloy

The Politics of Public Management: The HRDC Audit of Grants and Contributions, David A. Good

Dream No Little Dreams: A Biography of the Douglas Government of Saskatchewan, 1944–1961, Albert W. Johnson

Governing Education, Ben Levin

Executive Styles in Canada: Cabinet Structures and Leadership Practices in Canadian Government, edited by Luc Bernier, Keith Brownsey, and Michael Howlett

The Roles of Public Opinion Research in Canadian Government, Christopher Page

The Politics of CANDU Exports, Duane Bratt

Policy Analysis in Canada: The State of the Art, edited by Laurent Dobuzinskis, Michael Howlett, and David Laycock

Digital State at the Leading Edge: Lessons from Canada, Sanford Borins, Kenneth Kernaghan, David Brown, Nick Bontis, Perri 6, and Fred Thompson

The Politics of Public Money: Spenders, Guardians, Priority Setters, and Financial Watchdogs inside the Canadian Government, David A. Good

Court Government and the Collapse of Accountability in Canada and the U.K., Donald Savoie

Professionalism and Public Service: Essays in Honour of Kenneth Kernaghan, edited by David Siegel and Ken Rasmussen

Searching for Leadership: Secretaries to Cabinet in Canada, edited by Patrice Dutil

Foundations of Governance: Municipal Government in Canada's Provinces, edited by Andrew Sancton and Robert Young

Provincial and Territorial Ombudsman Offices in Canada, edited by Stewart Hyson

Local Government in a Global World: Australia and Canada in Comparative Perspective, edited by Emmanuel Brunet-Jailly and John F. Martin

Behind the Scenes: The Life and Work of William Clifford Clark, Robert A. Wardhaugh

The Guardian: Perspectives on the Ministry of Finance of Ontario, edited by Patrice Dutil

Making Medicare: New Perspectives on the History of Medicare in Canada, edited by Gregory P. Marchildon

Overpromising and Underperforming? Understanding and Evaluating New Intergovernmental Accountability Regimes, edited by Peter Graefe, Julie M. Simmons, and Linda A. White

Governance in Northern Ontario: Economic Development and Policy Making, edited by Charles Conteh and Bob Segsworth

Off and Running: The Prospects and Pitfalls of Government Transitions in Canada, David Zussman